THROUGH UNKNOWN TIBET

THROUGH UNKNOWN TIBET

M. S. WELLBY

The Kushok's Cook.

ILLUSTRATED

GYAN

Published by

Gyan Publishing House
5, Ansari Road
Daryaganj, New Delhi-110002
Phone: 011-47034999, 9811692060
E-mail: books@gyanbooks.com

Distribution Network
gyanbooks.com
India, USA, Canada, UK, Australia, France

ISBN : 978-81-212-4107-6 (PB)
First Published, London, 1898

2nd Impression 2020

Printed at: Gyan Press, Delhi.

Through Unknown Tibet
Author: M. S. Wellby

TO

OUR BROTHER OFFICERS

PREFACE.

In publishing the following account of a journey across Tibet and China, it has been my object to describe in a simple manner all that I did and saw from beginning to end, in the hope that some future traveller may learn, not so much what he ought to do, as what he ought not to do.

Those who have experienced the charms of a nomad's life, will, I trust, be once more reminded of happy days of freedom, will sympathise with us in our difficulties, and share the pleasures which they alone can appreciate. Should others, by chance, find some little interest in perusing these pages, and be tempted to taste for themselves the sweets of wandering through little known lands, they will be recompensed for doing so, and I shall have found my reward.

To those who patiently read to the end and close the book with a feeling of disappointment, I would appeal for leniency. Begun as it was at Lucknow, amid the distractions of polo, racing, and field-days, continued at Simla, India's summer capital, and finished in the wilds of Waziristan, it can lay no claim to literary or scientific merit, but only to being a plain story plainly told; and as such I give it to the public.

For the chapter on the Mohammedan rebellion in China, my thanks are due to my friend Mr. Ridley, of the "China Inland Mission," who lived in the very midst of the scene of trouble, and who kindly allowed me to make every use of his notes. They are likewise due to Sir Claude and Lady Macdonald, whose kindness and hospitality in Pekin can never be forgotten, and lastly, to those three faithful ones who stuck to us through thick and thin.

The names of Duffadar Shahzad Mir, Lassoo, and Esa Tsareng—known throughout as "Esau"—will always call to my mind three men without whom this journey could never have been accomplished, and in saying this I know that I am also expressing the feelings of my companion, Lieut. Malcolm.

M. S. WELLBY,
Capt. 18th Hussars.

WAZIRISTAN,
November, 1897.

CONTENTS.

LIST OF ILLUSTRATIONS.

LIEUTENANT MALCOLM.

THROUGH UNKNOWN TIBET.

CHAPTER I.

PREPARATIONS FOR THE JOURNEY—MALCOLM GOES ON AHEAD.

About the beginning of March, 1896, whilst the Inter-Regimental Polo Tournament was being held at Umballa, an occasion when representatives of regiments from all parts of India are gathered together, Lieutenant Malcolm, of the 93rd Argyll and Sutherland Highlanders, and I, agreed to join forces in an expedition through Tibet. Our resolve was to traverse the northern portions of this little-known country from west to east, to find out, if possible, what mysteries lay beneath the word UNEXPLORED with which alone our latest maps were enlightened; furthermore to discover and locate the source of the Chu Ma river, which was supposed to be a source of the Yangtse Kiang; finally to cross the Tsaidam and end up our wanderings at the celestial capital of China. During the few weeks that remained before we should be able to take our leave, we were unfortunately quartered at different places many miles apart, consequently all our arrangements had to be carried out by post and wire. It was towards the end of March when we left our respective stations of Nowshera and Umballa. I remember well the mail train to Rawal Pindi one bright morning gliding from the latter station past the well-known grassy maidan, then worn to a dirty dusty brown by reason of the morning tramp of small mixed armies, and by the equally keen and destructive work of numerous polo players during the latter half of the day.

On occasions like this, the thought quite naturally arises in one's mind, "Is everything here? Has my faithful bearer left anything behind?" Let us see what was with me in the carriage. In one corner lay my rifles; these consisted of a ·303 with Martini-Henry action, and 300 rounds of ammunition with Jeffrey's split bullets, a sporting carbine with 200 rounds, a shot-gun with 300, and a couple of government cavalry carbines with 100. These latter we brought not in the hope of using, but rather to lessen the chance of a skirmish with any natives showing hostile intentions, by merely making a display of them. The knowledge of a caravan being well armed and equipped, however small it may be, is very often a battle half won amongst unsophisticated inhabitants of little-known countries. The other rifles, for game, we selected chiefly for their handiness and the lightness of the ammunition, although a double-barrelled express may be equally or more destructive. All the ammunition was placed in government tin-lined wooden boxes, with rope handles.

Here, too, were our scientific instruments: A three-inch theodolite and stand, a six-inch sextant, three aneroid barometers, a hypsometer, maximum and minimum thermometers, plane table and stand, prismatic compass, and field glasses. Besides this we had a drying press for flowers, skinning knives, with alum and arsenical soap, a butterfly net, and a kodak; also the best map of the country we could lay our hands on, and a few stiff books, such as the "History of the Indian Empire," where the dullest mind and imagination can find unlimited food, for there are times on trips of this description when bad weather or illness may prevent outdoor progress, and the brain will at once cry out for an innings. Close by lay a despatch box and medicine chest, containing, for man's ailments, quinine, Cockle's pills, chlorodyne, auberge for colds, antipyrine, antiseptic wool, vaseline, and kola nut, the last named being particularly useful, for a small piece the size of a pea has been known to sustain strength and energy at the most urgent times; there were also mustard plasters, which are always effective for sticking on natives of any uncivilized country, Tibetans themselves being especially partial to this kind of medicinal adornment. For the mules and ponies, whose chief and probably only ailment would be the suffering from sore backs, we carried sugar-of-lead ointment and cyona. There lay, too, a small chair, a bundle of warm blankets and waterproof sheets, and a box containing twenty chain hobbles with bolt screw. We had learnt from Bower, who had crossed Tibet some five years previously, that one of the greatest delays was caused by the straying of the animals at night-time, and against this annoyance we were resolved to protect ourselves. These were very simply made. By way of a portable kitchen we had laid in a box of cooking utensils, consisting of some steel degchies and a frying pan. The stores were placed in six boxes, each weighing about thirty pounds, and made up principally of tea, cocoa, Lazenby's soup squares, Brand's essences, candles, matches, some sardines and bully beef, with three bottles of good brandy. In the luggage van were also two government cavalry saddles, with carbine bucket, wallets, and wooden stirrups, for we had been led to believe that the cold would be intense, and that metal stirrups would probably produce a frost-bite. Lastly, though more precious, was my little fox terrier, Ruby, so full of life and spirits at starting, yet in happy ignorance of the undeserved fate that overtook her some seven or eight months later.

Unlike many Indian trains, where, too, the fashion would have suited me far better, this particular train landed me punctually at Rawal Pindi at 2 A.M. Despite this unearthly hour and the drizzling rain, I was a little surprised to find my special tonga awaiting me, though it proved insufficient for carrying all the luggage. Leaving my little terrier to take charge of this, I embarked on to a wooden springless box, pulled by a mule, and steered for the nearest serai, in hopes of being quickly able to find an ecka. Here I squeezed through some bars of the large wooden gates which were supposed to keep out night intruders, and any sleeping inmate who lay in the various rooms I prodded with my stick, and demanded an ecka. None of these, however, at such an hour, would accede with any kind of willingness to my proposals. Some absolutely refused to awake, while others who did, strongly objected to being roused and to helping me. The only arrangement that would suit any of these men at all was, that twenty-five rupees should be paid instead of the proper fare of eighteen. In that case, and providing that my luggage was brought to the serai, and that there were not too many things, they agreed to start for Baramula when they felt inclined. Bribes, threats, and even blows were of no avail, and finally, being opposed by superior numbers, I retreated, and sad to say not gracefully, for I had to squeeze through those bars again. Another ride in the box brought me to a second serai, where I luckily fell in with a choudrie, who produced an ecka with so stout a pony that he reached the station before I could in my mule box. Here the ecka was loaded and sent on in advance, shortly to be overtaken by my tonga, for a tonga will cover the journey of 160 miles to Baramula in two days, while an ecka takes about five. The only difficulty that arose this morning was the constant jibbing of the horses, and had they not the providential dodge of repeatedly collapsing and lying down, I should undoubtedly have rattled down some open precipice. Despite this delay, I reached the well-known

CLUB OF NORTHERN INDIA, MURREE, IN SNOW.

hill station of Murree for 10 o'clock breakfast. From here the road was heavy, and had not some gangs of long-suffering coolies, who were working on the road, come to our assistance, the tonga would be there now. That evening we reached Domel, where a tumbledown shanty had supplanted, for the time being, a well-built bungalow which had recently been washed away by heavy rains and snow. In one respect this was an ill-chosen spot to spend the night at, as the horses had to be taken away for shelter some three miles off, I was told, and to induce natives to bring the tonga ready to start by daybreak was as difficult as to squeeze blood out of a stone.

By 7 o'clock, however, we were once more rolling along in dripping rain, with the everlasting but somewhat monotonous roar of the river Jhelum below us, so that it was a decided relief to stop for breakfast, even at an inn like that at Chagoti, where I could hardly mount the slippery steps that lead up to the entrance, benumbed as I was by wet and cold, and cramped from several hours of the same position, for the constant downpour prevented any stretching of legs when changing horses at the various stages. In somewhat heavier rain we journeyed on through slush and mud, and arrived at Baramula about sunset. It was my intention to have embarked here at once on to one of the river boats and reach Srinagar as quickly as possible. But darkness and rain, and an inviting light from the adjacent dâk bungalow dissolved these plans, and I was soon ushered inside by a Kashmiri, by name Mahomed Malik. This man was to be our cook on the expedition; he was armed with several letters of recommendation, amongst others from Curzon and Littledale, and had doubtless travelled over a great portion of Asia, and we vainly congratulated ourselves on having managed to pick up a servant with so much experience. I was struck, too, by his pleasant appearance, his quiet yet quick and business-like way of doing things, little knowing at the time that he had at heart no real intention of accompanying us, but merely of buying the articles required for our expedition, and persuading us to buy a great many unnecessary ones, in order to reap a small fortune from the transaction.

From experience gained on this trip and on others, I prefer servants of all descriptions, with the exception of

VIEW TOWARDS FIFTH BRIDGE, SRINAGAR.

guides pure and simple, to be men who have made no previous journeys. Although the possession of letters explaining what good men they have been on previous journeys is a useful recommendation, still it can never guarantee what they will be like. Many of them, after receiving liberal and well-deserved pay for their services, become inflated with their own importance and vainly think that no expedition can manage without them. Besides, men of this description are far more expensive articles than the fresh and keener man, anxious to make his first essay. It is hardly worth while, too, to quote the proverb about the fish and the sea. The following morning, I found myself being towed up the river towards Srinagar, fairly sheltered from the incessant rain by the matting that forms a roof to these boats, or doongas, as they are

A MERCHANT'S HOUSE IN SRINAGAR.

locally called. The water was thick and brown, no view of the famous snow-capped peaks or pine-clad mountains could be seen, all was obscured in damp dreariness, and my thoughts fled back to those I had left to enjoy the sunny plains below. Nor was there any more inducement on the morrow to slip out from between the blankets and admire the wonderful scenery of these parts. I continued to prolong the night until my boat was suddenly boarded by one of the chief agents of Srinagar, a member of the

Sumud Shah family, so renowned for their Jewish appearance and ways, and for their partiality in buying and selling all kinds of goods, and for lending or borrowing money to any amount in any shape or form. There was a second invader, a moment afterwards, by name Ramzana, who was a chapliwalla, or seller of chaplies, which are shoes made of leather and straps, and are worn by most sportsmen who shoot in Kashmir; besides these he sold everything that man's imagination could conceive as being made of leather, but, it should be added, of an inferior kind. They brought with them some large brass plates loaded with white almonds, sweets, and dried currants, and placing them beside my bed as a friendly initiative to business, began to ramble on, with beaming faces, about the superiority yet cheapness of their own goods, and of their eternal willingness to provide me and my friends who might come to Kashmir with them, at all places and at all times.

About midday the clouds began to lift, and having lightened my cargo of these persevering Jews, I decided to take a muddy walk and finish the last eight or nine miles on foot. Part of the way lay along the Baramula and Srinagar road, along which tongas should certainly be able to ply the following year, and if the many heaps of flints that were lying alongside were beaten down into the road itself, there is every chance of its being able to withstand the traffic. On either side, too, was a row of dwarf poplars, or "pruss" as they are called by the Kashmiris, beautifully planted in line at about a yard interval, doubtless helping to make the drive pleasant and shady enough.

By the river side were men breaking up between two stones black, spikey nuts called tinkara; these are gathered from the bottom of the river, and the outside appearance belies what lays hidden beneath, for they are rather good eating. About dusk, Sumud Shah's shop came in sight, and having climbed up the steep stairs into his showroom, which overlooked the river with its many opened windows, I was surrounded and made much of by numerous Sumuds, each of them inquiring amongst other things whether I carried any banknotes, and if so, whether they

MOHAMMEDAN MOSQUE, SRINAGAR.

might take care of them for me. Soon afterwards they produced dinner, composed of about a dozen plates holding different coloured messes. Fortunately Malik came to my assistance and brought a mutton bone, and certainly saved me from an illness. I was glad to escape from so much civility and hospitality and descend the stairs again and wend my way to my bedroom, which was airy enough, for three sides could only be described as windows of perforated wood, whilst the fourth held two doors and no wall.

The first thing I learnt here was that, if I wanted breakfast at 8.30, it must be ordered for 6 o'clock, which lesson saved me a vast amount of trouble and impatience in doing all other business in Srinagar. My second lesson learnt was to believe nobody, however sincere they might appear to

HINDU TEMPLE, SRINAGAR.

be, for these vendors are for ever plotting and scheming against one another for the sake of gaining the merest trifle, and many of them, who are seemingly bosom friends, are in reality the most unscrupulous enemies, and *vice versâ*. My time was spent in bargaining and purchasing goods from men of this description.

It was our intention here to have collected, if possible, some good mules and ponies for transport, and send them up to Leh, which would be our starting-point. But the route was at this time of the year impassable by reason of heavy falls of snow. All our transport, therefore, had to be bought in Leh itself. There was plenty to do at Srinagar, nevertheless, in fitting out the expedition in other ways, and in endeavouring to pick up some muleteers, as it is not always easy to pick up good men at Leh to accompany one on a trip of this description.

One day I visited the Tibetan serai which lies a little lower down the river, to see whether I could get some Yarkandi saddles for our mules, although it seemed rather ridiculous to purchase these before the animals. I was under the wrong impression that they were not obtainable in Leh. They are made of coarse grass or reeds, covered with sacking, with soft munnah over the part that rests on the animal's neck and shoulder, costing from eight to ten rupees each when complete. They have the advantage over the wooden saddle, as mules can roll with these on their backs, and they are, besides, easily repaired, and can have holes cut into them, or otherwise shaped, so as to relieve any pressure on the tender part of a sore back.

Whilst engaged in getting these saddles mended up, I fell in with a man called Tokhta, who was clever at shoeing, and as he seemed willing to come with me I at once engaged him. He was a Yarkandi man, and had travelled in Turkistan.

It is a great saving of time and trouble on the march to have loads so arranged that they can be easily loaded and unloaded. Most of the things were therefore placed into yakdans, which are light boxes about 2 ft. × 1 ft. 3 in. × 1 ft., but can be made to order in other sizes. They are covered with leather, and fitted on the outside with a pair of buckles and stout leather straps. Our beds, too, were composed of yakdans, with two iron sockets in each, to hold two iron rings. Into these were placed the two bamboo poles that held the bed. These yakdans can be bought cheaper, stronger, and lighter at Peshawar. I also bought 120 sets of shoes with 1,000 spare nails, and shoeing tools for the mules and ponies, and for our followers four maunds of rice (a maund equals about eighty pounds), a maund of dal, thirty pounds of tea, salt, pepper, curry powder, and hot spices. In the shape of presents we bought watches, pistols, knives, rings, and some

ON THE RIVER, SRINAGAR.

saffron which is made from the dried stigmas of the *Crocus sativus*, and is highly esteemed as a dye by the Tibetans, especially by the Lamas. A few days later, Malcolm joined me, bringing his share of stores, etc., and together we bought the warmest clothing we could find, underclothing of lambs' wool, thick woollen socks, double soled and heeled, thick puttoo suits, fur-lined caps and cloaks, and fur-lined sleeping bags. We wore the regulation infantry ammunition boots. For shelter we bought five tents, all double twill

DUFFADAR SHAHZAD MIR, 11TH BENGAL LANCERS.

lined. Two of these were for ourselves, one for our cook and servant, one for our sub-surveyor, and one for the muleteers. These were small and light, and the whole of them would not have equalled more than a mule load. I have seen some tents lined with warm cloth such as puttoo, but this is not so effective in keeping out a keen wind as the closer-woven twill. We found iron pegs answered our purpose, excepting when the ground was too sandy; on these occasions we used to tie the ropes to one of the handles of an ammunition box or yakdan.

One morning, in the midst of making these preparations, there was a sudden rush and hullaballoo, for a fire had broken out in some adjacent buildings, and I was invited by many excited vendors to go and visit the scene. The police station was in flames, and thousands of natives were engaged in passing up from hand to hand chatties or small earthenware pots from the river's edge, whilst the bhisties or water carriers were running madly about in every direction with their skins full of water. The police, who had lost their wits, were idle onlookers, but standing on a brick wall forty feet high was a fine muscular man wielding a massive beam, with which he was beating the roof of the burning building, with what object it was impossible to say. I was nevertheless struck by his courage, and inquired who this hero might be, and felt somewhat anxious for his safety; but when they told me he was my dhobie, or laundress, my fear for him was lost in the greater anxiety for my clothes which he had only that very morning received, and I at once took steps to get him to a safer footing, and left the fire to burn out as it pleased. With Malcolm came one Shahzad Mir, Duffadar, 11th Bengal Lancers, a man who had travelled before with Captain Younghusband, and who had done work on the Pamir Commission. He was a great addition to our party, chiefly as a sub-surveyor, and was keen on the job. Through him I was enabled to pick up another man called Shukr Ali, who had also been with Captain Younghusband. He was a tall, dark fellow of cheery countenance, and was anxious to make a little money to support his family living somewhere in Ladakh.

SHUKR ALI.

During all this time we received every kind of assistance from the Resident, Captain Trench, who presented us with a huge watch-dog called Tippoo. Tippoo unfortunately had to be chained up day and night, for when allowed to go loose he invariably seized on the first native who came in his way. In consequence of this imprisonment he quickly became footsore when compelled to march, and took up a new home with the first Nomads we came across.

On April 5th Malcolm left me at Srinagar to complete the arrangements and to wait for the passport, about which there had been so serious a hitch that it seemed doubtful whether we should be able to start on our journey at all. He left with a small flotilla of three boats to carry some fifty coolie loads of luggage, together with Shahzad Mir and Tokhta, who bade many farewells, mingled with callings to their god, to the large crowd of friends gathered on the shore to see the start. It was calculated that on the following day they would reach the village of Gunderbul, lower down the river, and from thence collect coolies and ponies and make their way to Leh, the capital of Ladakh, and the starting-point of our expedition.

CHAPTER II.

BALTAL—LEH—I REJOIN MALCOLM—THE CHINESE PASSPORT ARRIVES.

Five days after Malcolm's departure, that is, on the 10th April, news reached me that the passport would shortly be forwarded; upon this I at once embarked with the intention of reaching Leh as soon as possible after him. All things had to be settled up before leaving, and Shukr Ali was installed as cook for the journey instead of Malik, who had declined to go but had produced his bill. Amongst the items mentioned in it was an iron brush, which at first was a puzzler, but after all it turned out to be not such a bad name to designate a "rasp." His last request was that I might give him some more backshish, for he said he had not even made a single pie out of the numerous articles he had bought for us! The following morning, awaking in the boat, I found we had arrived at Manasbal, where three ponies and ten coolies sufficed to carry the remainder of our luggage, and we were soon wending our way up the glorious Sind valley. The morning was still and close, with small light clouds resting on the hills, while a fine haze enveloped all which might have augured a bright summer's day or the reverse. After fourteen miles Kangan was reached, where our transport was changed for seven fresh ponies, and the village of Goond, another fourteen miles, that same evening soon after dark. Although no provisions were procurable at that time, I found shelter

THE GLACIERS, SONAMERO.

under a shed wherein to put up my bed, but sleep was a failure, as my two dogs Tippoo and Ruby saw or imagined they saw a stranger every moment and barked accordingly. Rain poured all the next day, so that I could not push on further than to Gagangir, and was glad to find a house there made of mud and wood to rest in. It would have been very hard for the coolies to have toiled further that day, as the road for the next six miles led through deep snow, where, too, avalanches were feared from the mountains which rose precipitously from either bank of the stream we should have to follow. I therefore made the best of a halt, and having purchased a sheep for two rupees and a hen for seven annas, made a royal repast. The next day, after a wet march, we reached the region of snow, and put up at a small hut at Sonamerg. This place, although consisting of only a few small wooden huts, nevertheless boasts of a state telegraph and post-office. From here the road was deep in snow, upon which locomotion became more difficult every hour. I stopped for the night at a place called Baltal, well known to the many readers of Knight's interesting book, "Where Three Empires Meet." Here I found that two officers had taken up their abode, having pitched their tents inside one of the stone and wooden buildings, the one of course which admitted least snow and water. There they were seated, with big boots, ulsters, and umbrellas, and had been practically in this position for the last three days, and in every likelihood would remain there for a good many more; worse than that, it was probable that I should be added to the party. I did not envy them when they boasted that they were the oldest inhabitants of the place. The coolies lay together for the sake of warmth around small fires beside the buildings, having to take turns to sally forth and collect the wood.

Baltal lies at the foot of the Zoji La pass, and these men had not any wish to attempt to cross it while the weather was stormy, for avalanches at such times are most dangerous in those parts, and they were warned by the death, only ten days previously, of two post runners. There seemed, indeed, small chance of starting on the morrow as I sat down to enjoy a much appreciated dinner given me by these two old inhabitants. As I retired for the night we were, therefore, surprised and rejoiced at seeing once again some stars, and still more did we rejoice when, at 6 A.M. on a perfectly clear, still morning, so refreshing after the last few days of storm and darkness, the three of us, leading the caravan and followed by some sixty coolies, began the ascent of the pass. It was certainly hard work for these poor fellows, who, with a load of some fifty or sixty pounds, had to climb over the masses of snow, the result of the recent avalanches, and make a road for themselves, when, as often as not, at each step they sank up to their waists, all, too, for the small prize of four annas! Although the journey to the top of the Zoji La was only about two miles, we took three hours to get there. That day we were twelve and a half hours in marching sixteen miles to Metaiun, having made a short halt at the small posting place of Machahoi. At night I found a small hut eight feet square, but was forced to wait outside in the cold while my dinner was being cooked, for in this abode there was no exit for the smoke whatever, and suffocation might have resulted had I remained inside. From hence we journeyed on through the snow to Dras, taking again nine hours to do the fifteen miles. At this important stage, provisions, fresh coolies, and all manner of things can be bought, and letters can be had at the post-office if they have arrived; but on this occasion none had been received for five days, at the end of which time the news of the death of the two post runners was corroborated. From thence fresh coolies were to carry the loads, and the poor fellows who had done the work for the last five days were

FIRST SIGNS OF BUDDHISM BEYOND LEH, AT MULBECK.

dismissed to return to their villages in their own time. This journey, too, they had done most pluckily and cheerily, over mountains deep in snow and a pass over 11,000 feet high, amidst almost incessant falling snow or rain, with no adequate shelter at night time, all for two and a half rupees apiece! At this small sum, too, they expressed much pitiful delight, for it was a rupee in excess of their real fare.

The fresh relay of coolies carried my baggage in two more days to Kargil, passing through Tashgam, a pretty little spot with a small plantation of willows, but the beauty of the place was somewhat marred by the snow that still lay about. At Kargil there is good accommodation, and supplies are plentiful; there are, too, some little nondescript shops. Thenceforth ponies replace coolies for carrying the baggage, each pony carrying a load of about 150 pounds. From Kargil the road ascends the hills and leads over rolling ground, while the adjacent hill tops become rounded, and the general appearance of the country is somewhat dreary. After twenty miles, the village of Mulbeck is reached, where one first sees the small monasteries of the Lamas perched on some pinnacle, and the piles of flat stones with their sacred writings, called mānés. From this point the road became heavy, owing to the mud, and soon after midday we came to the village of Kharbu, where I learnt that further on the mud was yet deeper and thicker, and on the rising ground I found the snow even worse. About five o'clock I arrived at another small village at the foot of a pass. Here the men demanded a halt, for they said it would be impossible to cross it that evening. Despite their earnest entreaties and clasped hands, I decided to push on. Soon after this darkness set in, before even we had reached the summit, and a biting wind, with driving snow, made our progress slow, so that at one time I almost regretted not having paid attention to their supplications. Just as we were about to begin the descent, one of the baggage ponies completely gave way and collapsed in the snow. This necessitated a redistribution of the loads, many moans and groans, and very nearly resulted in some frost-bites.

In darkness we stumbled down the mountain side, inwardly hoping that no other pony would collapse. As soon as we had descended low enough to be free from the clouds of driving sleet, we were helped by the faint light of the moon, and eventually at a late hour arrived at Lamayuru. Fatigue and a short night's rest disinclined the men for another early start, although the march from this place is perhaps the finest and most pleasant of any. The road follows a winding stream running merrily between grand massive cliffs and rocks, till at Khalsi it crosses the River Indus, where a small native guard is maintained, thence through Nurla on to Saspul. From here I had resolved to reach Leh in one day, so instructed my factotum, Shukr Ali, to urge on the ponies as fast as possible. This he certainly did with such a will that in four hours we had reached Nimo, while none of the pony drivers were able to keep pace; consequently at Nimo the ponies were without masters. Here we again changed animals, and starting on ahead of the loaded ones and mounted on a rat of a pony, about sunset I first gained sight of this redoubtable Leh. The first conspicuous object was the Lama monastery, and quite naturally too, for, as usual with Lama monasteries, it was perched on a hill of commanding position, while Leh itself, at first appearance, looked small and insignificant. With my goal in sight, I was not long in finding a way through the narrow winding paths, past the missionary quarters, to the rest bungalow, having been twelve days on the road. Here Malcolm was waiting for me, having arrived two days previously, and we at once set about buying our mules and ponies and in collecting our muleteers, for at present we had only Shukr Ali and Tokhta.

BRIDGE OVER THE SURV RIVER AT KARGIL, ON THE ROAD TO LEH. BRIDGE ON CANTILEVER PATTERN.

We were told by every one that at this time of the year it would be most difficult to buy mules, so we were extremely fortunate in falling in with a merchant who had lately arrived from Lhassa, and who was willing to sell us fifteen. Although they were not in as fat a condition as they should be at the commencement of a journey, they were nevertheless hard, and formed the nucleus of our transport. Besides these, we were only able to pick up seven other mules, one here and one there, and were compelled to be satisfied with ponies for the remainder of our transport. These we found in no way equal to the mules for an expedition of this kind. If ponies have to be taken, the best are those which come from the district of Lhassa. Of these we had two, while the rest were Ladakhis.

In Leh three distinct kinds of mules are obtainable, namely, Yarkandis, Ladakhis, and Lhassa or Chang Tanis; of these the former are by far the most taking in appearance, and are mostly very big, standing 14·2 to 15 hands. They are, however, unfitted for a long journey when grass is likely to be scarce, and only a limited quantity of grain can be carried. The majority of these mules are black in colour. The Ladakhi mules are mostly brown; they are generally extremely hardy, able to stand great cold, and to do a lot of work on inferior food. Unfortunately they are hard to obtain, as only a very small number are bred, and some are too small to be much good. The best of all are the Chang Tanis, bought in Leh; the very fact of their being there shows that they have been able to perform a long march with loads on their backs; they require little or no grain, and are very hardy. Yarkandi merchants, as a rule, give their mules loads of 200 lbs. to 240 lbs. and about 4 lbs. of grain daily; the Lhassa merchants put about 160 lbs. on their backs, and, when grass is plentiful, give no grain. Altogether we mustered twenty-two mules, costing on an average 129 rupees each, and seventeen ponies at about sixty-one rupees each. All of them we branded on the hind quarters to guard against any attempt at fraud after the purchase. In collecting these animals and our men we were assisted by Lala Bishan Dass, Wazir of Leh. He also helped us in many other ways, and as he spoke excellent English, matters were somewhat simplified. Besides the two men already mentioned, namely, Shukr Ali and Tokhta, we impressed into our service six other muleteers, four of them being Argoons, who are really half-castes, arising from the merchants of Turkestan making short marriages with the Ladakhi women; also two Ladakhis and one Yarkandi. Besides these eight men and our sub-surveyor, Shahzad Mir, we also took as servant a Ladakhi named Esa Tsareng, whom we simplified into Esau, and refer to him afterwards by that name. This man had for some little time listened to the doctrines of the good missionaries of Leh, but eventually had reverted again to the Buddhist religion. For all that he proved himself throughout to be a most faithful servant and a useful and clever man, for he could read and write the Tibetan characters. We had one other follower, an Argoon named Lassoo. He was a very neatly made little man, cheery at all times. Besides being an excellent cook, he was also a first-rate muleteer, tailor, barber, carpenter; in fact, there was hardly any capacity in which he did not shine.

The muleteers soon gave evidence of what sort of men we had to deal with. They were an avaricious lot of fellows, and in a body refused to come with us under twenty rupees a month each, and this amount in actual wages we were unwilling to give, for we learnt that former travellers had paid men of this description fifteen rupees, and we were anxious not to be accused by those who might come after us of "raising the price." Promises of high backshish to all good workers carried no weight with such men, till at last we dismissed the whole crowd of them. At this stage of our preparations the chances of our ever starting at all looked decidedly black—we had no men and we had no passport—still more so when we were informed that there were no other men in Leh who would go with us. Being thus cornered and time most precious, we were in the end

SHAHZAD MIR AND OUR TEN MEN.

most reluctantly obliged to take them at their own price, and having discovered in other ways the class of men we had to deal with, we inwardly reflected that the only way to meet with success would be to humour them in all they wanted, and we foresaw that if we acted otherwise no headway would be made. We also agreed to give them per diem two pounds of flour, rice, or parched ground barley, one chitak (equal to two ounces) of butter carried in skins, one-fifth of a chitak (equal to one tola) of tea, besides the curry powder, spices, salt, and pepper already mentioned, and meat when procurable. We also gave them warm clothes and boots, money to buy more, and cooking utensils. We took in all for our ten men and Shahzad Mir nine maunds of flour, four of barley, four of rice, one of dal, sufficient, providing there was no robbery, to last them nearly four and a half months. Having so far bought our animals and enlisted our men, we at once set to work to fit out all these animals, so as to be able to carry the supplies. The twelve smallest mules were provided with wooden saddles, while the remainder wore the palans; to each mule were three ropes, two for tying on the load and one spare. Each mule, too, was provided with headstall, nosebag, and picketing rope. To equip each animal in this way cost us about ten rupees a-piece. As regards food for our animals, we made sufficient bags to carry eighteen maunds of grain and twenty-eight maunds of bhoussa, or chopped straw, both of which we should be able to buy some marches out of Leh, and also at Shushal on the Pangong Lake, which we were told would be the last point where we could obtain supplies. We reckoned that on an average each animal would carry 200 pounds. Of course, some of the mules were equal to nearly 300 pounds, whilst it would have been unwise to put more than 150 pounds on some of the ponies. Thus engaged, we continued to buy our goods and superintend the work and preparations, still anxious in regard to our passport, which had not yet arrived. Amongst other things, we had to see to the cold shoeing of our ponies and mules. On the 27th April everything was in readiness to start, and we decided to send forward our caravan on the morrow slowly with easy stages under the command of Shahzad Mir as far as Shushal, twelve days' march from Leh, whilst we ourselves would wait a few more days for the passport, and follow afterwards on hired transport, making two or three marches a day. On the evening before their departure, it was arranged that a nautch should be given in the rest bungalow compound, to which entertainment we were not only invited to come, but were also requested to subscribe and provide refreshment for the performers in the shape of spirits; it ended in our giving the show and their coming to it. In front of the bungalow was a small green, and in the centre of this a pile of bricks was erected to hold a number of burning logs; on one side and a few yards from this, seats were placed for ourselves, with men standing with lighted torches on either hand of us; opposite us were the local musicians—would that they had been placed at a greater distance off! On the two flanks, the inhabitants of Leh arranged themselves in several rows with the front ones sitting. Directly on our left was the well-nourished Munshi Palgez, master of the ceremonies, who, squatting on the ground with a low bench in front of him to hold the refreshments, superintended the distribution of the chang, the meat, and the chupatties.

The show commenced with half a dozen women, dressed in gay finery and bangles, moving in slow time around the fire, keeping pace together in the varied waving of their arms and swaying of their bodies. After this, each man in turn came forward and displayed his own special dance; some were of gentle mood, whilst others were frantic in their actions, and apparently dangerous with a flashing sword. The real fun was only reached when one of our own retainers, named Usman, doubtless bent upon celebrating his last evening at Leh, began his wild and lively dance. In the midst of his performance, suddenly stooping down, he seized the large pot of chang from under the very nose of the stout and all-important Palgez, who, having enjoyed every luxury of life without interruption for many years, was very nearly ending his days on the spot from mere fright at this piece of uproarious conduct. Yet Usman, not satisfied with this mirthful deed, began to dance more wildly than ever, swinging the well-filled pot at arm's length around his head, besprinkling all the onlookers with the intoxicating liquid, till finally, being tackled by some stout men from the crowd, he was thrown heavily to the ground, and disarmed of his dangerous weapons. After this unexpected burst we retired, leaving the entertainment to wear itself out.

On the morrow, the day fixed upon for the departure of our caravan, several delays occurred; some small item was always found wanting by these dilatory men. So anxious were they to delay their departure till another day, that it was nearly 3 o'clock before we could give the signal to open the gates of the serai and let out the animals, where they had been fattening since we had bought them. Thereupon there was a mighty rush, and on reaching the main thoroughfare of the bazaar, where crowds of inhabitants had gathered to view the departure, terrible confusion ensued. Some discarded their loads altogether, others rushed madly into any open door or alley that came in sight, and as they were collected, loaded, and driven on again, the crowd grew thicker and noisier. Soon after passing through the bazaar, the road makes a sharp descent, enough to baffle any further following of the crowd, nor were the sorrowing relatives of the men inclined at this spot to accompany them any longer. Here our muleteers bade a fond farewell, little suspecting that this in reality would be the very last for some of them, while a few of the more generous-hearted cast small change to the young fry. We ourselves, after riding with them till more steadiness prevailed, turned our ponies' heads again to Leh. After so much confusion, arranging, bartering, and arguing, we lived in peace and quiet for the next few days, amusing ourselves in taking heights and latitudes, and enjoying the hospitality of the good missionaries, our only excitement being the arrival of the post, with the chance of its bringing our passport. On the 4th May, passport or no passport, our patience had ended, and we resolved to start, for it was not desirable

CHINESE PASSPORT, ONE AND A HALF FEET SQUARE.

that our caravan should remain many days in an idle state at Shushal. We had no confidence in our men, and felt there was nothing like humouring them in all their wants, but at the same time in giving them no time to think of forming and carrying out any plot that might upset our arrangements and intentions.

We hired six ponies for our remaining baggage, and ourselves mounted on two others, equipped with Government cavalry saddles, carbine bucket, wallets, and wooden stirrups, with poshteen in front and small suleetah behind, prepared to leave the bungalow. We had just been lunching with Vaughan of the Border Regiment, and Ward of the Middlesex, both of whom had come for shooting; with them we enjoyed the last hospitality, and the last conversation with our own countrymen, we were to have until the middle of next October. "Well," they remarked, as we mounted directly afterwards, "so you are off to Pekin!" "Yes," we replied, "we will start this very moment, and do our best to get there," not that we felt doubtful of our undertaking, for the bracing air, the pure clear skies, the grand and glorious mountains of Ladakh, would inspire any man with confidence and self-reliance. Fortune, too, seemed favourable that day, for at the same moment the postman entered the gate of the

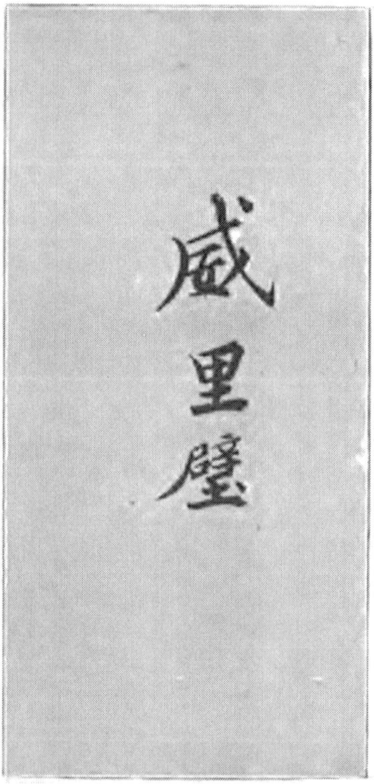

MY RED CHINESE VISITING CARD, FIVE INCHES BROAD AND TEN INCHES LONG.

compound, bringing our Chinese passport and Chinese visiting cards, the delay of which had cost us all our limited store of patience. The passport gave us free permission to travel through the provinces of Kansu, Shansi, and Shensi to Pekin, and through the New Dominion, at the same time enjoining all whom we came across to assist us and put no obstacles in our way. As we passed the kind missionaries' house, we received a hearty and last farewell, and entering the bazaar rode through it almost unobserved, for none knew of the exact time of our departure, and most of the inhabitants were enjoying repose at that time of day.

CHAPTER III.

FOLLOWING THE INDUS—EGU—WAITING AT SHUSHAL—A WARNING.

It was a warm afternoon as we descended the hill already mentioned towards the River Indus. We felt full of spirits in expectation of the journey that lay before us, for great is the charm of entering an unknown country in absolute ignorance of what lies ahead. We thought perhaps we might be fortunate enough to be about to open up a land rich in minerals or pasturage, or teeming with game, for none could tell us what existed over the border land nor who lived there. We might, too, be instrumental in discovering a new and easy route into China. All these thoughts and many others were foremost in our minds, while the glory of uncertainty and the pleasure of perfect freedom, added to the success we had met with in overcoming all the initial preparations, made our hearts light that day. On the other side of the river we saw the straggling village of Shushot, and at the time I thought to myself what miserable wretches the people must be who live there with no thought of ever going beyond its precincts, such as could never attempt to make a trip like ours, or even dream of it.

On one side of the river we passed by several chortens or monuments, and the village of Shey with its ruined fort, an almost indelible sign of its former importance. This village straggled on into Tickse, which was to be our first halting-place. Throughout this valley we had been travelling, the young grass was just beginning to bud, and we fondly imagined the richer grass we expected to find when we crossed the frontier a few weeks later. In the fields around Tickse, men and women were busily engaged, but ceased from their labour to watch and salute us, apparently glad to see Europeans. On the hills were the houses of the Lamas. We put up at the rest-house and bought two maunds of bhoussa for one rupee and filled three of the bags we had brought with us. We used a patent weighing machine of our own, which, of course, the men of Tickse could make neither head nor tail of, nevertheless they trusted us implicitly, for they said we never cheated, but remarked that if they had had the weighing machine and we had been unable to understand it, they would have done their level best to defraud us of as much as possible. From Tickse we continued to follow the River Indus, or Tsang-po-chu, as it is called in these parts, through a large open plain and still blessed with that fine blue Ladakh sky. After easy riding for nearly ten miles, we came to the small village of Chemre. At this spot there is a road which bends sharply to the left, passing over the Chang La, La being the Tibetan word for Pass. At this time of the year, however, the pass was closed, for the snow was deep. We were therefore compelled to take a more circuitous road but still following the river.

A short distance beyond Chemre is the village of Maserung on the other and left side of the river, and almost opposite Chemre itself is the Hemis nullah, famous for its great yearly festival and still more important gathering every twelve years. The monastery up this nullah can be seen from the other side of the river just after leaving Chemre.

About noon we reached the village of Egu. The people about here and the headmen of the different places we came to had received news of our coming, partly from our imposing caravan having passed through a few days previously, and also through rumour, which in these parts travels in a miraculous way, and, being friendly disposed and anxious to aid us (for they were under the impression that we were tremendous swells), were awaiting our arrival headed by the chief man and his attendants, all ready with their humble salutations. On this particular occasion my dignity had a great fall, for when we had approached within twenty yards of this gathering and were riding up in pomp and circumstance to receive their homage, my pony put his foot into a hidden hole, sending himself and rider spinning on their heads.

I think this unlucky coincidence somewhat damped our lordly reputation, for we had great difficulty in getting sufficient baggage animals after it, and were compelled to take yak, a slow conveyance even compared to ponies at the walk. Over the ground we were about to traverse they never made more than two miles an hour.

After another eleven miles, we came to the village of Sherwos, having about half-way noted the village of Upchi on the other side of the river, a spot worth knowing to sportsmen, for it lies at the mouth of the Gya nullah, so famous for its ovis ammon and burhel shooting. To-day we saw our first game in the shape of a few wild duck.

Anxious to push on from Sherwos, yet unable to get as far as Lickse that evening, for there were two little bridges that had to be crossed by daylight over the river, we determined to make neither of them our halting-place for the night, but to journey on and bivouac when darkness stopped us. It was a grand march, for the river here became very narrow, perhaps only ten yards broad, with a swift and busy torrent rushing through the gorge, while almost from the water's edge arose precipitous rocks some hundreds of feet, the grandeur being magnified by the uncertain light of the moon. At night-time we made our bivouac close by the waterside, and found this cleaner than some of the rest-houses we had of late frequented. From here we crossed two bridges and reached Lickse after two and a half miles, and once more re-crossing the river came to Herma, having come ten miles altogether. Here we changed our yak for new ones, ponies again being very scarce. These were the slowest going yak that ever did work for us. After six miles we passed through the village of Cunjian, as we were unable to change them there. We continued our slow march, a very trying one for these thickly-clad animals. The sun beat down with pitiless vigour upon the loaded brutes as they struggled up and down a narrow stony pathway, completely sheltered from any welcome breeze there might have been. So toilsome became the march that one poor yak carrying the instruments was actually slipping, and would have rolled down the rocky edge to destruction, had he not completely collapsed from exhaustion in a heap on the very brink. It was some time after dark before we could find a place called Gya to stop for the night, having only come eight and a half miles in six and a half hours. Here was a little cultivation, and just room to pitch tents, but no village close at hand wherefrom to get any supplies.

From here for seven miles the road is bad, stony, and hilly, and at this distance the village of Kera lies on the other bank of the river. One mile further on our yak were once more replaced by new ones at the village of Yakiki. On paying the drivers of the last lot of yak, we gave them eight annas each, that being their correct pay, yet to our surprise they showed much delight at receiving what was only due to them. This was probably owing to the fact that the few sportsmen who go up there for shooting allow their Kashmiri shikaris to pay these yakmen, and these latter being of timid and simple nature are afraid to complain, and are probably threatened with all sorts of punishment should they dare to tell the sahib that only half the money has been given them. After leaving this place the gorge becomes broader, and the road in consequence improves.

At six and nine miles we passed the villages of Ni and Keisir, and at the latter place were met by the Lama of Chumatang. Although this man was of portly mien, and mounted on a stout pony, he was kind enough to agree to an exchange of animals. Two miles further on we saw the village of Tiri on the other bank of the river, and a little later reached Chumatang. Supplies here were plentiful enough, and we took up six bags of bhoussa, a sheep, flour, and milk. The people were simple, kind, and ready to help us in every way. We had intended to change animals again, but, as sunset was close at hand, it was arranged that, to save time in changing the loads, we should drive on our own yak till darkness, and that the good people of Chumatang should bring on the animals we were to have the following morning, as well as some donkeys laden with wood, and a number of other articles in their own hands. We grew that evening into a large and mixed rabble; everybody was carrying or driving something for the two miles we marched, before halting for the night on a small patch of grass close to the river.

Thus far in our journey we had only seen a few gulls and some duck, so in hopes of seeing more I shouldered my gun the following morning. Plenty too, indeed, we saw, but all of them persisted in flying down the centre of the river or over the opposite bank, so that shooting them would have been a waste of birds and ammunition. This was aggravating, to speak lightly of it, when Malcolm agreed to fetch any I might shoot, should they fall on the other bank of the river. A few minutes later over came the duck again, and one falling midstream was soon carried away, but a second falling on the opposite bank awaited Malcolm. He, true to his word, was soon swimming in the icy water to the opposite shore, which he reached without mishap. He soon seized the duck with the intention of throwing it across to me, but falling short of his aim, the duck fell in the water, and was soon floating away after the first. To plunge a second time into the Indus and swim across it, at this time of year, and at this height, cannot easily be described, but Malcolm's frozen state on return gave me some idea of what he had undergone, all, too, to merely throw a dead duck into midstream. There was no compensation in the shape of a good supper for his swim, but we both agreed, at any rate, that shooting duck along the banks of the Indus was but a poor kind of amusement.

That morning we reached the little village of Maie, which did not seem to hold more than half a dozen men. Although no transport animals were procurable, yet supplies were plentiful. At this spot there are two roads that branch off to Shushal, the shorter or left hand one leading over the mountains. We fancied we could see the pass over which the road went, and there appeared to be but little snow there. Yet every one told us the pass was not open, and we had reluctantly to take the longer one. We came upon a herd of eight kyang, who are pretty sure heralds that there is good grass somewhere in the neighbourhood. They appeared unable to understand what we were, and allowed us to come within a hundred yards of them. After making an easy ascent, we saw a few miles off on our left hand the village of Numa, conspicuously seated on a rock, quite an important place with its numerous ponies and yak, and plentiful supplies. We loaded up the yak first, to send them on ahead of the ponies, for they won't travel as fast, especially in the middle of the day. It was a sharpish morning.

After going some ten miles the Indus became broad, resembling a lake, and about here pigeons were fairly plentiful. We agreed that we could never afford to waste a single cartridge so early on our journey, and decided to economise by endeavouring to make every shot do double execution. A chance quickly presented itself. There were two pigeons close together on the ground. "Fire away," I cried, "now's our time." "I really couldn't," said Malcolm, "they will be blown to pieces." "Never mind that," was my encouraging reply, "we shall be able to collect the bits." Immediately afterwards, off went both the barrels, and terrible to state, off went both birds too, safe and sound, only a little bit startled.

Seven miles further on we bade farewell to the river, which flowed away to the right, while our road branched off to the left, taking us to the black tents of some nomads. Where there are nomads, good grass will also be found for the grazing of their large flocks of sheep. We spent the night close to one of their encampments, and found them pleasant and hospitable enough, receiving from them dried apricots, nuts, butter, and milk. These nomads, too, have a knack of always finding a sheltered nook with a flowing stream. Although we were on that night over 14,000 feet high, we did not feel the cold at all, doubtless because we were well protected on all sides from any wind.

After leaving these people on the 10th May, we crossed over an easy pass, and then descended to more black tents, always finding the nomads civil and friendly. A little before noon we reached Shushal, the final starting-point of our expedition. Shushal lies back against the hills, five miles or so from the Pangong Lake, which is not even in sight. In the serai we found Shahzad Mir, who thus far had brought our caravan without an accident. Some of the muleteers were there, too, while the remainder were watching over the mules and ponies out grazing in an adjacent and well-watered valley.

SHOWING STAGES FROM LEH TO SHUSHAL.

	Miles.	
Leh to Tickse ..	9	
,, Chemre ..	9½	
,, Egu......	12½	
,, Upchi	17½	on other side.
,, Sherwos ..	23½	,, ,,
,, Lickse	31	,, ,,
,, Herma ..	38½	,, ,,
,, Cunjian ..	44½	,, ,,
,, Gya	62	,, ,,
,, Kera	69	on other bank.
,, Yakiki ..	70	,, ,,
,, Ni........	76	,, ,,
,, Keisir	79	,, ,,
,, Chumutang	87	,, ,,
,, Maie	99½	,, ,,
,, Numa	112½	,, ,,
,, Ralma	135½	Champa encampment.
,, Donlung ..	138½	,, ,,
,, Shushal ..	156½	,, ,,

The first thing for us to find out was the shortest and best way over the frontier. We learnt that the ordinary route over the Marsemik La into Chang Chenmo was closed by snow, and would not be open for at least another month and a half. With the exception of this road and another one that went to Rudok, nobody knew of any other, or more correctly speaking, would own that there was another road. Rudok lies at the south-east corner of the Pangong Lake, and we knew that at Rudok a large Tibetan guard was maintained, who jealously guarded the main road to Lhassa, under the condition that should they allow any foreigners to pass that way, they would have to pay for the negligence with the loss of their heads. This year, too, they were more than ever prepared to oppose any attempt at crossing the frontier in that direction. This we considered due to the fact that only the previous year the Littledales, in their famous expedition, had camped for some days within fifty miles of the capital. To dream of taking an easier road to Rudok, and crossing the frontier at that point, was soon dismissed from our minds. Looking at a map of the country, the Pangong Lake appears to consist of two lakes joined together by a narrow strip of water, about half-way on the road to Rudok. We saw no reason why we should not be able to find a crossing over this stream, thence on to a village called Pal, and thus avoid all encounter with the Rudok men. All the headmen and any other men of Shushal who had travelled at any time in that direction were summoned to our presence and questioned about this road to Pal. For some time all vowed they had never heard of a place called Pal, but seeing that we were bent upon going there at all costs, they finally agreed that they had heard of the spot, but that it was impossible for us to get there, for the water that joined the two lakes was far too deep to ever think of crossing. Unwilling to believe any of their statements at all, we dismissed our servant Esau with a companion to ride out to this water, some twenty miles away, and find out whether it was fordable or not.

Whilst waiting for this information we laid in our stock of grain for the trip, buying it at thirty-two pounds for a rupee, and tied it up into coarse sacking, which we had made into suleetahs. We also packed our bhoussa into a smaller compass, and doctored up the few backs of the animals that had been touched up during the march from Leh; in fact, saw after every little detail we could think of.

That same night, and somewhat to our surprise, Esau returned with the news that he had been stopped some way before reaching the water by a body of twenty armed men, who sent their salaams, begging us not to try and come that way, for if we did, there would certainly be trouble. They had already heard of our departure from Leh, and knew that we were waiting in Shushal, and were prepared to oppose any attempt we might make to cross the frontier in that direction. Under these circumstances (there was no alternative left us), we should have to journey back in a north-west direction along the shore of the Pangong Lake to Ludhkong, situated on its north-west extremity, thence travel eastwards to Niagzu, and so on by hook or crook across the frontier. We had by this time arranged our loads, and had fitted and mended the saddles where required, and were ready in all other respects to leave Shushal.

We gave orders to start for Ludhkong at 7 o'clock on the morning of the 12th, and, in order to save our own transport as long as possible, we hired seventeen more yak and ponies, making a total, with our own, of fifty-five animals. On the morning above mentioned, the baggage lay outside the serai in heaps and anyhow. The serai itself was a small, square yard with rooms built around it. We had hoped, having placed everything outside where there was oceans of room, to have arranged the loads systematically. This, unfortunately, was not in accordance with the way of doing things amongst our muleteers; but as we felt there was still a discontented mood prevailing underneath a smiling surface, we, too, smiled outwardly in return, and allowed them for the present to do as they chose.

Each of the muleteers had under his own charge five ponies or four mules, and each of them, with the willing help from the people of Shushal, seized upon whatever baggage he fancied the most and loaded up his own animals. Although all this was badly done, it was certainly done quickly, and we had very soon made a start.

CHAPTER IV.

MUN—LUDHKONG—TOUCHING FRIENDSHIP OF MULE AND PONY—NIAǴZU.

THE road for the first couple of miles was fairly good over rising ground when the lake first came into sight, and an extensive view permitted the taking of several bearings to distant hills. The lake looked blue, clear, and inviting, bounded on the further side by a fine range of mountains running into snow-capped peaks.

Besides obtaining a view of the lake, we also saw our flock of sheep, which had left Shushal the day previously, and very shortly overtook them. We were surprised and somewhat disheartened at finding the condition they were in. Two of them were already being carried in the arms of the shepherds, which will at once prove that our mutton was not of the fattest description. The remainder of the flock were going along so weakly that it seemed doubtful whether we should see any of them again. This disaster was a great blow to our commissariat arrangements. We had at one time even reckoned that our sheep might carry loads of about fifty or sixty pounds, but finding that would be impracticable, we decided to drive them along with us day after day, keeping them as a reserve, only making use of them when our own supplies began to run short and game was scarce. But now two of them were knocked up after going only a couple of miles. At this time of the year, sheep are naturally in poor condition, for they have picked up but scanty feeding during the winter months.

On this morning there was a strong north wind blowing in our teeth as we rode on ahead of our caravan, and after five more miles followed the sandy, stony shore of the lake.

As we were anxious not to be too far away from our caravan, we sought a sheltered nook by the edge of the lake, and, dismounting, allowed our ponies to graze on the little grass that grew close by, while we ourselves, seizing the opportunity, pulled out the kettle from our saddle-bags and soon had the water boiling for our breakfast. The kettle might as well have remained where it was, for here we learnt our first lesson in regard to many of the lakes of these regions, so pleasing to the eye, but deceptive as to their use. Our tea was so brackish as to defy any attempt at drinking it.

In the meantime our baggage had passed by, so we rode on over somewhat heavy and stony ground to overtake them, and before nightfall reached Mun, a small village with some cultivation around it, forming a kind of oasis in this stony, sandy country. We found here a good serai wherein to put our animals for the night, and a room for ourselves and men. There was no more transport to be had here, but the usual supplies being plentiful, we gave our animals two pounds of grain each and as much bhoussa as they could eat.

The following morning, although we were able to better arrange the loads, yet there was nothing satisfactory about them. Still favoured with the north wind we continued along the shore of the lake. Thus far we had found the water absolutely devoid of life, but after twelve miles we came to the end of the lake, and found there the only inhabitants living on it, a few gulls and a single Brahmini duck. At this spot, too, the place is called Kaba, and there is another more direct road branching off to the left to Leh.

Three more miles over deepish sand brought us to Ludhkong, the end of our march. This was the last place where any kind of supplies could be got. There was no grain here, but we were able to get plenty of bhoussa, some milk, sheep, goats, and a limited number of hired yak. The place consisted of a few stone houses built by the banks of a small fresh-water stream. Around on all sides were hills and snow-topped mountains; the land was barren, for there was no grazing ground at all.

The baggage arrived in good time, and we were glad of the afternoon for overhauling everything, doctoring our animals, and taking heights. We had, besides, to make up our minds as to which way we were going next. This was our great difficulty, and at first we could induce nobody to show us. We knew passes would have to be crossed, but as to their height, and as to water, grass, and camping grounds, we were in total ignorance.

Towards evening we learnt that, should we decide to proceed further, we could only go by one road and in this case should have to cross two passes, and that we should find no grass or water until the third day on arrival at Niagzu. This was certainly gloomy intelligence, and a bad lookout for our mules and ponies. Here they were about to go three days without grass or water before even they had crossed the frontier into Tibet. How could they ever cross the whole of Tibet and China? It was absolutely cruel to think of it. In addition to this, our hired animals had only agreed to come with us as far as Ludhkong. The only solution out of the difficulty was to persuade the owners of them to come on further with us, and this they were unwilling to do, for none of them relished three days without water and grass. By promise of higher rewards we finally overcame their scruples, and with the assistance of the Kadir who, by orders from the Wazir, had come all the way from Leh to smooth matters for us, we were enabled to hire more yak at Ludhkong itself, making a grand total of thirty-four hired animals. These were to come with us to Niagzu. As to our sheep, we came to an agreement with the men of Ludhkong, by which they were to take possession of our flock of sheep, which were coming on behind us, and were to fit us out with a fresh flock of sheep and goats, receiving an adequate remuneration for the bargain.

Things now began to look rosier for us. We arranged to put full loads on these hired animals and allow them to travel to Niagzu in their own time, while we ourselves, putting small loads on some of our own animals and none on others, would journey on in advance and cover the distance as fast as possible.

We reckoned that by leaving Ludhkong early one morning we could reach Niagzu the following evening. There we knew both grass and water were plentiful, and our own animals, while awaiting the arrival of the hired ones, would be fattening up and enjoying a rest. After seeing that all was ready for an early start the next day, we turned in for the night with light hearts.

On awakening the following morning, the first sight that greeted our eyes was that of our original hired yak being driven back in a body the way they had come, without any one attempting to stop them. It was fortunate we had woken up in good time that morning, as we were in time to prevent their straying far. We soon had them back again, and to prevent further attempt at desertion, at once set about the loading up of the two lots of transport. In spite of our instructions and arrangements the previous night, there was considerable confusion, and with the class of men we had to deal with, it was unavoidable. All as usual seize upon the nearest animal to load it up with the baggage nearest at hand, entirely regardless as to whether the load is suitable in weight or size to the animal, or whether it is required to go on with the party in advance.

Until the muleteers were quite under our thumb, it was impossible to make them do otherwise.

We carried a glass lantern to hold a candle, and being anxious to save it from being broken, it was carried in the hand by one of the hired yakmen, but as to one of our own muleteers carrying a lantern for a few miles! why, he had never done such a contemptible thing in all his life, and wasn't going to do it now!

To avoid the chance of our hired transport making a second attempt to turn back, we left Shahzad Mir and Esau to bring them on, as well as our two most reliable muleteers, Bakr Hadji and Shukr Ali, and after saying good-bye to the Kadir who had done so much good service for us, and to the kind people of Ludhkong, we started on our waterless march.

We soon took a turning half-right, over some good grazing land, and then began an easy ascent of the Porandu Pass for about five miles. When we had nearly reached the summit, we stopped to boil our kettle with some snow at hand, and to have our breakfast. Below us we could see first of all our own mules and ponies, while right away in the distance our glasses showed us our flock of sheep and goats and our hired yak, and Shahzad Mir with the man carrying the plane table.

It was not encouraging, after having crossed this pass, to find the road bending still more round to the right, following the direction of the shore of the Pangong Lake, and we calculated that if we continued to zigzag in the way we had done since leaving Leh, we should stand a chance of reaching China in two or three years' time.

Our muleteers manifested anything but a willing spirit. As we were riding on ahead, we were annoyed to find the caravan had halted some way back, of their own accord, and from their general demeanour we concluded they were contemplating whether the journey they were about to launch forth on was really good enough or not. We, too, halted; this seemed to be a turning-point in their plans, for they soon began to move on again.

As we ascended the stony nullah, sleet began to fall, encouraging the darkness before its due time, and compelling us to take the best shelter we could find for the night. Close by we found a suitable place—a sudden dip in the nullah bordered by heavy overhanging rocks, with a fair stretch of level ground at their foot. Here we drove four stout pegs into the ground, with strong ropes fastened to them, making two parallel lines; to one of these lines we picketed the mules, and to the other the ponies, with the exception of a certain black mule and a certain white pony. This couple had lived together practically for all their lives; in fact, at the time when we were buying our transport in Leh, we had to be satisfied with taking both of them or none at all, for the merchant who owned them was as fond of them as they were of one another, and rather than see them separated he would lose the chance of making his profit on one of them.

This remarkable pair also found a warm spot in our hearts, and we did all we could to keep the white pony in health and strength. They always marched together, grazed together, and were never apart. On one occasion when the pony was showing signs of weakness, we decided to ride it, for by dint of walking a good deal and stopping two or three times during the march, in grassy spots, we managed to save our riding ponies considerably, and, we thought, the black mule would manage without his friend for a few hours; but nothing of the sort—as soon as we rode away with the white pony, immediately after him came the black mule, load and all. We felt more convinced than ever that should the white pony die at any time from exhaustion, his faithful friend would soon follow after him; this doubled our anxiety to keep up the strength of the white pony, for he was in no way equal to the black mule. To tell now of the fate of this dear old couple would, perhaps, be anticipating events.

Near our camp there was not a vestige of grass, so we had to fall back upon our limited supply of bhoussa and grain. Of course the mules and ponies had to go waterless, although we were able to collect sufficient snow for the use of our men and ourselves.

We had already turned to our left again, and had ceased to follow the Pangong Lake, but had continued to make a long ascent. On leaving our encampment by the rocks, up, up we went; a blinding sleet blew in our faces, making it hard to see more than a few yards. At the top of this pass, which was called the Ann Pass, sickness from the unaccustomed height in no way sweetened the temper of some of our men, and we found no pleasure attached to the operation of finding out the height of this pass with the hypsometer, with a temperature just about freezing-point. We hurried down the other side of this comfortless pass, and for the rest of the day marched along a rocky, stony pathway, amidst a continuous snowstorm, when suddenly, on a bend to our left, the whole aspect was entirely changed. The heavy clouds gave way to a warm and genial sun. Thick brushwood and green grass replaced the sharply-angled rocks and those countless loose stones that lay about everywhere, as though they were a bore to themselves and to all others. A clear stream, too, ran merrily through this pleasant spot. No wonder the kyang and antelope had chosen this as one of their favourite districts to wander into, and the hares had grown fat and multiplied.

At this stage we had come nearly forty-five miles from Ludhkong, and this was Niagzu, a place well worthy of note, for it neither lies in Ladakh nor in Tibet. We had thus reached the border of the land we were anxious to traverse. Having pitched our camp, we looked forward to the morrow with composed feelings. First of all, we knew our mules and ponies would enjoy a complete day of rest and freedom, wandering through the fresh green grass or by the clear, trickling stream. We felt our success depended in no small measure upon their welfare. We rejoiced, too, that thus far we had managed by tact to prevent our men from turning back, and reckoned that, could we only manage to go a little distance beyond the

ON THE BORDERS OF TIBET; OUR CAMP AT NIAGZU.

frontier, they would be in our hands and not we in theirs. We had, in truth, overcome what we considered as difficulties such as made us more sanguine for the future. The day we waited at Niagzu for the arrival of our hired yak was an ideal one, when much could be done in rearranging the loads we had with us for the continuation of the journey. The numerous hares, too, afforded sport and provender for ourselves and our men. How anxious they were to hallal this small game in the orthodox manner, little dreaming that a few months later hunger would cause all these religious scruples to be put aside and forgotten for the time being!

While waiting here we experienced our first annoyance with relation to the straying of animals by night. Although at Niagzu we enjoyed good shelter, grass, and water, yet on the following morning few animals were in sight, and it was midday before they were all recovered. We almost dreaded to think of what would happen should we chance to halt where there was no grass, and where we intended marching early the next day. They would quite naturally wander during the night to an indefinite distance. Our chain hobbles, though most effective, and with which we had been so pleased, were at a discount with our men, for they hated an innovation, and infinitely preferred a long search of some miles after a strayed mule to the two minutes' work necessary to fasten on securely one of our chain hobbles.

We learnt from some of the hired yakmen, who had travelled still further inland to collect salt, that there was another pass of considerable height to cross over before we should have journeyed very far east of Niagzu. Such being the case, it was evident that the trial of crossing a high pass so early in our expedition without hired assistance would be most detrimental to the well-being of our transport, loaded as they would have to be up to the brim. We determined, therefore, to bring forward every inducement in persuading some of the owners of the hired yak to lend us their animals as far as the other side of this pass.

The day following our arrival at Niagzu there was no sign of our baggage at all, but the day after this, about noontime, our anxiety was relieved at seeing some of the laden yak just turning the corner to come up the Niagzu valley. From the higher ground above our tents a fine view down the whole of the valley was obtained, as well as of the range of snow mountains far away in the distance. The transport came in by driblets, as also did the flock of sheep, and it was quite clear that these latter would not last out for many more marches.

The day on which our yak arrived chanced to be a Sunday, so we were glad to be compelled to rest on that day. We clearly foresaw that in future, Sunday or no Sunday, we should be forced by circumstances to waste no single day. This last Sunday of rest was in consequence doubly appreciated, and it was some months before we were enabled to enjoy another.

CHAPTER V.

MORTALITY AMONG SHEEP—LAKE TREB—THE NAPU LA PASS—SICKNESS OF BAKR HADJI—RUDOK OFFICIALS COMMAND US TO RETREAT.

Early on the morning of the 18th May all was hustle and bustle at Niagzu. First of all we were sending off our sheep, followed by our hired yak. We had persuaded the owners to lend us twelve yak and three ponies as far as the other side of the pass called the Napu La. By sending these sheep and slow travelling yak ahead, we made a handicap of the march. We ourselves, after seeing nearly all the mules and ponies loaded up, followed next, leaving our own men behind to bring them on. Little did we dream that these same men, as soon as we had disappeared, were about to remain where they stood for two hours, idly waiting with all the animals loaded up and tied together in groups. Still we knew that just at present we had not sufficient power over them to rebuke them for their unwarrantable laziness.

Our road all day lay through stony valleys, enlivened by two cosy nooks called Mitpah Yungmah and Mitpah Conmah, where bright green grass flourished, and where a clear rivulet trickled over a sandy bed, sheltered by rocks and steep hills from the severe winds. At these two small camping grounds the officials from Rudok sometimes place a detachment of soldiers to prevent any foreigners from entering the country from that quarter. Although ignorant of it at the time, we discovered afterwards that we were in reality lucky not to have already met with opposition to our journey.

Far snugger than these two spots was the place called Nurtse, where we halted for the night. From here onwards our flock of sheep began to give way, and we had to sell fourteen cf them to our yakman for seven rupees. Our men might have eaten mutton all day long, and yet would have failed to keep pace with the death of the poor sheep.

We passed over a good deal of snow, the remnant of the winter, yet nothing sufficiently bad to impede us at all. We saw very little to shoot excepting a few kyang which were, of course, of no use to us. The kyang or wild ass of Tibet and Ladakh usually stands about fourteen hands; he is of a light brown colour, with white throat, belly, and legs; rather heavy in neck and shoulders, he is, nevertheless, a graceful mover, and there are few prettier sights than a herd of them scampering over some wide plain. Perhaps they have been startled by the unwonted sound of a rifle; off they go, full gallop. Soon curiosity outweighs fear, and back they come to have a look at the intruder. All standing in line they gaze at him from a hundred yards or so, apparently considering whether he is really dangerous or not; then, at a word from the leader, they wheel round and are off again, only to repeat the performance a few moments later, a performance that has ruined many a well-planned stalk before now.

Our guide, who in his time had been a salt collector, and knew the lay of the country, proved himself to be invaluable. Without him, the route we took would have been very hard indeed to find, and to him we owed the steady progress we daily made, not that we went at any rapid rate, or as a rule for any great length of time each day, but we were marching in the right direction, we were travelling east. By reason, too, of the assistance we received from the hired yak, we were able to ride ponies, and it was our wont, after starting off our sub-surveyor in front of every one else, to start ourselves ahead of the caravan, with our cook, Lassoo, likewise mounted. We carried our rifles and ammunition, while he carried in his saddlebags our cold breakfast with some tea leaves and a kettle to boil them in. As soon as we considered that half the march had been covered, we would halt by a stream, if there were one, or by a patch of snow, and boil our water. During these operations the caravan would catch us up again and march on ahead of us. In this way we were enabled to keep an eye upon our men without appearing to do so and thereby raise their suspicions.

On the third day from Niagzu we made our breakfast halt by the side of a valley close to some white stones. From this point two more lines of white stones lay at intervals, separated at an angle of some twenty degrees, and ran right away across the valley and over the opposite hills. We were told that this was a gazelle trap laid by the nomads. As soon as they can contrive to get gazelle into the space between these two lines, they drive them along between them. The gazelle being afraid of the stones continue to be driven on to where the stones meet, where they are easily captured, and sometimes a big haul is made. Although we saw plenty of gazelle about here, they were very timid, and as we had no time to go in for a recognised stalk, we shot none at this period, nor did we drive any between the two lines of white stones!

On the same evening, after crossing a waterless, stony plain for several miles, we reached Lake Treb, so famous for the salt that is taken away from its neighbourhood and carried into Ladakh. Salt, in fact, is collected from any spot within a hundred miles of Ladakh wherever it can be found. We had been marching twelve hours upon arrival at this lake, and it was already dark. Our chances of finding fresh water were very small, for our guide informed us that there was none to be had till we reached the other side of the lake, another four miles. Certainly there was no water running into the lake from this side, and the guide's statement would have been correct, had we not luckily found two small patches of snow and a little grazing close by.

Marching after sunset is without doubt a mistake, for when a halt is made the animals are unloaded carelessly and the loads are thrown about in any fashion; the men become tired and short-tempered, and should there be no moon, there is necessarily much delay in searching for the things that are required, especially when candles are at a minimum. The animals' grain is wasted as well as the men's rations, tents won't pitch, the water won't boil, animals stray, and everybody is blaming some one else.

All such petty annoyances, however, are very soon forgotten again, when, after a sharp frosty night, a glorious morning like that we experienced at Lake Treb announces the commencement of another day. Everything, even the crystallised salt, sparkled in those first brilliant rays, nor was there the remotest breath of wind; all was perfect stillness.

Far away south of us lay a towering range of snow peaks. Their distance seemed to increase their overpowering grandeur and one could with difficulty cease to gaze at each outline of this pure white magnificence. To east and north of us lay Lake Treb, backed by more ranges of mountains. Even Lake Treb itself, which on a dull day would have probably produced a suicidal despondency in the gayest of hearts, seemed to throw aside its natural gloom and rejoice like its grander neighbours at the cheer and brightness of the sun's first rays.

We were almost tempted to try a swim in the salt water, but on close examination we found the shore sloped down in terraces to the water's edge, where it became soft and treacherous. All this distinctly showed that the size of the lake must have been for many years gradually decreasing, and one is led to believe that such is the case in regard to most salt lakes in Tibet. The water, we were surprised to find, was not nearly so brackish as the surroundings would have induced one to believe. The only life we saw about it were a few Brahmini ducks and a couple of geese, which latter did not settle on the lake.

CROSSING THE NAPU LA (18,500 FEET HIGH).

Throughout Tibet we never saw any kind of game on any salt lake, with the exception of the Brahminis. At the east side of the lake lies the foot of the Napu La (pass).

All the way, a track leads up a narrow, stony, and rocky gorge, an almost impossible road after a fall of snow. To have taken our own animals over this pass carrying heavy loads would have been ruination to our plans, and we more than ever congratulated ourselves on having engaged the assistance of these fifteen extra hired animals. During these few days too, a certain amount of grain and bhoussa had been eaten, so that our mules and ponies on this occasion were not really heavily laden. At the top of the pass was the usual pile of stones and sticks which always have been erected in these regions, to denote that the summit is reached. The stones had been piled up in the centre of the col, while a little snow lay on the adjacent heights, which it connected.

A snap shot with the Kodak at some of our poor animals after a four hours' climb was an opportunity not to be lost, for the pass was nearly 18,500 feet above the sea level.* After descending for a short distance, we saw below us a fine glacier sloping downwards from north to south; to have attempted to cross it would have been madness itself. Around its southern edge we found a narrow and very steep track, which we followed, and as soon as we had found some fair grass, lower than and beyond the precincts of the glacier, we halted for the night, the place being called Tanjun. Although our own animals had managed thus early to cross this pass, yet it was not until the following afternoon that the hired yak arrived.

At this stage we began to taste of difficulties and casualties. First of all our hired transport would go no further, and henceforth we were entirely dependent upon our own animals. One of our men, too, Bakr Hadji by name, a Yarkandi, declared that he could proceed no more. He lay on his back, and, rolling his eyes, moaned continuously. We pitied him, for he seemed a fairly decent sort of fellow, but we had no desire, so early in our trip, to be encumbered by a sick man. We concluded that he was suffering from mountain sickness, though all the Argoons came to us protesting that Bakr Hadji was a Yarkandi, and like all other Yarkandis had a "chota dil," or in other

* Captain Deasy, who marched over this same pass a few weeks later, calculated its height to be over 19,000 feet.

words, was chicken-hearted; they maintained that they themselves were of very different kidney, and prepared to follow us wherever we might choose to go. It was, at any rate, manifest that our men had no intention of turning back just at present, for with the return of the hired yak-men an easy opportunity was open to them, and in all probability it would be their last. Our guide, who had served us so well, agreed to come along with us one more day.

Our road lay through a broad valley, which stretched away eastwards, with a small stream which took its rise from the glacier running down its centre. On either side were small grassy nullahs, suitable spots for encampments. The guide told us that in two or three days we should find ourselves amongst men living in a district called Rundore, and that we should have met men before had not a great many of them been summoned to strengthen the post at Rudok. He himself was anxious to turn back before coming amongst the men of Rundore, for he was convinced that he would meet with but scant civility for having been the cause of bringing us that way.

After we had marched down the valley for about a dozen miles, we overtook two nomads, and having supplied them with some tobacco and other small articles we thought they would appreciate, we entered into negotiations as to their willingness to come along with us and show us a road that ran eastwards, receiving in return for their services food and money, and some small present, such as a knife. They became in time ready to accept these proposals, and promised to show us the way to Mangtza-Tso (or lake) where they said we should arrive in four or five days. They, however, feared the Rundore men, and said that they would undoubtedly stop our progress, should they happen to learn that we were in their vicinity. Yet they hoped before meeting with any opposition to take a turning up a certain valley to the left, and thus escape observation.

Throughout this valley we found sand-grouse, kyang, yak, and the heads of several dead ovis ammon; doubtless some of the adjacent ranges abounded in game. But at the present time we were still living on our sheep, nor had we time to waste in shikar pure and simple, for however fine a head we might have knocked over, we could never have

OUR THREE RUNDORE GUIDES.

dreamed of carrying it with us; besides, we valued each cartridge, and had no inclination to waste any on a useless errand.

It was remarkable that although we were over 16,000 feet high, above the sea level, yet we were glad to cast aside our lambskin waistcoats and thickly-lined puttoo coats, and bask in the sun over our breakfast in our shirt-sleeves, while some of our men became ill, partly on account of the warm climate during the day, but chiefly from the excessive amount of mutton they ate. At night-time there were well over twenty degrees of frost.

We had not marched very far with our two guides before they pointed out to us two roads. One road continued down the valley we were in for a few more miles, and then turned up to the left hand along another nullah. The second road led over the hills into the same nullah, cutting off a corner. We had already discovered that with baggage animals the longest way round is the shortest way there, or in other words, that a dozen miles of level marching is easier for them, and takes less out of them, than half a dozen miles of steep climbing, which almost invariably did harm to one or more animals. We therefore sent on the mules to make the detour, while we ourselves cut across the hills. Even during this short climb we saw both ovis ammon and goa, and hitting off the nullah before the arrival of our caravan, we sat down by the stream that wound its way to the main one, and, having found some dry droppings, made our fire and the water boil.

As time wore on, we began to grow anxious about our caravan, and suspected that something adverse must have happened. We were just about to retrace our steps, when the leading mules made their appearance round the corner, and in less than an hour we were once more amongst our followers. The only deficiency was the absence of the two guides, who having pointed out this route, had refused to go any further.

Now we saw the folly of having left our caravan even for that short period, for had we been present we should never have allowed the guides to leave us in that fashion. We now began to suspect there was something in the wind, and decided that our best plan would be to march as far as we could, and perhaps avoid contact with anybody.

Our road unfortunately began to wind too much to our left, and, not wishing to run the risk of taking our animals in the wrong direction, we called a halt, resolving to explore further ahead, and find out whether there was not some other nullah that ran more eastwards, before launching forth the whole of our caravan along an uncertain route.

Shortly after we had unloaded, and while the animals were picking up what little grazing they were able to get, our two guides suddenly reappeared accompanied by several other men, and, during the evening, others continued to flock in from Rundore. We invited the headmen to our tent and endeavoured to persuade them to allow some one to show us the way to Mangtza-Tso. At first they would not hear of such a proposal; they denied the existence of any road, and even hinted at opposing us. Thereupon we adopted fresh tactics, and quietly told them that if such were their game we should retrace our steps down the nullah we were in and march down the main nullah right through the Rundore district on to Lhassa. This produced a consultation resulting in their willingness to show us a road that would take us direct to Mangtza-Tso. Everything was finally settled agreeably to both sides, and we became friends for the time being.

On their departure from our presence, we were congratulating ourselves upon the good fortune that continued to follow us, when to our astonishment some officials from Rudok rode in in hot haste, and throughout the night and following morning we constantly heard fresh arrivals, the rapid jingling of the bells which were hung round the ponies' necks proclaiming how hurriedly they were riding. It was dark, and we could hear men's voices from the stream that ran down the centre of the nullah, while we ourselves had encamped close to the mountain side. We could see they had lit some fires and were sitting and standing around them, occupied in eager conversation. From the light of the flames we could see their matchlocks standing up against one another on the ground. Our hopes, which only a short time ago had been so sanguine, had now received a severe blow, and we wondered, yet guessed, what the intentions of these men might be.

In order to solve this mysterious gathering we sent and invited the chief men to our tent. Two of them were before very long ushered in by Esau, intelligent-looking fellows enough and open to hear all we had to say, yet staunch in their determination to obstruct our further march onwards up the nullah we were in. Threats, bribes of money and goods, as well as every other kind of argument, entirely failed to carry any weight with these Rudok officials, for they very wisely remarked that "if we allow you to go this road, we shall for such an act of disobedience undoubtedly lose our heads, whereas if we stop you we shall receive a reward." They maintained that they would rather risk being killed in attempting to oppose us than meet with certain death for negligence of their work in letting us go through. Argue as we might, nothing would alter their determination, namely, that the only road open to us was back by the road we had come. It was by this time growing late, and the officials took their leave of us.

Throughout the still night we could hear the loud talk and peals of laughter that rang out from the groups of men who had bivouacked by the stream.

At daybreak we discovered that more men had swollen the gathering, but nevertheless we began to load up as usual, and having distributed our sporting rifles and guns amongst our muleteers, tried to impress upon them the necessity of having to fight our way through, should we meet with opposition.

A few hundred yards from our encampment, in the direction in which we were anxious to go, was a stone wall, built probably as a shelter against the wind, and behind this the Rundore and Rudok men had taken up a position, and from their demonstrations it was evident that they did not intend to let us go by easily.

As soon as our last mule had been loaded and we had begun to move towards the wall, our opponents rushed forth and began to drive our animals back, meeting with little or no resistance from our faint-hearted followers, who had no pluck to face superior numbers, whose actions and feelings were those of fanatics. A loaded revolver pointed

× WALL BEHIND WHICH THE TIBETANS FORMED UP.

at a few paces distant at the chest of one of them had no other result than to induce the man to tear aside his garments, and, showing his bare flesh, point to us to shoot at it. Such frenzied determination on the part of these Tibetans proved to us that we should never make any headway in the desired direction, and that our only chance of being able to do so would have been to shoot the most determined of our obstructionists. But inasmuch as we had not started on the expedition with the remotest inclination to shoot Tibetans, we stayed our hands. Even supposing we had shot some of them, it would have been a very hazardous step to have risked a serious scrimmage almost on our very frontier. We also reflected upon the results of such an affair; not only would it bar any future travellers from peaceably entering the country from this direction, but we ourselves would be pestered for many days to come by an increasing force of Rundore and Rudok men following in our rear.

Therefore, after we had been driven back some distance and were left alone again, we pitched a fresh camp with the intention of remaining another day, in hopes that something or other would turn up in our favour. Perhaps we might get round these officials after all, or perhaps others of more influence would in the meantime arrive from Rudok and allow us to go the way we wanted, when they became convinced that we had no intention of making an attempt on Lhassa.

Such were our faint hopes as we commenced unloading, for we dreaded beyond measure the very idea of having to recross the Napu La a second time, being alone dependent upon ourselves for doing so.

Throughout the morning we tried every means we could think of to be allowed to march up this nullah, which they called Kerambutabuk. The officials informed us that no other Englishmen had ever been there before, and that, had their men, whose duty it was, been properly on the look-out, we ought never to have been permitted to come so far. These officials were quite reasonable and sensible men, and hoped we would not fight, for they said that war between the English and Tibetans would result in consequence.

It was a very cold and raw day we spent in this Kerambutabuk nullah, and most of the time, too, sleet was falling. The only noise we heard, besides an occasional sudden blast, was the firing off of the Tibetan matchlocks further up the valley, and the tinkling bells on the ponies of fresh arrivals as they trotted past a few hundred yards from our tents. There had been so much ringing all day long that, by the end of the day, quite a small army had been amassed.

We told our friends that we wished to go into Turkistan, but the upshot of all our war meetings ended in our having to retire by the same way we had come, namely, over the Napu La, thence northwards to the frontier pass called Lanak La. They agreed to give us four men to show us the way as far as Lanak La, but did not see the force of giving us any help with our transport.

CHAPTER VI.

OUR RETREAT—CROSSING THE BORDERLAND OF TIBET—A STRANGE ACCOUCHEMENT—SPORT—PONIES SHOT.

On the following morning we commenced our retirement, followed by a large body of Tibetans, armed with matchlocks and spears. Most of them were very dirty-looking little fellows, with long black locks, strongly reminding one of some of *Punch's* "Prehistoric Peeps." Their guns, which we examined, consisted of a long smooth-bore barrel, roughly fastened on to a stock, with a wooden prong on which to rest the gun when firing.

At the corner of this nullah, where it joined the main Rundore valley, was a small nomad encampment called Kerinagar. These people lived in some very dirty and dilapidated old tents, and possessed a small amount of grain and a few sheep, but the prices they demanded for them were high. Close by was a hill called Chotenchenbo, conspicuous amongst a chain of others. The hill is probably volcanic, as these nomads informed us that every month much noise was emitted from the summit, which has so worked upon their imaginations that they hold it in the deepest veneration, and on the 15th day of each month numbers of people from the surrounding district come to worship and propitiate the spirit of the mountain.

We found it heartrending work having to retrace our steps to the Napu La again, and in order to waste as little time as possible, and reach new ground, we made long marches, testing our animals to the utmost. Certainly there is a shorter road to Lanak La crossing over the Serai La and cutting off a corner. But here again we were foiled, for the men we sent on ahead to discover the possibility of going that way reported the pass to be deep in snow and absolutely impassable for ponies and mules. As we marched along this valley we had more leisure for shikar, as our surveying, etc., had already been completed. Malcolm knocked over an antelope, and being alone at the time, hallaled the animal himself; but our followers, being filled with pride and mutton, declared that nothing on earth would induce them to eat the meat, for it had not been hallaled by one after their own religion. Little did they dream at the time how, before very long, they would have to change their minds and be a little less particular. Our four nomad guides thoroughly enjoyed their frugal feast, as they sat round a fire of droppings, boiling what meat we gave them in a small pot, while the bones themselves, after having scraped off every particle of meat and skin from them, they broke between two stones, and ate the marrow raw, just as it was, without any boiling or stewing.

This was the last occasion on which we saw anything of our big dog Tundu. He wasn't going over that Napu La again, and having had a royal repast over portions of the slain antelope, he perhaps imagined that if he remained where he was there would be an equally big meal every evening. Nearly a year after this desertion of Tundu we learnt, when we were back in India again, that this dog had turned up one day at the Residency in Leh, where Capt. Trench was living, in somewhat reduced condition. He must have found his way back of his own accord over three hundred miles. Our little fox terrier bitch Ruby had no hesitation in re-crossing the Napu La, for nothing on earth would have induced her to remain with the nomads, amongst whom she had made her presence most obnoxious.

We made a long, toilsome march over the pass again, down to the entrance of the gorge, close by Lake Treb. There we found two small pools of fresh water close to our camp, but no grass whatever, so there was nothing left for us but to lessen our loads by doling out a pound of grain all round and three bags of bhoussa.

During the recrossing of this pass, there were a few of the animals who were unable to keep pace with the majority, necessitating one of the men being left behind to bring them on. This was the first experience of many such delays we were about to meet with during the next few months.

In this gorge we picked up some curiously-pointed stones, relics, perhaps, of a bygone age.

Owing to the great care we took of our animals when recrossing the Napu La, they were better off as regards sore backs and galls than we could have anticipated. Their chief ailment showed itself in the shoulder, at the point where the front ends of the saddle terminated. The shoulders used to swell from the irritation caused, and matter would form, yet there appeared to be but very little pain attached to it, and after the swelling had broken, and the place had healed, the animal never suffered again from the same cause. When possible, we used to change the palan with the wooden saddle of another animal, and in some cases averted the evil altogether. There is no doubt, with properly padded palans so as to prevent the ends from pressing against the shoulders, or if the ends themselves were bevelled off, there would be none of these sore shoulders at all. Our sore backs up to the present time were practically nil.

As we marched northwards along the eastern shore of our old friend Lake Treb, shut in on one hand by the mountains, and on the other by the water, the sun's morning rays beat down with surprising warmth at this height of just under 16,000 feet, and finding no fresh water running into the lake we were tempted to test the water of Treb itself. It turned out to be far less saltish than that on the other side of the lake, and on giving our ponies and mules free access to the water's edge they drank the precious liquid eagerly. The four guides informed us that the nomads frequently bring their ponies to the lake to drink the water for its medicinal purposes. It was more than ever a wonder to us to find the water very nearly fresh, for along the banks there lay a white crust of saline particles resembling snow, and when the wind blew, a cloud of this fine white powder was raised, not at all unlike sea spray. In some places close to the edge was a layer of ice.

At nightfall we halted by the northern edge of this lake by a fresh water spring. Here we found numerous Brahminis and a few geese, and a fair amount of antelope dwelt in the hills close by.

That evening the wind blew with sufficient force to create considerable waves in the lake. The water itself was of dark Prussian blue, its colour being intensified by the background of snow mountains and the last rays of the setting sun. This grand sight, together with the clouds of fine salt, reminded one vividly of the sea itself. Our ponies and mules were let loose all the night long, but as no other grass could be seen, excepting what was close to the spring, they had no occasion to stray; besides, they had really not recovered from the effects of the useless double crossing of the Napu La.

We left the lake behind us blessed with another brilliant morning, the sun again becoming intensely hot about 8 or 9 o'clock. At this time, we used to find this the hottest hour of the day, before the wind had come; then, with the rising wind, clouds were very often blown over too, making the middle of the day sometimes quite chilly. After sunset again the wind would drop, and every star would shine out clearly and brightly.

This same day, the 29th May, we reached the foot of the eastern side of the pass, called Lanak La, the very same pass that Bower had crossed some five years ago, when, first of explorers in this direction, he made his famous journey across Tibet, passing a few miles north of Lhassa. We found fairly good grass growing here, the best, in fact, we had come across since leaving Niagzu. We decided, therefore, to stop a day and give our transport a chance to recover their strength, especially as on that very evening two ponies and one mule had failed to reach camp. Our casualties were already beginning in earnest.

It was now a full month since the day when our caravan, under Shahzad Mir, had started from Leh for the Pangong Lake. They had only traversed 397 miles and were already beginning to give way, yet we had only just reached the borderland of Tibet, for Lanak La separates Ladakh from Tibet, and our journey across this country only commenced from here. Our store of grain and bhoussa was now reduced to thirteen maunds of grain and twenty maunds of bhoussa, while nearly a month's rations of the men had been consumed. That evening there were twenty-four degrees of frost, and little Ruby, who during her life had only felt the severity of an Indian winter, begged for a warm seat, and was allowed one on my knees beneath a thick fur-lined coat, while we made our evening repast. Her appreciation of this comfortable bed she signified by giving birth to five pups. Three of these little beggars we soon put out of their misery, and after the first day Ruby would have nothing to do with the remaining couple. They were placed in a box well protected from any wind or cold, placed between some bags of bhoussa on the back of a quiet mule. Ruby, however, would only condescend to cross Tibet in this lordly fashion for one day. Her nose was outside the box all throughout the march, with no consideration for her two little pups. On the second march she jumped out altogether, for she far more enjoyed trotting along by our sides and putting her nose into every little hole with the chance of finding shikar.

On the morning after our arrival at the foot of Lanak La, we woke up with the astounding news that our four nomad guides had deserted; with what object it was difficult to imagine. We had intended before parting with them to have given them some slight remuneration, for they had been willing helpers, and had proved themselves useful to us in many ways.

On leaving this place, we wanted, if possible, to strike off a route which is called the Polu road, running in a northerly direction into Turkistan, and after following this road for a few days to strike due east again.

Our men, however, seemed more in favour of crossing the Lanak La into Ladakh, and finding a way from thence into Turkistan, and thence across to China. An idea of this kind we would not entertain for a moment, inasmuch as we should have at once given up the object of our expedition. They enumerated the amount of supplies that had already been consumed, and were anxious to travel as far as Khotan, and lay in a fresh store before making for China. We explained to them the distance we were from Khotan, and the idiocy of adopting such a measure, and reassured them that as long as we had guns and ammunition there was no need to fear of ever running short of food, and even if we did that we could easily strike north again at any moment, and reach Turkistan in a very short time. Fortunately, that same day, when Malcolm was away spying out the country, he shot a yak, and as one of the muleteers was at hand to hallal the beast, he and his comrades were enabled to feast on all the tit-bits they fancied to their heart's content, helping considerably to put them in a better frame of mind.

At daybreak, the man who remained behind with the

mule and two ponies, came into camp with the former, declaring that the ponies were too weak to go any further. Not wishing to lose any animals so early in our trip, we sent back other men with grain, but they too returned, corroborating what had already been told us by the first man. As we could not leave them to die slowly in that cold, bleak land, a poor return for the good service they had done for us, we sent Shahzad Mir on a stout pony with a carbine to go and shoot them. His journey was, however, unnecessary, for he found that both the ponies had already died.

Whenever a mule or pony lagged behind it was our custom to leave a man or two men with them, as well as clothing and food for both; but in nine cases out of ten this arrangement was a waste of labour, for if an animal is incapable of carrying a load any further, the most satisfactory and economical way is to shoot the poor brute, unless there is at one's disposal time to halt for three or four days by some good grass, giving it a chance of recovering some of its lost strength. Without being able to do this, an animal will be driven along for several days carrying no load, and at the same time, it must be remembered, he is being fed up with more than his full share of grain, which the other animals are carrying, in the hope that he will recover sufficiently to earn his keep. When once they have given in, and there is no chance of a halt whereby to recoup, it is false economy to drive them along any further. Yet we did this over and over again, to our own detriment, for one forms a great attachment for such patient and long-suffering animals as our mules and ponies proved themselves to be.

The district of Lanak La is a good shooting-ground for yak and antelope, and it would well repay a sportsman shooting in Ladakh to quietly pop over the frontier and enjoy his sport in secrecy.

CHAPTER VII.

A COLD NIGHT — DEATH OF MULE — A FRESH-WATER LAKE — BAD WEATHER—DEATH OF THE FAVOURITE WHITE PONY— BY A SALT LAKE — ILLNESS OF TOKHTA — I SEARCH FOR MISSING ANIMALS.

WE left our camping ground at Lanak La on Sunday, the 31st May, and failing to find the sign of any track running northwards, we tried to make out by which route Bower had gone, but our only map was drawn to such a very small scale that we could decide on nothing with any certainty. Riding ahead on our ponies, we found our easiest way was to continue up the nullah we were in, which led over an easy pass, from the summit of which we looked back over the Lanak La.

In spite of our extensive views, we could discover no route running in any direction whatever, and having come so far, we decided to give up all searching for routes and to find a way for ourselves, marching due east as much as possible, and, failing that, north rather than south. Quite naturally, therefore, we descended the other side of the pass just the same as any one else would have done, and then we found a range of mountains north of us, and another range south of us, compelling us to take to a rather narrow nullah which eventually debouched in the early afternoon into a broad valley some miles across, running in an easterly direction, and bounded north and south by ranges of snow-tipped hills. Thus the actual finding of our way was not such a difficult undertaking as one might have expected. We could see the valley stretching far away to the east, and calculated that we had some days of clear sailing before us.

We trotted on ahead in search of grass and water to halt by. Straight in front of us, we noticed what we took to be snow in the middle of the valley, but the nearer we came to it the farther off it appeared to be, and we were most anxious to reach that snow, for otherwise we saw no chance of finding any water. We finally concluded that it was a hopeless job to try and get there; and as the sun was setting, and a short distance in front of us we saw some antelope, we knew there must be some grass close by and probably some water too. Such proved to be the case; there was a small stretch of very short growth with two little pools of rain-water, as good a camping ground as we could have expected to find that night.

A strong wind was blowing from the south-west, enough to cut us in two, and as the skies clouded over pretty quickly, we had no chance of taking any observations. I really felt inwardly thankful that the clouds had come up so thick, for it is no joke observing stars with twenty-five degrees of frost and a keen wind. Unless the clouds absolutely obscure the view and one slips in between the blankets without attempting observations, one's conscience feels a prick of guilt.

Our mules and ponies must have suffered from the cold that evening, and seemed to find but little amusement in nibbling at the short grass. Throughout the night we heard some of them becoming entangled in the guy ropes of our tent in their endeavours to find some small amount of shelter from the blast. And it was a marvellous thing how the tent managed to stand at all.

Despite these and other divers annoyances, we both fell off to sleep till daybreak, when all seemed clothed in perfect stillness—the whole atmosphere was calm. It was difficult at first to collect our thoughts and to remember where we were and what had befallen us. Why was it we could hear no sign of man or beast? Something unusual must surely have happened. In another moment we were up and outside the tent; the wind had completely died away, and everything and everywhere was covered with a fresh layer of snow. The men were silent in their tents, some of our mules lay without moving, others stood with drooping heads, and, on counting their number, we found that several were missing. It was not very long before we found one of these latter; there he lay stretched out close to our own tent, as dead as dead could be. We felt sad for the poor brute, for little had we thought whilst we had been abusing him for fiddling with our guy ropes, that he had been actually dying from cold or from some other painful cause. We turned away from the corpse, and tried to forget our own selfishness.

At this moment the sun was just appearing and omened a fine and warm day, arousing us to the fact that the snow would soon melt, and if that happened, we should have no small difficulty in tracking the animals that had strayed. We at once turned out our men and sent some of them off on our stoutest ponies to search for the deserters.

This morning's disastrous work undoubtedly laid the seeds of many more deaths to come. As to our own riding ponies, which had been ridden by the muleteers in the search, so much was taken out of them that we were only able to ride them for a very few more days, and ever afterwards were solely dependent upon our own feet. The five delinquents were eventually found about five miles back in the nullah we had come from the previous day, but they were in so exhausted a condition that one of them could scarcely drag itself along, let alone take a few pounds' weight of luggage, in fact, he never reached another camp.

Even at this early stage there was no use blinding ourselves to the truth that there were a goodish number of the animals that could not possibly last out many more days. Had we been able to find good grass and water together, our best plan would have been to halt there for a few days; then, again, it must be remembered that during that period the men would be eating their rations all the same, and probably more, without making any onward progress at all.

It was almost noon before we were off, and by that time all the snow, excepting on the tops of the hills, had completely thawed, for the day was warm and pleasant. Again we fortunately had easy marching down the valley, and we went towards the patch of snow we had been so anxious to reach the previous day, but we never seemed to get there; the illusion was caused by vapour or steam rising up from the salt ground and hanging over it like a white sheet, and when we conjectured we were on the very spot, we could see nothing at all.

After fourteen miles we came to a fresh-water lake completely frozen over, having been seven hours over the march. Knowing how deceptive the distance is across such lakes at this great height, namely, just over 16,000 feet, we decided to halt where we were; besides, there was fairly good grass, and a bright moon for observations, but no water for the mules. The man, too, whom we had left behind to bring in the exhausted pony, had not turned up, and despite our discharging our guns pretty frequently, he never reached camp that night at all. In addition to all this, my own pony, which had made the march riderless, had some difficulty in struggling in. We here gave our beasts three bags of bhoussa, leaving us only thirteeen more, and allowed them to graze till 8 o'clock the following morning. At that hour the sun had begun to thaw the lake, and on reaching the further side, after a most slippery walk, we found a small stream had just commenced to trickle, a great boon for our beasts.

That same evening, after marching over a stretch of undulating ground, with a certain amount of grass in some of the nullahs, frequented, too, by antelope and kyang, we came to a large salt-water lake. There was but poor grass around, but a stream of good fresh water. Ahead of us, on all sides of the lake, the land appeared absolutely barren and arid, possibly on the southern side there might have been a little hidden grass; but then, again, had we marched south, we did not know that we might not meet with another show of opposition, so stuck to our original plan of steering north when in doubt. We began at this early stage to recognise the superiority of the mules over the ponies, for three of the latter could only just crawl into camp at a late hour in a very weak condition.

Another snowstorm prevented us from making a fresh start before 11 o'clock, and as the snow had put a stop to the grazing, poor as it was, we prepared some bhoussa for our remaining thirty-five animals, yet only thirty-four came hurrying up for this much appreciated food. There stood the thirty-fifth, a few hundred yards off, gazing at the remainder, who had their noses hidden deep into the chopped straw. Poor brute! he could not reach the spot, his condition was so weak and impoverished; there he stood, resembling mostly a bag of bones, a grievous sight for us: for this was the very white pony who had been such a great friend of the black mule, and he had struggled hard for some days to keep up with the caravan. After he had been shot, we were glad to leave the spot to try and forget the sad event.

By reason of the late snowstorm, the going along the edge of the lake was heavy in the extreme, so much so that we lost a small black mule from exhaustion, the only advantage gained by this disaster being that fewer animals were left to eat up the grain. The land was barren and useless to a degree, with no chance of finding any fresh water or grass; the former difficulty was overcome by collecting some snow, and the latter by being extravagant with our bhoussa. The ground fell in terraces from the hills that rose up some distance from the lake, and was split up by several deep, narrow and harsh nullahs running into it; nor was there any sign of life, with the exception of an occasional startled hare.

Although there were twenty-four degrees of frost that night, yet at 6 o'clock in the morning we were eating our breakfast with comfort in the open, by the edge of the salt lake. There was not a single ripple on the dark blue water, whose colour was only rivalled by the magnificent sky, nor was there a sound excepting the murmurs that came from our own camp. Although enjoying this peaceful scene for a few minutes, we were all the time getting most anxious about our inability to find grass, as another few days of this kind of marching would have been most disastrous. As far as we could see, a barren salt land extended due east, and we were therefore very likely following a regular zone of salt country, and, to get clear of this belt, it was advisable to strike north.

At the eastern extremity of the lake, we found a nullah running in that direction. This we followed, a gradual ascent between two ranges to the top of an easy pass, where we found a very small stream and fairly good grass. It was freezing hard by the time our animals reached this spot, defeating us in our hopes of being able to water them properly. Three ponies and a mule failed to reach camp, and we grew more anxious than ever to hit off a suitable place for a day's halt.

It was a grand, hot morning as we commenced the descent of this pass, so much so that we were somewhat puzzled to know really what amount of clothes we ought to put on to suit the extraordinary variety in the temperature. As soon as we had come down a few hundred feet, we came to a more hospitable-looking country. Grass grew in some of the valleys, and water, too, was to be had, while a herd of antelope close by gave us an easy chance of knocking some of them over. Early in the afternoon we came to a stretch of fairly good grazing, and in the sandy nullah close at hand, a foot or so beneath the surface, flowed unlimited water. Antelope were plentiful and tame around this spot, and having fallen into such clover, we agreed to remain there over the following day.

During this necessary halt our time was by no means wasted. Men and animals had to be doctored up, the shoeing had to be seen to; there was mending, repairing, washing, sketching, mapping, and writing to be done; above all things, we began to overhaul our impedimenta to see if there were not a few articles we might dispense with. As it was, we had only been making some nine or ten miles a day, and even with this care we feared to think of or to count our losses. At this spot we left a yakdan, with some horse-shoes and a book or two inside. Whoever may happen to come this way will find something worth having. One of our muleteers, too, named Tokhta, was so ill that he could do no work; he had swollen to an abnormal size, more resembling a balloon than a human being.

Looking ahead of us, it seemed as though a range of mountains barred our road, and our only chance was to follow the sandy nullah from whence we had obtained the water. It was now covered with snow and ice owing to another storm during the night. On our left hand were some very heavy craggy-looking rocks, and through them was a very narrow gorge, only a few yards across, sorely tempting us to follow it through and see what would be disclosed on the further side. It almost invited one to enter and explore, but we feared marching too far north, and followed instead the nullah we were in, which eventually led to the summit of a pass. The way was steep and rocky, and the sun so powerful that we slung our coats across our arms and loitered on the top for the breeze and the caravan. Snow lay there in heaps, a welcome quencher to our thirst. This was a stiff climb for our caravan, the height of the pass being nearly 17,000 feet. Having waited till they were nearly at the top, we began to descend again the other side.

Quite suddenly we seemed to be transplanted into a new zone, for a cutting snowstorm blew straight in our faces. We were almost frozen, and any portion of the head we exposed suffered severely. We looked for some overhanging rock that would serve for a shelter, but there the cold became so intense that we preferred to fight the elements and keep in motion. As soon as we had completed the descent we found a broad valley stretching east and west, apparently to eternity. We walked along this, for our ponies had become too weak for us ever to think of riding them again, and sought grass and water for making a halt by. Having found a fairly suitable spot, and waited for a considerable length of time, we were perplexed to hear no sign of the caravan. They would have to come thus far, for until they did they would find no fit place to camp in.

Darkness and cold came upon us, and we kept up an intermittent fusillade till eight o'clock, when a distant shout in reply revealed to us that they were at length coming. But alas! although some of the mules walked in fit and strong, others came in wretchedly weak, and, worst of all, six animals and three complete loads had been abandoned altogether.

This was a crushing bit of news, coming as it did just after our day's halt, when we had expected to make such good headway. The men, too, declared that these six animals had all died; but we suspected, from their demeanour and the way they spoke and behaved, that very likely some of them had been left behind in good condition for a reason, namely, that should any of the men take it into their heads to turn back, they would have the assistance of one or two stout animals to carry what they wanted. We knew they had been taking but little care of the transport, even in the proper adjustment of their loads.

In order to satisfy our suspicions, we arranged that Malcolm should remain in camp, or, better still, shift the camp a mile or so further on to a better spot, while I should take a man and go back in search of the mules and ponies that had been left behind. After a five-mile tramp, we came to a dead black pony, and another mile further on found a single mule grazing, to whom we gave some of the grain we had brought with us. In another nullah close by was a second dead pony and another mule, which must have very shortly died had we not hastened on his end with a revolver. The fifth, a grey mule, we found grazing, apparently enjoying himself. The sixth, a dun-coloured pony, we could discover nowhere. He was a useful pony, and had probably wandered a long way in search of good grass. We returned triumphant to camp with the grey and black mules, the latter especially doing good work afterwards for some weeks to come. Had one of us not gone back we must have lost the services of two strong mules, which would have been due solely to the men's laziness, and we could not help thinking that they, the dun pony, and the three loads of food, had been temporarily abandoned with the intention of helping some of the men on a return journey to Ladakh. My satisfaction was, however, marred on return to camp by the news that my own riding pony had succumbed in the night.

CHAPTER VIII.

LAKE LIGHTEN—INTENSE HEAT—AN OLD FIREPLACE—SERIOUS ACCIDENT THROUGH OVER-HASTE OF MULES TO DRINK—A COUP D'ŒIL—THE FIRST FLOWER—OUR PET SHEEP—ANOTHER FRESH-WATER LAKE—A PLEASANT BATH—DEATH OF ANIMALS AND DEARTH OF GRAIN.

WE were now reduced to twenty-eight animals, and we knew our muleteers to be so careless and untrustworthy a lot, that we resolved that henceforth one of us should always remain with them and the mules—never, in fact, let them out of our sight. This would ensure the animals being properly cared for, and would be a prevention against the muleteers forming any scheme for desertion. We decided, too, to make very easy marches. We continued to see snow mountains in all directions, and somehow or other managed to steer our way amongst them, either east or north-east, over valleys and plains or stony nullahs, but we were most unfortunate as to finding good grass. It must have been too early in the year, for in many places it was just beginning to sprout.

Owing to the heavy loss to our transport we could only march some four or five miles the next day, which brought us to a big fresh-water lake, completely frozen over, resembling a large white sheet. Here we resolved to lighten our loads, and left on the ground a number of cartridges, horse shoes, cooking utensils, clothes, candles, etc., besides giving the mules and ponies a feast of forty pounds of flour made into bread. Some old pistols, rather heavy ones, which we had brought with us as presents for natives, we allowed the men to carry themselves, on the condition that should we require them as presents we would buy them back from them, otherwise they might retain them for ever. Every one, too, carried a certain number of cartridges, the men doing so under the proviso that we would lend them a rifle when game was close to camp.

LAKE "LIGHTEN" (WE LIGHTENED OUR LOADS HERE).

To celebrate the occasion we christened this lake "Lake Lighten." The size of this frozen water was deceptive. Our direction took us over a portion of it which we reckoned to be about a mile across, but in reality this turned out to be six miles. On the other side we found good grass, and in a snug corner a very tiny fresh-water lake, or what we should call at home a duck-pond. Here were geese, antelope, and kyang, so we were able to make a substantial addition to our larder, which at that time was in the same state as Mother Hubbard's cupboard. This spot, too, became famous in its way for two events. First, it was here discovered that one of our carbines had been left behind the day before, and the men were so unwilling that none would go back to fetch it. To do more than they were obliged to do was quite against their grain. Secondly, another mule had to be shot, for he was too weak to rise and march. The next day another pony met the same fate, and we began to think our ammunition was more useful for this purpose than for killing game, which, as a rule, was scarce. Our march took us another six miles over the ice, and on the way we narrowly escaped losing one of the best mules, who dropped his hind legs in a crack; luckily, he was extricated unhurt, but he might easily have broken a leg.

On the 13th of June we camped by another salt lake. From the top of a pass we had been rewarded with a very fine view of it, for the water under a cloudless sky was of a wonderfully bright blue, backed as it was by massive snow mountains, but detestable when near for its uselessness. As we marched along its banks, the heat was intense, the maximum thermometer registering 105° in the sun, and although there was no fresh water to be seen, we found some by digging, though not enough to satisfy our mules, and on making our tea, its constituency was, to say the least of it, thick; perhaps Esau's description of it was nearer the mark, for he said it was like jam. On warm days like this we were always glad to discard our heavy boots, and coats, while our little terrier Ruby could only lie and pant for breath. Such heat in the Chang at a height of between fifteen and sixteen thousand feet may seem to some people incredible. Its effect upon our animals was most disastrous, sapping their strength in no small degree, and on this account we decided in future to make an earlier march.

In this little nullah we found three stones which from the way they were placed showed that they had been used for a fireplace, but not at any very recent date, more likely two or three years ago. This was the first sign of mankind since leaving Lanak La, and had probably been made by some nomads who had wandered in this direction. We here consumed two more of our remaining three bags of bhoussa, thereby still more lightening our loads.

According to our intention, camp was astir at 3.30 A.M., and we were well off before 5 o'clock, and even at that hour it was so warm that our gloves were not even wanted. It was a grand morning, and as we faced the glorious rising sun, we were blinded by its brilliancy and found it most difficult at first to see precisely where we were going. After passing into a fairly grassy valley, the home of the kyang, we descended to a fresh-water lake. At the time when the caravan was approaching this water, we were both some distance off, shooting and taking observations, and blamed ourselves afterwards at having left the muleteers. These men knew the animals had been short of water lately, yet took no step to prevent the calamity which naturally occurred at the sight of a clean fresh-water lake. They, poor brutes, forgetful of the loads on their backs, with one accord made a simultaneous rush to satisfy their thirst. The water, although only two or three feet deep, concealed a treacherous bottom of several feet of soft mud and as they plunged in further and deeper, a general collapse ensued, and the mules and ponies lay in a heap unable to extricate themselves, with a good chance too of being drowned. Nor did any of our baggage benefit by the soaking it received. Each animal as he lay had to be unloaded separately, no easy undertaking, and then pulled out of the mud on his side by head and tail, by four or five men. Furthermore the weight of each load was considerably increased by this disaster, and as the going along the edge of the water was not of the best, there were more stragglers than ever into our new camp, two of them not even getting in at all. Around the lake were several antelope, while geese and Brahmini ducks were fairly plentiful.

There appeared to be no outlet, and from the nature of the soil for some distance round the lake, we judged that its size varied in accordance with the rainfall. From this lake two routes were open to us, one running in a somewhat northerly direction through a good, grassy, watered valley, which we should have liked to have taken; but as the other route led almost due east, we took it, and perhaps made a wrong decision, for we came to a dried-up country, with small salt lakes, and had to dig deep in a dry river bed for water. The antelope we had slain made its mark upon the men, for the quantities of meat they ate made them lazy and late in making a start the next morning.

As we moved off at six o'clock, there was a light mist hanging over the land, with no breath of wind to dissolve it, a pretty sure sign of a hot day. We began ascending for some miles, and then dipped into a dry river bed. This looked a likely place to find water again by digging, and as fair grass grew around, we decided to halt. We had only marched seven miles, yet there were stragglers, and four loads had to be abandoned. This loss we could ill afford, so agreed to halt another day, when we could send back some of our stoutest mules and recover the baggage. We had no fear whatever of a stranger turning up during the night and running off with some of the goods. As we intended remaining another day at this spot, it was indispensable that we should contrive some means for watering the animals properly. We found water flowing three or four feet below the surface, but a single hole was very quickly emptied, and then we had to wait until it had refilled, so that watering in this kind of way would have taken half the day. Every one, therefore, was set to work to dig water-holes. We carried with us a large waterproof sheet, and having made a trench in the sand, in the shape of a trough, we spread the sheet over it, and then filled it up from the various holes. In this way the mules and ponies could come and drink as often and as much as they liked, and they probably would have drunk more than they did, had not the water been somewhat saltish, with certain purging qualities. We also set about lessening the loads again, and many of the articles which we had imagined before to be absolutely necessary were here discarded. Two

17TH JUNE. THREE OF OUR TENTS ARE ABANDONED AT THIS SPOT.

of our five little tents were abandoned, and we took the opportunity of photographing our last entire camp. Other things, too, were left, for our animals were dying at an alarming rate. Out of our original thirty-nine only twenty-one remained, including the riding pony of Shahzad Mir. Our own riding days had before this come to an end.

Yet we had only come 150 miles from Lanak La, but our hopes of coming across nomads, from whom we might either purchase yak or exchange some of our own worn-out mules, strengthened us in our determination not to entertain for a moment the idea of turning back. The men, too, were so confident that we should ere long fall in with nomads that they became lavish with their rations. Instead of continuing the practice of doling their allowance out to them every three or four days, they had latterly been permitted to have the full run of it, after being made well aware how long the rations should last if they never exceeded the amount agreed upon. This plan was instituted because in spite of all our endeavours to regulate the consumption of food, yet in the dead of night they would undo and take out whatever extra they fancied, even when the foolhardiness of such a procedure was carefully explained to them. Nevertheless, we reaped one advantage from their avarice, namely, that the loads grew lighter in a shorter time than they otherwise would have done. One man, Mahomed Rahim, annoyed at being upbraided for his laziness and sulky temperament, threatened to turn back. This we gave him full permission to do, much to his astonishment, and on second thoughts he withdrew his threat, and even our own persuasion would not induce him to go.

During our halt we were able to overhaul all the luggage. Some of it had suffered from the immersion in the lake, notably the contents of our dispatch box, for all our papers inside it had had a thorough soaking, and each one had to be put under a stone to be dried again, and to save it from being blown away by the strong wind.

About half a mile from our camp was a solitary hill rising up between eight and nine hundred feet above the level of the camp. I climbed over the rocks to the summit of this to spy out the land, and see which would be the most favourable route to take. South-east of us lay a fine range of snow mountains, and I reckoned that if we could manage to steer just north of these, there would be no more difficulty about water to annoy us. All the ranges, large and small, seemed to run east and west, and it struck me how much more difficult, for this reason, it would be to traverse Tibet from north to south. Directly south of us, some sixty or eighty miles off, was another magnificent snow range with enormous white peaks. Some six or eight miles south-east was a dark blue salt lake, with two other smaller ones nestling close to it, and in the nullah immediately south of us grew grass which, for this country, was rich. Far away to the north again loomed another mighty snow range. Our own way eastwards, as far as I could make out, would take us past a small lake, and then, skirting round some low hills, turned up a nullah half left, where there seemed, through my glasses, to be good grass.

On account of the heat we delayed our march till early in the afternoon. During a part of the morning we tested the skill of our muleteers in rifle shooting. We thought that, should we come across nomads who showed any signs of hostility, our men would have more confidence in their arms, and perhaps would not show the white feather. None of them could hit an empty bottle at forty yards, so the confidence in their aim received rather a demoralising shock.

Two days after leaving this camp, we crossed over an easy pass of some 17,000 feet high, and about the top of this found a small white butterfly and a yellow flower, the first we had seen, and it was satisfactory to think that our flower press had not been carried along all this way for nothing, for it nearly shared the same fate as other things thrown away. A few miles further on, we camped in a grassy nullah, close by some heavy, craggy rocks.

Finding the morning again too hot for the mules to march, we shouldered our rifles and set forth in search of game, and to try and find out the lay of the country ahead.

We had completely run out of meat and had no wish to slay our single sheep, which for many days had marched along with us, the sole survivor of our flock. He had now become inured to hardships, was never fatigued, and was looked upon as our very last reserve in case of starvation. Although we actually found no game, yet we saw tracks of antelope, kyang, and one or two entire skeletons of yak.

We were rewarded for our tramp in another way, when, from some high ground, we saw below us a fresh-water lake

WE CAMP IN A GRASSY NULLAH.

with rich grass growing around it, and we wondered why nomads did not go and live there if they knew of the spot. We hurried back to camp with the good news, so as to march to such a paradise as soon as possible, and halt there another day, to give our animals the opportunity of thoroughly enjoying the luxurious spot. Poor brutes, strive as hard as they might, there had been more casualties amongst them and we were reduced to nineteen, less than half our original number.

On arrival at this lake, we found the centre portion of it was frozen over. By the edge of the water were a number of geese; but they might as well have been living in another country altogether, for they would give us no chance of shooting them, and we began to meditate the slaughter of our pet sheep, when, coming over the crest of a grassy rise, we spotted a herd of antelope. They were certainly timid, but, with a lucky longish shot, Malcolm knocked one over, saving us from hunger and our dear old sheep from an unmerited death. How often we looked at our living mutton with hungry feelings, it is hard to say, and how often an antelope just saved him from the slaughter-house would be equally hard to relate. We admired him, too, for his pluck and endurance, for he had long outstayed every other member of the flock. Our affection for him was great, and we even meditated his triumphal entry into China, and he would undoubtedly have accomplished it, had not an unforeseen mishap later on demanded his flesh and blood. Poor beast, if he had only known how we admired him, he would willingly have given us a dinner long ago.

It was a great treat for all to get good water clear and fresh, for latterly the water we had been digging up had been mostly muddy and saltish. We were blessed with a perfect day for repose, the mules and ponies grazed along the edge of the lake, sometimes standing up to their fetlocks in the still water, a day of thorough enjoyment to them. All their swellings and sores too were doctored up and the shoeing looked to. Considering what they had undergone, their backs were in a very satisfactory state. Tents and clothes were mended and a general clear-up was organised, so much so that about mid-day, we and Ruby were bathing in the lake itself, and although the lake was partly frozen over with ice, and we were living at a height of nearly 16,000 feet, the water was quite enjoyable, and we could remain splashing about in it for half an hour, and afterwards bask naked in the sun. So much pleasure did we derive from this bath that we ordered all the men down for tubbing. They went, certainly, but the amount of washing they executed would not have been sufficient for some people.

A climate like this at such a height struck us as truly marvellous. After seventeen degrees of frost by night, we found ourselves basking in the open in a temperature of 106 degrees, showing a variation of ninety degrees in the twenty-four hours. At 7 P.M. again, the thermometer registered as much as forty-eight degrees Fahr. Our route, as

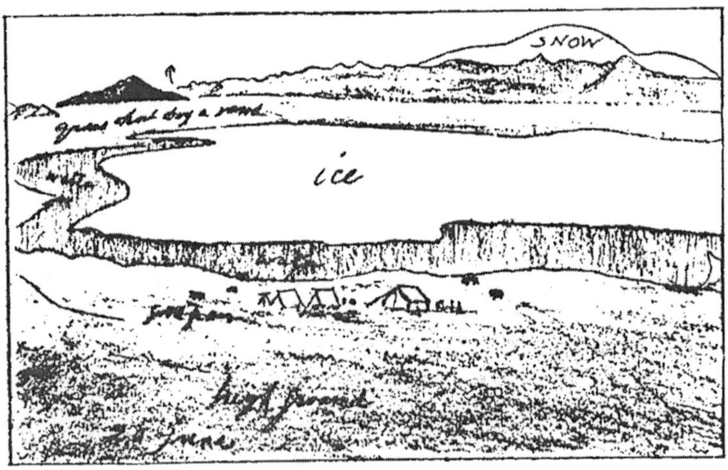

A DAY'S HALT BY A FRESH-WATER LAKE.

far as we could make out, lay over a large open plain with but scanty grass, and far off we could see a hill standing out alone conspicuously, a useful landmark for us to march on to. Without a distinct feature to make for, the caravan would very often zigzag down a broad valley and perhaps cover a mile or two more of ground than was necessary.

We were off before 5 o'clock, with a keen morning air in our faces, but after a couple of hours the heat became so unbearable that we would fain have halted. We had, however, to march ten miles before we could find a spot at all suitable, where, too, we had to resort to digging for water. Around here we shot sand-grouse, excellent food. Owing to the impossibility of marching with the sun so powerful, we decided to make two short marches each day, one of three hours in the very early morning, and the second during the afternoon. The drawbacks to this method were the uncertainty of finding grass and water twice in one day, and the fatigue involved in doubling the work of collecting the animals and loading and unloading them. But to march ten miles straight away in one morning as we had just done would have been suicidal. We reckoned that by making these two short marches, we should cover rather more ground each day, about twelve miles.

Whilst resting the animals, that they might recover from the results of the hot morning's march, we sent Esau on in front to spy out the land, who brought back the favourable news that lakes and grass were ahead of us, and no mountains to climb. It was bitterly cold as we moved off at 4.30, but no doubt a bracing morning for our animals, but as soon as the sun rose, the heat again made itself unpleasant, and we were glad to find a suitable camp before 8 o'clock. One of the mules, a big black one, could only carry his load a few yards, and had to be shot. Although at the end of the first march we had found a good halting place in a clean gravel-bedded nullah, with running water from the snow mountains, and fair grass, yet the second march ended by moonlight with no grass at all, and two of the ponies were left behind. Our second attempt at a double march failed.

During the early morning we hit off a rivulet, which, as we continued to follow it, increased in volume, but on issuing from the nullah into a large open plain, this rivulet became a river, some ten yards across, and two feet deep, and wound away northwards. As our course took us due east, we reluctantly had to leave it, with the hope of meeting it again further on, and of finding its size still larger, so that we might be able to map out its course for a considerable distance. For some time afterwards we could see a silver streak in the distance, and beyond it an enormous range of snow mountains.

As soon as we left the river and marched east, our route lay across a sandy gravel plain, and our chances of ever finding water and grass again seemed very small, when, fortunately, from one of the hills I climbed, I noticed a hidden dip in the ground, with grass, and here, as usual, water was found by digging. The number of our animals was still decreasing, and the strength of the survivors was growing weaker and weaker. We had to economise every cupful of grain, for that was the way we always doled it out. There were six bags remaining, in all about 480 pounds, and we reckoned that each bag would last out for eight marching days if we gave to each animal two cupfuls of grain *per diem*. There were only sixteen survivors. One of the mules showed an obstinate and mutinous frame of mind, for when loaded with his fair due, he absolutely refused to march; as soon as we gave him a light load, he trotted along gaily and felt no effects from the march. He was about the fattest and strongest mule we had, thereby convincing us that his inability to carry his proper amount of baggage was a mere sham, and in order that he should not get the better of us, we gave his grain to others who did his work, until he saw the folly of his obstinacy.

On viewing the country from a neighbouring hill, I found that if we marched due east we should meet with obstacles in the shape of innumerable steep nullahs of red, sandy soil, but that by marching north-east we should travel over undulating grassy ground skirting round a small range of hills. This latter route we decided upon, with the hopes of marching due east again before very long. We also made up our minds to try and find a good camp where we could halt for two days, so that during that time we could send off men north and south, with food to last them, in order to search for signs of people. Even if the men were not successful in their object, still we reflected that the animals would be gaining strength and a complete rest all the while.

At 3.45 A.M., 23rd June, Camp 36, we were drinking our cocoa with chupatty in the open, without feeling any discomfort from the cold, preparatory to marching. We required neither gloves nor coats, and we almost imagined we were about to start for an early morning shoot in the Indian plains. For the next two days we made successful double marches, inasmuch as there were no transport disasters. As usual, we dug for water, and found it brackish for our labours.

Towards the end of the second day, we came to a small nullah with beautifully green grass, and two tiny pools of water almost fresh. Imprinted on the moist sandy soil were marks of kyang, antelope, and yak. Evidently we had hit upon a favourite drinking resort of game, and accordingly pitched our tents just out of sight but close to the pools, expecting to get as much food as we wanted, for it was no easy matter to keep ourselves supplied in meat. Although we stopped here a day, the only game that came for his drink was a cock sand-grouse, who suffered the penalty of death for his intrusion, while just above the camp was an old hen, who sat undisturbed upon her nest. We should have had to be a good deal hungrier than we were before we could have found it in our hearts to kill her.

CHAPTER IX.

TERRIBLE GUN ACCIDENT—WE SEND OUT SCOUTS.

We were still favoured with wonderfully fine weather. About this time the wind would blow from the east in the morning, and afterwards from the west, if there were any wind at all.

During our halt, we sent out men to the north and to the south, to try and find some signs of nomads, while we ourselves sallied forth in search of game. The total result of all our exertions was *nil*. The men who went south spoke only of a hilly country with grass and no water, and the northerners reported that after crossing a broad grassy valley they came to a range of hills, and that on the other side flowed our lost river, then consisting of a small stream running south-east in the centre of a very large sandy nullah ; that still further off was another range of hills but no grass. We could not put much faith in the assertion of having found our lost river, which must have been still further north.

There is a place marked as a town in our map, called Barkhalu, which we intended to try and steer for by keeping as nearly as possible on the line of its exact latitude. From our present camp we reckoned that it was about a week's journey off. With such expectations, we endeavoured to keep up our men's spirits, and to induce them to double their exertions. It was always a difficult task to get them up of a morning in time to load the animals for an early start, and upon their doing this our success greatly depended. In order to make a start at 4.30 A.M., the camp would have to wake up very soon after three, and unless Malcolm or I awoke, the camp would go slumbering on till sunrise. But when we knew it depended upon ourselves, one of us generally managed to wake up in time. As the men had returned unsuccessful from their search for people after one day, there was no need to stop two, especially as all were eager to get on to Barkhalu. At our first halt for grass and digging operations, the sand-grouse came over in fair numbers and did well for our breakfast. Ahead of us a range of hills obscured an extensive view, although they did not appear of a very formidable nature, differing from those ranges to our north and south. The very feeling of not being able to see our onward course made us all the more eager to surmount the obstacle, peep over the other side, and see what lay in store for us.

On the 27th of June, Camp 39, we marched up the hills that hid our view and camped near the summit, where the water was brackish and purging. We inspected our men's rations, and found there was only sufficient to last them twenty-five days more, and as to ourselves, our consumption would have to be curtailed to one pound a day between the two of us, so as to last out for the same length of time. We all hoped to reach Barkhalu and there lay in fresh supplies, and we felt that if we could not find the place, our difficulties would be hard to overcome. From this summit we made a very early start at 4 A.M. I went on ahead, as it was my turn, finding it fairly plain sailing, considering it was not yet light. It was my intention to reach some point of vantage, whence I could get a good view as soon as there was sufficient light. Below me was an expanse of uneven, barren, sandy country, and the haze prevented me from seeing at all far.

As I was finding a way over these low mounds, I looked

back, as was my wont, to see how far the caravan had come, when I noticed that Esau, a long way off, was coming towards me all alone, but, thinking little of it, I went on again to another bit of rising ground. There was Esau still alone, and on using my glasses I saw that he was first walking, then running; no doubt he wanted me. I waved my handkerchief and waited. On he came faster than before, so that when he reached me, he was so breathless from his exertion and feverish agitation, that it was some minutes before he could come out with even a single word. His first utterance was, "Shot—gun." It struck me that something terrible might have happened; all sorts of things entered my head, and the worst thought of all—had Malcolm met with an accident? I made Esau sit down, and as soon as he had grown calmer, he told me that our cook, Lassoo, had been carrying a shot gun, and that Mahomed Rahim had tried to take it from him. Whilst they were struggling for the loaded weapon, off went the trigger, and the contents of the cartridge had blown away the lower half of the face of one of the muleteers, by name Sulloo, who was marching only a couple of yards off at the time.

I hurried back as fast as possible, only hoping that Esau, like many other people, had been carried away by his own imagination, and greatly exaggerated the truth. I thought it quite possible that the man might have been wounded, and at first sight that Esau had on the spur of the moment concluded that half the man's face had been blown away. I soon met the caravan, still coming along with most of the men, but their long faces and downcast looks told me too clearly that there had been some sad mishap. They told me that Malcolm had remained with Sulloo to doctor him up and give him brandy, and had sent on the caravan, with orders to halt at the very first spot where water could be got. It seemed to me that at the place where we met water could be obtained by digging, so the animals were at once unloaded and set free.

On my way further back to the scene of the disaster I met Malcolm coming towards me. He explained to me how the poor man had completely lost the lower half of his face, and how he had done his best for him in the way of bandaging and doctoring. It was impossible for him to walk or ride, so the men took back one of our bamboo beds, whereon to bring him into camp. Whilst they were away on this errand, Malcolm and I set to work to dig for water, the toughest dig we had had, and as the water could be only taken out by cupfuls it was a very tedious business before the animals had had sufficient to drink. The water, too, was very brackish, and almost undrinkable.

In the meantime Sulloo had been brought in, and we found the most effective solution in the way of soothing his pain was cyona and water. The poor fellow was most plucky over it, and implored to be merely left where he was to die. His only thought was that somebody owed him twenty rupees, and he wanted this money to go to his brother, and not to the woman he had married the day before he had set out from Leh! And there was no one else he cared about. We had certainly fallen into a most distressing fix. We could not help wishing that it might be so willed that the unfortunate man should die quietly that same morning. We could then have buried him, and marched away from the sad calamity to fresh scenes. As one of our men, Shukr Ali, philosophically remarked, it would only be his "kismet." Should, on the other hand, the man live, for all that, it was not in our power to remain where we were, for in that case the small store of rations would have soon been eaten up, and when they were gone there was nothing to follow, as far as we could see, but starvation. "We must shove on and find people" had been our daily axiom for some time, and to halt more than was absolutely necessary for the strength of the mules would be entirely fatal. Yet it was our duty, if we possibly could, to keep the man alive, and we knew it, too. We were in a most unpleasant situation; whichever course we adopted was equally hateful to us.

After seriously considering the pros and cons, we decided to remain where we were, Camp 40, for the day, and on the morrow to strap the man to a pony, with a muleteer walking on either side to support him. The idea of carrying him on a stretcher certainly entered our heads, but its execution was an impossibility.

It was indeed a very gloomy day, most of the time being spent in trying to get enough water from the holes we had dug. The unhappy Sulloo was fed through a small opening, by holding back his head and pouring down brandy and water or mutton broth.

One sad event seldom comes without a second. As we had no meat with us, and it was imperative that Sulloo should have something in the shape of beef-tea, for solid food could never be his fare again, we had to slay our dear old sheep and make the soup from his bones and what flesh there was. We wondered all the time what possible good we could be doing the man. He would never be able to eat again, nor even speak, or, as Shukr Ali put it, "What's the use of troubling about him? *Admi kabhi nahin banjaega!* He'll never make a man any more."

Our caravan was very depressed as it moved off the next morning at 4.30, marching for five miles over a most barren, sandy, and desolate country, when there was some improvement, and we were able to call a halt, again managing to get brackish water by digging. Poor Sulloo was brought into camp later on, and seemed to be doing well, for the bleeding ceased when he was placed on the ground and rested from the motion of the pony. He would lie huddled up in a heap on the pony's back, and if the pony happened to take an uneven pace or make a sudden jolt over an unlevel piece of ground, the jar to the man must have been almost unbearable. The second march was accomplished, too, without any casualty to man or beast.

The following day we had two stragglers, and Sulloo came in late, for even the two miles an hour was too fast for him. The land we marched over was remarkable for its various

OUR MULES BEING WATERED.

coloured stones; there were different shades of blue, red, green, yellow, black, and white, all perhaps indicating the presence of a multitude of minerals. The fine range of mountains to the north was still kept in sight, and we conjectured they must be a part of the Kuen Lun. Towards evening we came to a sandy nullah at the foot of an easy pass, and as water was good and plentiful a foot below the surface, and the animals had had none that day, we halted and made our drinking trough with the waterproof sheet.

The wind blew hard and bitterly cold that evening from the north, and as we had no meat we tried one of Lazenby's pea-soup squares. These were excellent, and quite equal to a meal; would that we had brought more of them. After the strong night wind, we had a perfectly still cloudless morning as we began the ascent of the pass, whose summit we reached almost simultaneously with the rising sun.

We were sorely in need of meat, and although there was good grass round and about, yet there was no water visible above the surface, and this was how we accounted for the remarkable absence of any game. During the latter part of the day things improved, for an antelope was shot, but as none of the men were at hand to hallal the beast the entire meat fell to our share, so we made the most of our opportunity by carrying enough to last us for five or six days. And if we were lucky enough during that time to shoot another antelope, we promised the men they should have the whole of it, provided one of them came up quick enough to hallal it.

During the night of the 2nd July some snow fell, and caused some of our mules to stray in search of grass and better shelter, and, what was worse still, forced upon us a late start. We passed through a very barren, sandy country, so much so that it was no surprise to us at not finding the remotest trace of any one ever having been there before. We calculated by our dead reckoning and the plane-table that we had just crossed the eighty-fourth degree of longitude, and if that were the case, we knew by the latitudes we had taken that we must be about forty miles south of the village of Iman Mula, which lies just south of the Kuen Lun, or it would be more correct to say, the place according to our map would be there, if in reality such a village existed. At our first halt there was a hill, quite close, completely covered with loose round stones of a fossil-like appearance, or the equal halves of them, about the size of Tangerine oranges, one of which we brought back with us. There was good water in the black clayey soil that lay just below the surface, and we were able to satisfy the most thirsty of our animals. During the day there was thunder and a shower of snow. It seemed as though there was about to be a breaking up of the grand weather.

The men wanted us to give Sulloo some medicine which would make him insensible, so that they might then sew up a portion of his face. This we did not feel inclined to do, as we did not know the proper amount of laudanum to dose him with, and an attempt at sewing up his face on the top of this would probably have done for the man. He had, undoubtedly, gained some strength, for he was able to keep up with the caravan on his pony.

Another snowstorm coming from the north, that blew through the night, made the ground in heavy condition, so that we had to make a late march. We passed through a sandy, stony country, with low ranges of hills on either hand, and further off another large range running as usual almost east and west. Our difficulties throughout the day were increased by the scarcity of water.

On the 4th of July we found ourselves marching down a fine grassy nullah, with several others running into it from the north and south, and we could not help thinking that we had struck a nullah of some importance, that perhaps it would eventually lead to the source of some river. About a foot below the surface we could always get as much water as we wanted and of a very fair quality. It was a happy event to have some means of raising hopes of finding people in the men's minds again. They were becoming lazier and inclined to be insolent, and any kindness or consideration we showed them was looked upon as so much weakness on our part. Our only way of getting any real work out of them was by behaving towards them with sternness and severity, and showing a pretty sharp temper, much as we disliked doing it. Towards evening the aspect of the country underwent a change. Although there were still grassy valleys, several of them and the intervening country were adorned by curiously-shaped hills of sandstone.

Far away, some thirty or forty miles, in an east-north-east direction, we saw a fine snow mountain range and peaks, and decided to steer for the south side of them. On climbing a hill it was obvious that the nullah we were in ran straight away towards these mountains. This was certainly encouraging. There would be no more trouble in having to find a way, and there would be no anxiety about our water and grass supply. The chances, too, were that we should pick up a better supply of wild game droppings for our fires, instead of having to dig up so much boortsa each day, and on some occasions we had hardly been able to collect enough to make a fire at all. We argued, with regard to the range we should come to, that if there were grass, streams from the snow, and shelter from the hills, why should not there be wandering inhabitants of the place?

Some time back a muleteer, Ghulam Russul, had taken the post of headman in place of Tokhta, degraded for incapacity. Ghulam Russul had been on a previous trip with the Littledales, and knew the likely sort of country where nomads love to dwell in. We had been warned against this man by the Wazir of Leh, but then we considered him the most suitable, out of a poor lot of men, for the post of head muleteer. The sight of this range added to Ghulam Russul's opinion that people might be living there, and the knowledge that we must be somewhere near Barkhalu, if there were such a place, induced us to make the following plan. We arranged to send Esau and Mahomed Rahim south, and Ghulam Russul with Shukr Ali north, each man with enough rations to tast for two days; this we were able to do, for fortunately an antelope had just lately been shot. We furnished them with the simple instructions to find people, get assistance in the shape of some baggage animals, and return again into camp a little lower down, but in the same nullah we were in. We agreed that we might just as well not lose an opportunity of making a few more miles, by marching the first day without these four men. Before, therefore, these two exploring parties sallied forth, they helped to load up. We thought we could manage to drive them by ourselves for one day, seeing that the way was clear, although our numbers would be very small. Of a truth, when these four men went off, there only remained, besides Malcolm and myself, Lassoo and another man, called Usman, to look after the caravan. This is really not enough, for one man must lead the way in front; whenever, too, a load during the march falls over to one side, the mule must at once be reloaded, to prevent any chafing from a badly-balanced burden. While this is occupying the attention of two or three men, the rest of the mules will stray in any direction, unless there are some more men present to keep them together. Sulloo, as usual, would come along behind, with one Juma to look after him, whose special employment was as cook for the rest of the men. Shahzad Mir, of course, would have to attend to his plane-table work. Usman was a tall, black, powerful fellow, but not fond of work; when Shahzad Mir's pony died he was generally told off to carry the plane-table. This duty suited him admirably, for he could put in many a snooze throughout the day on the top of various hills. He used to say he had travelled before, with a Russian through Turkistan. As for Tokhta, who had swollen to a tremendous size, resembling a large, over-ripe gooseberry, or rotten apple, he had been sent out in the very early morning to look after the ponies, for he was equal to no other greater exertion, but when it came to the hour of starting there was no Tokhta present, nor could we discover what on earth had become of him. In the end, we moved off without him, knowing that when he awoke, for he was probably slumbering peacefully in a sheltered nook, he would find it no hard job to track us down the nullah we were going along; besides, we intended halting all that afternoon and the whole of the following day. Tokhta was a regular drain upon us, for, although he had made up his mind that he was unfit to do any more work, still he had to have his share of the rations, much to the disgust of his brother muleteers, who under such circumstances soon lost all affection for one another, and had no scruples about letting a man starve as long as it suited their own ends. Having loaded the animals, we all started off together, the men who had been selected to the north and south, and we ourselves down the nullah.

About 9 o'clock we decided to halt, as already one of the mules had collapsed half a mile back. After unloading, we first of all dug a number of water holes, so as to have an abundant supply for all. We next found out that some of the animals required re-shoeing. We had leisure to see to all things. Our little camp table had come to ruin, or rather its legs had, but their place was taken by a couple of yakdans, which served us equally well. Our two camp chairs were still holding out; the most durable one that can be had in India is from the Government workshops at Roorkee. Most other chairs generally last for two or three weeks, when they require nailing and binding up, only to give way again shortly afterwards. Even at this early stage of our journey, when we were buoyed up with the empty hopes of our men finding signs of people and of Barkhalu, and of bringing in yak, ponies, and provisions, we began to anticipate the pleasures of our voyage across a portion of China, down the Yellow River from Lancheo to Pao T'eo. With so many men, we argued that this would be quite the best way of getting through China, as well as an inexpensive way, for we could pack the whole of them on one boat, and ourselves on another; or, better still, perhaps one boat would hold both the men and ourselves. Leisure and a clear night enabled us to take latitudes again from north and south stars, showing us to be about 35 degrees, 20 minutes.

During the afternoon of the following day Ghulam Russul and Shukr Ali turned up, without any news whatever of people. They told us how, after climbing a range of hills, they had been able to see an immense distance, but that there was nothing more than a continuation of grassy plains without any water; this, too, with the help of field-glasses we had provided them with. As Esau and Mahomed Rahim had not turned up by sunset, we began to entertain hopes that they had really found people, and that their delay was caused by bargaining and persuading them to come to us. Tokhta, too, had not turned up, and must have been having a splendid sleep. It was blowing hard with sleet the next morning, and this, combined with Esau's absence, kept us imprisoned in our tent.

CHAPTER X.

I SHOOT A YAK—DEATH OF ANOTHER MULE—"HELMET HILL"—WE LEAVE TOKHTA AND SULLOO BEHIND—REDUCED TO TWELVE ANIMALS—A MULE'S ADVENTURE.

About 8 o'clock all these excuses for repose came to an end, for the sun began to shine, and with it Esau returned, bringing Tokhta, whom, as we had rightly surmised, he had found snoozing peacefully in a nullah. We could not help feeling somewhat disappointed at the sleeper's return, for the chief reason that the food he ate was like having so much wasted. Nevertheless, had he not come in, we had arranged to send back a search party for him. Esau had been equally unsuccessful in his wanderings, and the only excuse for his absence he could offer, was that he could not get back sooner!

We all moved off, once more reunited, down the nullah, soon after 9 o'clock, and as I went ahead to feel the way, I came to a spot where the nullah bifurcated. Here was actual running water, and at the point of separation was a hill on which grew fine green grass, and running half-way up it were two long lines of white stones, piled up in small heaps of three, showing me that at some time or other people must have been there.

Whilst reconnoitring the surrounding country from the top of the hill, I spotted in a valley about two miles away a single yak grazing. Seeing by the lay of the land that the caravan would have no difficulty in finding their way, on arrival at this spot I went off on a little stalk, taking

Ruby with me. I had to cross a broad expanse of sand, where some antelopes had come to drink, before reaching the grass land where the yak was feeding. After cautiously crawling up to a crest from where I had calculated I should be quite near enough to the yak to shoot him, to my dismay there was no sign of the animal, but as I had not seen him make off, I concluded he must have moved on over some other crest, which now hid him from my view, during the time of my stalk when he was out of my sight. This proved to be the case, but it was only after crossing several crests that I at length found him fast asleep in a dip of the ground. Creeping up silently on tiptoe to within 100 yards, I woke him up rather harshly by placing a ·303 Jeffery bullet into a fatal part, and as he rose to learn the cause, I knocked him over with a second bullet, much to little Ruby's unbounded delight, who was soon scampering, snapping, and barking around the dying body, worrying as only terriers can. To cut the flesh off a dead yak is no slight undertaking, so I retraced my steps to get assistance from some of the men, but, on reaching the hill, there was no sign of them. I climbed to the top again, and found they had marched down the left branch of the nullah, so soon made tracks for them. After about a mile tramp, I came upon Mahomed Rahim and Shukr Ali asleep, and by their side a little black mule on the point of dying. Seeing they were doing no good, for the mule was too far gone, I sent them on to catch up the other men and bring back another mule, so that they could go to the dead yak and fetch in some meat for Malcolm and myself, and for themselves too, if they cared to eat it, in spite of it not having been hallaled. The death of another mule had now reduced us to fifteen.

The next day we still followed the same nullah, which became so soft and so full of water that we suddenly found ourselves bogged, and had no small trouble in extricating the animals and baggage out of such a mess on to the left bank, which was nearest to the catastrophe. Despite our misfortune, we could not help thinking that so much water must surely lead to a fresh-water lake, and to more favourable country. Very great, then, was our disappointment on climbing to the higher ground to find the land was absolutely barren and desolate, and what was more disheartening still, after going a few more miles, to learn that this water

WE CAMP IN A WILDERNESS AND STEER FOR "HELMET HILL."

ran into a lake so salt that even the mules refused to drink it. All around was an arid, stony desert; not a blade of grass, no droppings nor roots wherewith to make a fire.

In the direction we intended going we could see a distant hill in the shape of a helmet with a spike in it, so we christened the curious eminence "Helmet Hill." As we moved off towards this landmark we agreed that few things are more detestable than having to march along the borders of a salt lake, where the surroundings are absolutely barren and lifeless; such land as this always seems to have a depressing effect on men and beasts, and one wonders why there are such places. At night we most luckily found some fresh water below the surface, in a sandy nullah, and in a small valley close by grew some boortsa. This food the animals generally preferred to grass, and there is no doubt that in this coarse kind of short heather there is a deal of moisture and sustaining power. As long as the mules could get plenty of boortsa, they wanted but little water.

Such adverse and inauspicious times as these made their mark on our men, who lost heart and became lazier. We consequently made a later start from the sandy nullah than we should have done, and on coming to the end of the lake, the sun being hot, we called a halt where we fancied we should get water by digging. In this expectation we were unfortunate, much to the annoyance of our muleteers, and to make them feel that the misfortune was brought about by themselves, we explained to them that had they only risen and marched earlier we should by this time have been some miles further on, and reached a place where water could be obtained.

At this waterless camp we had to shoot a big, grey mule, who could not possibly have done another march. He had carried a load for many days, and we felt his loss severely. This death reduced us to fourteen animals, including the one that was kept spare for carrying Shahzad Mir's plane-table.

We felt we must come to a standstill unless people came across our path before long. As the country was so barren and desolate, we wanted to cover as much ground as possible that same afternoon. I went on ahead, and so bare was the aspect that it looked as though we should never see any water or green again; everywhere the ground was incrustated with salt; all the nullahs were white with it, and to all appearance we were leaving bad for worse.

At sunset, after which time it would have been impossible to proceed and when most had given up hope, we came to a nullah running down from the north, and to the surprise and delight of all we found good water a few feet below the surface, and a small quantity of boortsa on the adjacent hills. A strong north wind blew hard during the night, which made us wonder how our tent ever withstood the tension. Two or three miles further on from this place, we came to the bed of a salt lake partially dried up. Here again misfortune overtook us, for some of the animals got bogged, and nothing but an absolute desolation of salt land still loomed ahead of us. The going became so heavy that poor Sulloo on his pony, being unable to keep up, was left miles behind. It is impossible to picture such a barren land as we were in, and it seemed as though there would never be an end to it as long as we pursued our eastern course. We therefore struck a more northerly one, and after eventually getting beyond the salt belt marched east again. In some places we noticed a large amount of yellow soil and in others of bright red. In spite of our manœuvre we came to another dried salt lake, a disheartening obstruction, and when our doubled exertions seemed to be hopeless and our trials at their worst, we saw through our glasses, some considerable way off, a small patch of grass on a bit of rising ground. We were at once inspired with new life and marched straight for this harbour. The grass we reached grew at the foot of a nullah that led over an easy pass, so we allowed the mules to enjoy a few minutes' grazing before commencing the ascent. This grass was quite green, and the joy of the animals at meeting with such food was clearly manifest by the avaricious way in which they tore it off, and the marvellously quick way in which they ate it. Later on we came to a broad, sandy nullah, with abundance of good water just below the surface. The nullah, too, was itself well sheltered from the cold winds by the higher ground on all sides, where splendid grass was sprouting. Antelope had made no mistake in choosing this as one of their haunts to wander into. In order to counteract the results due to such depressing and demoralizing country as we had just passed through, and as Sulloo and Tokhta were still in the

MALCOLM AT BREAKFAST WITH ESAU.

rear, we determined to make the most of our opportunity and halt for half of the following day.

This was now the 10th of July and we had reached Camp 51. We were well repaid for our decision, for the following morning was perfectly glorious—not a cloud, not a breath of wind was there to mar the quietude that man and beast at this time so much needed. To commemorate the occasion, I photographed Malcolm enjoying his breakfast just outside the tent, with Esau standing by the other side of the table, holding in his hand a dish of luxuries!

About midday, Tokhta, Sulloo, and the pony walked slowly into camp. They persisted that nothing on earth would induce them to travel onwards another step; poor fellows, they had reached what seemed to them a perfect haven of rest; they must have felt thoroughly worn out, for all they wanted to do was to remain where they were and quietly die. It was quite certain that it would have been madness for us to remain with them, for only a few more days' rations remained, and our only chance of getting through the country at all lay in our coming across nomads from whom by hook or crook we could get supplies. We did think of leaving some men behind, while a small party marched on as fast as possible with light loads in search of people, but these men did not relish being left, and supposing there were no people to find, our situation would have been still more critical. We ended our problem by leaving the two sick men with a pony and a supply of food and drinking utensils, etc., so that if they felt inclined they might follow after, for they would have found no difficulty in tracking us. We buoyed them up, too, with the hopes we entertained of shortly finding people, when we would at once send back assistance to them. We also endeavoured to persuade them to make an effort in reaching a fresh camp each day, by marching and halting according to their inclination, for we told them we should only make short marches, and at each camp we would leave a supply of food for them and some grain for the pony. It was a sad thing having to leave these men and the pony as we did, and when we halted for the night and the sun began to set calmly over these vast solitudes, there was no sign of their coming, look back as we might to the far-off hills for some tiny, distant, yet moving, speck. The darkness of night soon gathered around, and we could only wonder how close they might be to us. The next day we saw new life, for Malcolm had a shot at a wild dog, while I saw two eagles; such sights as these at once set our imagination at work, for we argued as to how could these creatures exist unless people were living somewhere close. At the same time it brought encouragement to all.

Towards evening, after making two short marches during the day, we camped south of the snow range we had been steering for, but there were no signs to tell us that the three abandoned ones were following. More food and grain was left here, and we moved off soon after 4 A.M. It is, as some will know, chilly work sallying forth before sunrise when the minimum registers over twenty degrees of frost; and as one tramps along, marching only two miles an hour with the animals, one eagerly watches for the first tip of the sun to appear, meanwhile warming the hands alternately inside the coat, for we always made a point of carrying a rifle each.

It was my turn to go on ahead to-day, and after a brisk walk of five miles I came upon a most inviting spot. There were two tiny fresh-water lakes, surrounded by grassy hills, with the snow peaks on the northern side feeding the hills below with a daily supply of water. Fearing disappointment in that the water might be salt, I hastened on to the two pools, and, as I expected, they were fresh, so I hurried back to climb some rising ground, from whence the caravan would be in sight and earshot. There the firing off of my gun announced to them, according to previous arrangement, that water and grass had been found.

Whilst enjoying our midday halt a couple of antelopes and sand-grouse came to drink, and fell victims to our guns for their greediness. We all revelled in the abundance of such good things, and would have much liked to lengthen our stay; but on inspecting our supplies we found the men had only fifteen days' rations left. We tried hard to persuade them to subsist on half rations, as we ourselves had been doing, and although at the time they finally expressed their willingness to do so, and saw the expediency of the plan, still they made their promise when filled with immense meals of hallaled antelope and heavy chupatties, and we doubted their power of abstaining. If they could have managed to show more self-control over their food, we reckoned in thirty more days on half rations we should cover another three hundred miles, and we considered the fact of travelling

WE CAMP BY TWO FRESH-WATER POOLS.

that distance further on, without meeting anybody, was an absolute impossibility; besides, the general appearance of the country was improving, and on that very evening we actually encamped on the grassy banks of a small running stream. It was an enticement to us to follow up this rivulet, but the extreme southern course it took outweighed our wishes. The men already began to grumble that they could not work on half rations, this too when they had vast supplies of meat from the antelope. The only advice we could give them, was to eat up their food as fast as they could, and then, when it was all gone, they would have to exist on still less than they were now doing, if they wanted to live at all. Whatever argument we brought forward had no weight with such men, who would only think of appeasing their wants for the time being. Although we spoke to them harshly, still it was our fixed intention to strive our utmost to shoot game for the men, so that they might save a little of their rations, and sometimes at our midday halt we would sally forth with rifles to try and bag something before the afternoon's march. Even then it was only in a grumbling frame of mind that a man would accompany us to hallal the animal.

The muleteers, too, began on some occasions to quarrel amongst themselves, and to threaten all kinds of punishments to one another; but the mere threatening, and actual carrying out, are very different things. Still, there was a kind of feeling in the air that unless we got assistance some calamity would befall us. Whilst on the march a big black mule died, and as the pony with Sulloo had not come in, this reduced us to only twelve animals, a very small number indeed for the men to load and look after, and a very small cause for them to complain of overwork.

At midday halt the spirits of the muleteers became more discontented than ever, for no water could be found for a long time, nor would any of them bestir themselves in the matter; so unreasonable had they become that we doubted our ever being able to forget and forgive their failings when we came to the end of our journey. Towards evening we saw a fresh-water lake, and camped a mile or so east of it, choosing a spot by some good grazing. As the animals had had no water that day, we drove them down to the lake, but the banks all round were treacherous to such a degree that one mule only just escaped drowning, so difficult was it to drag him out of the heavy mud; and when we eventually did, he had been so long in the water and was so benumbed, for the sun had set and a bitter blast was blowing, that when we got him back to camp he was too far gone to think of eating. He was a fine, powerful mule, and his loss would have been severely felt by us. All our warm putties, etc., were given up on this occasion, and the frozen mule was bandaged up almost from head to foot. The following morning great was our relief at finding he was none the worse whatever for his lengthened drink at the lake.

CHAPTER XI.

SHOOTING AN ANTELOPE—SNOW—A MYSTERIOUS TRACK—THE BED OF AN ANCIENT LAKE—EMOTION OF MAHOMED RAHIM—VARIABLE WEATHER—MORE ANTELOPES SHOT—THEODOLITE BROKEN—EXTRAORDINARILY SUDDEN WIND—HUNGER *v.* CEREMONY—NEW FINDS.

BEFORE starting forth again we upbraided the head muleteer, Ghulam Russul, for his chicken-heartedness and bad example to the rest of the men. He denied a grumbling spirit, and said he was brave and ready to undergo any hardship, and follow us anywhere, but as to the other men, he said they were a discontented lot. Knowing as we did how he influenced them, his statement bore no weight with us. We made a double march over undulating grassy country, intersected by some broad gravel nullahs, running almost at right angles to our course. South of us lay a range of hills running east and west, making it appear as though a river were running along at their base, and for this reason we intended to steer gradually for them.

At night we found a well-sheltered nook, with water close at hand, and such splendid grass that we were induced to remain half the next day and feed up; besides, there had been no signs at all of Tokhta and Sulloo, and we considered this the last hope of ever seeing them again. Henceforth we would make no more provision for their coming, in the shape of leaving food and grain behind. It was fortunate we had fixed on a half day's halt, for at daybreak there was a strong wind blowing from the north with driving sleet. The grass at this camp, No. 56, had far more nourishment in it than any other grass we had come across up to the present, and Ghulam Russul remarked that if we saw more grass like it we were sure to come across nomads, so all were, for the time being, in a more hopeful frame of mind. The melting snow had made the marching somewhat heavy, and there was no lack of water.

Soon after starting, Malcolm, who had gone on ahead, came hurrying back to me, with the request that I would come with him and shoot an antelope, for he had seen a great number of them. Shortly afterwards we saw a large herd grazing or playing about as antelopes do, but one of them, without the slightest provocation, came trotting towards us; perhaps he was wondering whatever could have brought such queer-looking creatures there as we were. We sat down to make ourselves still more mysterious and to receive him, when suddenly his instinct seemed to tell him that there was just a suspicion of danger attached to us, for he started off at a gallop, crossing our front at about fifty yards distance. We both fired simultaneously at so inviting a mark, and both hit. It was a sight worth seeing, an antelope retreating at top speed in a second bowled over quite dead, so much so that when Mahomed Rahim, who was at hand, rushed up to hallal him, no blood would flow from the operation, and the men declared it was not fit for them to eat. In one way it was satisfactory to hear them say this, for we were convinced that up to date they had not been suffering from hunger. If they had, no hesitation, through religious scruples, would have arisen about eating the antelope's flesh.

We halted by a lake whose water tasted very nearly fresh, but the banks were so treacherous that it was a hazardous undertaking to get close to it, and after our previous experience we preferred digging instead. This very likely accounted for the absence of game in the neighbourhood, that they could not get to the water; but it is difficult to account for the absence of birds on the lake itself, for there was not even a Brahmini duck. A bright night, and we made preparations for a very early start the next morning, but the ill luck that sometimes accompanied us had brought another storm, so that the ground bore a very white appearance, and all idea of marching, for the time being, had to be abandoned. By noon, although the ground was still heavy, we ventured forth again, and hit off another large lake containing water very nearly fresh.

Throughout the day storms continued to rage around us amidst the adjacent hills, but, fortunately, none fell actually over us; we could not help reflecting how all this snow must have entirely baffled Sulloo and Tokhta in their tracking us, that is, if they had attempted to do so. Everywhere the country was beautifully grassy, and occasionally we picked a new species of flower. Another large lake was situated to the north of us, and during our march down the valley the hills that lay both north and south were gradually closing in. As we proceeded, the going became more difficult. In addition to another snowstorm which had fallen during the night, the valley became split up by irregular nullahs and hills running in every direction, with no defined features.

We continued making our double marches, and as the loads were becoming lighter we hoped to cover fifteen miles a day. One great continuous anxiety was the task of finding enough game to shoot, that we might all live. At one time it would be plentiful enough, at others for days we could find nothing. On some nights we registered over twenty degrees of frost, and still remained over 16,000 feet above the sea level, and at this great height we actually saw a brown butterfly.

On the 20th of July we began to notice the days were

growing shorter, as the sun would rise just a few minutes before 5 o'clock; but the whole country appeared to be changing for the better, which in no small degree alleviated our fears of being able to get across this high plateau before the cold weather should set in. Generally speaking, everywhere there was more grass growing, and, instead of the coarse tufts we had been accustomed to see, their place was taken by short crisp grass, the kind of growth that is so much sought after by the nomads. We were, too, making a very gradual descent, and felt convinced that, with such natural signs, we must before very long hit off streams which would lead us to some sort of civilization.

At our midday halt the men's spirits were more cheerful. We had stopped in a fine broad nullah, running nearly due east, with pleasant-looking grassy hills sloping down on either side, and, with a cloudless sky and no wind, we were glad to sit in our shirt-sleeves, whilst our twelve veteran mules, with their saddles off, rolled in the sand before enjoying the rich grass and water. We began to pick fresh additions to our flower collection, the specimens being chiefly of a mauve or white colour, and up to the present time we had only found one yellow flower. At 7.30 P.M., in Camp 61, at a height of over 16,000 feet, the temperature was forty degrees Fahrenheit, and during the night there were nineteen degrees of frost. Fine grass and fine weather still favoured us, while the presence of a number of sand-grouse indicated that water was at no great distance off.

Just after leaving Camp 62, we were all struck with wonderment at finding a track running almost at right angles to our own route. It was so well defined, and bore such unmistakable signs of a considerable amount of traffic having gone along it, that we concluded it could be no other than a high road from Turkistan to the mysterious Lhassa, yet the track was not more than a foot broad. Our surmises, too, were considerably strengthened when one of the men picked up the entire leg bone of some baggage animal, probably a mule, for still adhering to the leg was a shoe. This was a sure proof that the road had been made use of by some merchant or explorer, and that it could not have been merely a kyang or yak track, or one made use of only by nomads, for they never shoe their animals in this part of the world.

Such a startling discovery as this bore weight with the men, and nothing would have suited their spirits better than to have stuck to the track and march northwards, and they evidently thought us strange mortals for not following this course; therefore, instead of being elated with joy, they became more despondent than ever when they found we were still bent upon blundering along in our eastern route. But it was our strong belief that we should for a certainty find people in a very few days' time, and this being the case, we did not see the force of travelling in a wrong direction, and put aside the objects for which we had set out, just to suit the passing whim of a few craven-hearted men, especially when we knew that the cause of their running short of food and consequent trouble was entirely due to their own dishonest behaviour. We did, however, send one man, Mahomed Rahim, supplied with food, with instructions to follow the road north as far as he had courage to go, thinking that when he had crossed a certain range of hills he would discover the whereabouts of people. Furthermore we explained to him the way we intended going, so that there could be no chance of his losing himself.

A mile or so further on we came to the dried-up salt bed of a very ancient lake. The salt was in every shape and form of crustation, and the whole lake for several miles across was divided up into small squares with walls one to three feet high, rugged and irregular. The going across this was troublesome and arduous, first stumbling over one wall, then crossing a few yards of crumbling, crystallised salt before another had to be scrambled over. Thus it went on for mile after mile, and the length of the lake being most deceptive it seemed as though we should never, *never* cross it. As the sun rose higher some of the salt composite melted, and then we found ourselves first in slush, then on a bit of hard, rugged going, most liable to to cause a sprain to any of the mules. It became evident that unless we were pretty smart in getting off the lake altogether, we should find ourselves bogged there for the rest of the day; thus our first idea of going straight ahead across the lake had to fall through, and we steered for the nearest shore, which was on the southern side, all the time the ground getting worse and more treacherous. When, only in the nick of time, we did stand on a sound footing again, we congratulated ourselves that for once only had we deviated a short way from our course. Although this salt bed had proved such an unforeseen obstacle in our line, still it was useful to us in another way. The salt was of an excellent quality, and we were able to replenish our store of this most necessary article, of which there was so little left that we were carefully economising it.

During the morning's march next day we shot an antelope and a kyang, and not wishing to delay the mules or to overload them, we left two men behind, Ghulam Russul and Shukr Ali, to cut up the meat and bring it in, whilst we continued in search of a suitable spot for a midday halt. This was a plan we frequently adopted, and there were always volunteers to stop behind, for by doing so they took good care to light a fire and feast on the tit-bits to their hearts' content, and well fortify themselves before carrying the load of meat to their fellow muleteers.

We had halted, and were expecting the arrival of these two men, when Mahomed Rahim, who had been sent to follow up the track, rejoined us, and as he approached we could see he was weeping bitterly. On asking the man what ailed him, he sobbed out that he had lost his way. He was a ludicrous sight, for he was a great, big, strong fellow, and we asked him, if he wept like this at finding us again after only being absent a day and a night, how would he weep had he not found us at all? We fed up the great baby with some unleavened bread, which he ate voraciously amidst his sobs. Some kyang came trotting up to camp with a look of wonderment at our being present there, and as we were about to move off some antelopes also came to inspect us.

The men carried quantities of cooked meat about their persons, wrapped up in their clothes, and as they tramped along they munched almost incessantly at the tough food tending to make them very thirsty, so that when we halted for the night they suffered considerably, for the water we dug out was too salt for drinking.

The following morning we came to a most dreary-looking region, ornamented only with a big salt lake, without any vegetation or kind of life, making us eager to get across such a solitude. At the east end of the lake we marched over rising ground up a nullah about a couple of miles before we came to some fairly good grass, where we called a halt, never dreaming that we were doomed to an unpleasant disappointment. On getting up some water from below the surface, we found it to be the worst we had tasted, quite impossible for man or beast to drink. Two of the men, however, did gulp some of it down, and suffered in consequence for their indulgence. Their thirst became far more acute than was that of the rest of us. We were afraid that should we find no water by the evening, it would go badly with all. Some of the animals were too thirsty even to eat the grass. We, therefore, made an earlier start than usual, sending on ahead a couple of men to search for water in in some likely-looking ground that lay some distance on in front on our right flank.

As we were marching along in silence, we suddenly saw the two men were coming towards us, and as soon as they drew near enough for the other muleteers to see by their animated appearance that they had found water, they made a general rush towards them, forgetful of what became of the mules, or whether Malcolm and myself had any water at all. Their one and only thought, as usual, was themselves. A few miles further on we found two pools of good water, and resolved to remain there half a day to give the animals a chance of regaining their lost strength.

During the night our tent had great difficulty in withstanding the wind, that blew with much violence, while the temperature fell to twenty-one degrees of frost. As we had run short of iron pegs, we found a most efficient substitute in fastening the ropes to our tin boxes of ammunition. On other occasions, too, the ground was so sandy that pegs were entirely useless, and each rope had to be fastened to a yakdan, or to one of our bags of grain.

During the afternoon we marched along a broad, grassy, and somewhat monotonous valley, steering for some snow peaks we had seen the previous day. We found no game, excepting sand-grouse, which, by their unmistakable notes, made their presence known in the mornings up to 8 or 9 o'clock, and after sunset.

On the 26th July we left Camp 66, moving off by moonlight, for the going was easy. On halting for breakfast, two antelopes ventured to come and have a look at us, and, of course, paid the penalty of death. Such an opportunity as this was not to be thrown away, and laying them together, I photographed them, and afterwards cut them up, carrying as much meat as we possibly could manage—enough for three or four days' consumption. The afternoon was hot, like a summer's day in England. Some yak, resembling big black dots, could be seen in several of the grassy nullahs: a trying temptation to have a stalk after them, for the ground was of such a nature that with care one might have come up to within a hundred yards of some of them without being seen. But then it would have been useless to slaughter them, so we contented ourselves with watching their movements, and with making out what we could have done had we been merely on an ordinary shooting trip, or had we been hard up for meat.

TWO ANTELOPES ARE SHOT CLOSE TO CAMP.

We met with a great misfortune that afternoon, for one of the mules had been loaded so carelessly that its baggage, consisting of two yakdans, fell off with a crash on to some ground as hard as rock. One of these yakdans contained my theodolite, and on opening up for the evening's observations, I found the top spirit level was broken, and from that time I had to be dependent only upon the sextant.

As usual we were off by 4.30 A.M., and going on ahead, I

climbed up some hills to spy out the land. It was pleasant walking, for grass grew everywhere, and in the lower-lying ground were flowers and water. On crossing a certain ridge I saw two yak grazing quietly, as they probably had done without any interruption ever since they had been dependent upon themselves for picking up a living. I sat down silently, without, however, attempting concealment, to enjoy the sight of watching carefully, at so short a distance, the habits of these massive, dark-haired cattle at home in their wild state. At length the caravan, which had been marching along on much lower ground, over grassy valleys, came in sight, a signal that I must push ahead again and reconnoitre. I rose, therefore, and walked up towards the two yak, and one of them was so tame and eager to make out whatever on earth I was, that he allowed me to walk up to within forty yards of him, so that, had I chosen, I might have given him a very telling shot. As it was, he merely trotted off a short way and started grubbing again.

Ahead of us was a range of mountains, an imposing sight, with grand snow peaks, the very ones we had been steering for. From the high ground it seemed as though there was a pass leading over them between two of the peaks, but entirely without vegetation. It was impossible to make out how far the pass went, and what would be in store for us after we had reached the point as far as we could see. We calculated that the climb in our present condition could not have been done in one march, and wondered how we could strengthen our animals sufficiently for the second march, if there were no grass at the end of the first. We knew from experience that an ascent of this description would have taken more out of our mules than several days of ordinary marching, and therefore determined to abandon the idea of surmounting the pass, or rather what appeared to be a pass, but to strike north, finding a way somehow or other round the entire range.

As we steered for some extra good-looking grass and water by which to make our midday halt and give the mules their midday graze, a couple of inquisitive yak actually came trotting after us, keeping at a distance of two or three hundred yards. Such boldness augured well for a plentiful supply of good meat in the future. We were glad to pitch our tent in this pleasant spot for a few hours, and even under that shade the maximum thermometer registered seventy-five degrees.

Having breakfasted off our antelope meat and some good tea, we were busy with our maps, and drying flowers, etc. Everything was spread out—for such frail specimens it was a splendid opportunity; the men were sleeping, too. The mules, having eaten their fill, were standing still enjoying the rest and perfect peace; all was absolute silence, with the exception of our own chatting to each other, as we amused ourselves with our hobbies, when without a moment's notice a powerful blast of wind caught us with such violence that the tent was blown down and many things were carried completely away, and our camp, which only a second ago had been the most peaceful scene imaginable, became a turbulent one of utter confusion, as every one jumped up in an instant, anxious to save anything he could lay hold of, or to run frantically after whatever had escaped—for some things were being carried along at a terrific rate. Fortunately the loss, compared to the excitement, was trifling; but we made up our minds not to be caught napping in this way again.

That same afternoon, after marching north, we crossed a river that took its rise from the snow peaks; the bed was sandy, about half a mile across, with several small, swiftly-flowing streams about a foot deep, which had to be crossed barefooted. This was the largest body of water we had as yet come across, and there was much speculation amongst us as to where it would lead, and we thought we should at any rate not lose sight of its course. Splendid green grass and flowers were flourishing everywhere. Vegetables, too, were a valuable addition to our table, for besides the "kumbuk" and "hann," we here first found the wild onion, which afterwards formed the chief staple of our food. Onions cut up into pieces and fried in yak's fat, was a dish appetising at these great heights in the absence of other food, besides being very sustaining and an excellent medicine for all internal complaints. On some nights the mules and ponies were wont to stray, but with such good grass close at hand, and the presence of water in more than one place, as a rule they did not go very far; but, as we could not run the risk of a long delay, the first thing in the morning, they were nearly always watched throughout the night in turn by the men. We found a nullah with a small stream in it running eastwards, rising all the time, and marched up it, leaving the river to wind its way north; we had no real fear of losing it, for we could see it turned east again later on. At the top of the pass we found another nullah running northwards, and followed this down to a prairie-like looking valley, thence on to a beautiful lake. At the western extremity we could see it was fed by the river we had crossed the day before. All around the valleys and hills were green, and on many of them the grazing yak were dotted about in great numbers.

As we were now running short of meat I instituted a stalk against one of them, and took a vast amount of trouble and exertion in order to come to a close range before firing, little knowing that it was a waste of labour, as one could have approached them with taking only ordinary precautions. Close to the yak were several kyang, who were the more watchful of the two, for they were the first to notice my crawling along and at once stood up in bewilderment, but beyond that they did nothing more, so that I was enabled, without in the remotest degree disturbing the yak, to get within sixty yards of them. There I took my shot and bowled over with a single bullet the one which I considered to be the juiciest-looking one in the herd. The rest of them merely raised their heads for a moment at the unwonted noise, and then began to graze again, making no attempt to escape. I, too, then rose, and it was only after a deal of shouting that they grasped that it really was rather dangerous to remain where they were, thereupon off they trotted across the valley, far, far away. Not so the herd of kyang, who appeared the most disturbed at first; they continued to manœuvre around the whole time we were there, as though inviting us to try our skill on them, but one dead yak is oceans of meat for a much larger caravan than ours, for many a day.

As soon as one of the men had come up, I told him to look sharp and cut its throat for it was not quite dead, although in reality it had breathed its last some ten minutes ago. He at once set to work, but so tough was the hide, and so blunt his knife, that he could not cut through it, and merely first pricked it with the point; and although no blood exuded, he nevertheless told the other men that he had properly hallaled the brute, and they by this time having become less scrupulous with regard to their religious custom, made no bones about arguing as to the meat being unfit for them to eat. As a matter of fact they were beginning to learn what real hunger was. Some of them came to help cut off the meat in a business-like sort of way, pretending not to examine the throat at all.

As we made our midday halt only a hundred yards from the carcass, all fed right royally, and carried off large lumps of the flesh as well. The men, too, were in high spirits, for they had found a very old chula, or fireplace, consisting of three stones, and what was still more joyful tidings, close to the dead yak ran a narrow track actually in the direction we intended going.

About here we also saw some new creatures—large marmots, butterflies, and hoopoos. I skinned one of the latter. Such fresh sights, and the discovery of the track in addition to the improvement in the climate, the grass and abundance of water, made all eager to be off again in expectation as to where the track would lead us.

CHAPTER XII.

A FOOTPRINT—SHAHZAD MIR INDISPOSED—DESERTION OF MULETEERS—A RAINY NIGHT.

It was now the 28th of July, and we had reached a spot between our night encampments 69 and 70, the day camps not being recorded in the map. Since leaving Lanak La on the 31st of May, we had been daily finding our own way across country, over mountains and valleys, along nullahs and beds of rivers, etc., and at last we had found a track we could follow. Such a sensation was novel to us. We could scarcely grasp that there was no need to go ahead to find a way. We had simply to follow our nose. We thought that our troubles were nearly finished, and for the rest of our journey that there would be easy marching, and every moment we quite expected that the dwellings of mankind would heave into sight. Especially, too, when one of the men picked up a stout stick, three or four feet long, which must have been carried there by somebody or other, for since leaving Niagzu the highest species of vegetation we had seen was the wild onion. Some of the men also declared that they had found a man's footprint. Personally we did not see this sign of civilization, but the men maintained there could be no mistake about it, for they said it was the footprint of a cripple!

Besides all this comforting news, there was no need to be tramping over the hills in search of game for food. The antelope, yak, and kyang were plentiful and easily shot in all the valleys, and, had we been so disposed, we might have shot a dozen yak during the afternoon's march. When we halted for the night one of the wild yak actually came and grazed amongst our mules!

We camped at the entrance of a winding nullah, along which grew rich grass, and being tempted by the shelter, some of the mules wandered up it during the night and thus forced upon us a late start the next morning; but as there was a strong wind blowing, this somewhat counterbalanced the otherwise too over-powerful heat of the sun.

Our track led up a fine grass valley, where we could actually smell the wild flowers, but as we continued the track became less defined, till eventually there was no track at all. We spread out to the right and left hand, but without success. Whether it had turned off to north or south it is impossible to say. For the moment we were disappointed at the overthrow of all our hopes, and instinctively felt that our journey had not quite come to an end.

We had been marching uphill, and at the top of the valley found a fast-running rivulet taking its rise from the snow mountains that lay south of us, the same range that had blocked our way and compelled us to make the detour. Added to the work of once more having to find our own way, the country took a change for the worse. Although there was no difficulty about the water, still there was less grass, the soil became slatey, and in places barren. Storms began to brew around us, but we were lucky in being favoured with only some of the outlying drops. We had a perfectly still night with one degree of frost.

It had been our custom, especially on dark nights, to make the men take their turn of guard over the mules, to watch and see that they did not stray. They were far too precious to lose, and by marching in the early morning, felt less fatigue.

On this particular morning, 30th July, Camp 70, no

mules were forthcoming at the time when we wanted to load up, and it turned out that the man, Usman, who should have been on watch, was fast asleep in some secluded corner. It was only the previous night that this very man, after unloading the mules, had been sent to fetch some water for the other men and ourselves, but as we waited and there was none forthcoming, another man was sent to see what was the matter. He found Usman, having had a good drink himself, contentedly sleeping with the empty water-skin by his side. We therefore had no inclination to go in search of him on this particular morning, but after collecting the mules from all quarters, loaded up without him.

Our twelve mules with fairly light loads seemed to be stronger and fitter than they had been for a long time, no doubt due to the excellent green and sufficiency of water they had of late enjoyed. We had besides become better acquainted with the carelessness and laziness of our men, whom we used to watch very closely, never trusting them entirely.

After marching about a mile, we crossed a narrow track running north and south. Here again we were much tempted to take the northern route, but as our mules were so fit, we still stuck to our eastern one, daily expecting more than ever to find people.

Another inducement for doing so was that of late there had been little difficulty in keeping all well supplied with meat. It thus happened that when everything was in our favour, we were sanguine of accomplishing our journey without any further mishap. We crossed over several cols and saw fresh-water lakes, while yak, kyang, antelope, and sand-grouse were plentiful.

Storms had been threatening a great part of the day to break over us, but were held in check by some extra high peaks. In the evening, however, we had crossed a broad sandy bed of a river, wherein a shallow stream was flowing, and had just pitched our tents in a small sandy nullah, well sheltered from the wind, when down came the rain in real earnest.

We were sorry to find that Shahzad Mir had not come in, though very shortly the man who was carrying the plane-table walked up, saying that Shahzad Mir had stopped the other side of the stream with a pain in his stomach. We knew quite well what was the cause of this. He had been taking some chlorodyne and afterwards had eaten enormous quantities of meat. As there was nothing to be gained by getting anybody else soaked, we sent back the same man to fetch him in. The night was very dark and the rain turned to snow, still neither of them came. Fearing that on account of the darkness they had gone astray, we popped outside and fired off our gun at intervals; still the ammunition was wasted. Nothing but daybreak brought them back, when it turned out that they had been so ridiculous as to sleep in a nullah only a few yards from our camp. They had even heard the shots, but still could not find us. Neither of them was any the worse for the outing, in fact the result had been beneficial, for the stomach-ache from which Shahzad Mir had been suffering was completely cured. They caused a good deal of merriment amongst us all, and we all thought they might have selected a more suitable night for sleeping out of camp.

The ground was covered with snow, so it was out of the question to think of marching early. We were rather anxious to cover a few more miles that morning. It was the last day of the month, and since leaving Leh we had marched very nearly a thousand miles, and we thought we would like to start a fresh thousand on the 1st of August. To our delight the sun made an appearance quicker than we had anticipated and the snow was very soon thawed, allowing us to move off again at 11 o'clock.

The day was fine and warm, and as I went on ahead to explore, I saw below me some grassy hillocks, and, grazing in their midst, a fine yak. I thought it would be interesting to make a stalk just to see how close it was possible to get

SHAHZAD MIR AT WORK.

without disturbing him. I walked down the hill I was on and dodged in and out between the hillocks, always keeping out of sight, still getting closer and closer, till at last there was only one small hillock that separated us, not more than half a dozen yards. But when I stood up before him and he raised his head, for he was intent upon grazing, and saw me, his look of utter bewilderment was most amusing to see. He was so filled with astonishment, as the chances are he had never seen a human form before, that it was some moments before he could collect his thoughts sufficiently to make up his mind and be off.

Further on were many streams, forming their own course over a very broad, sandy river bed, all swollen on account of the recent rain. Although we were at an altitude of 16,000 feet we felt no discomfort in taking off our boots and stockings and paddling across and about the streams, collecting bits of stick wherewith to make a fire for our breakfast of venison and fried onions.

To-day we were only making a single march, and in the afternoon halted by a pool of rain-water on some high ground, well sheltered on all sides from the wind by a number of sandy mounds. From here we had magnificent views of the massive snow mountains that surrounded us, looking grander than ever from the fresh supply of snow.

In the direction we intended marching there seemed to be abundance of water, but whether rivers or lakes were in store for us it was impossible to make out. We rested the following morning, enjoying the warm sunshine and the glorious scenery, and would fain have remained there when the time came to load up and continue our journey.

The water, about which we had been unable to make up our minds, proved to be a large shallow salt-water lake. We found it best to march round by the southern shore. In some places there were tiny rivulets flowing into it, which caused us some trouble in crossing, for the bottom and ground around was muddy. Otherwise the going was good, and we marched on till it was almost dark.

Our men that morning had behaved in a peculiar way, for each of them had come to make his salaam to us; not that we attached much importance at the time to it, still it flitted across our minds that they were becoming very faithful muleteers all at once, and perhaps intended doing better work for the future. That evening we impressed upon them the necessity of making double marches again, as the last two days we had only made single, and told them how impossible it was to march much further without meeting somebody, and gave orders for them to commence loading at 3.30 A.M.

On waking up the following morning we found no attempt was being made to collect the mules, and it was 5 o'clock before they could be induced to bring them all in from grazing. Then we noticed that muttering was going on, but no attempt at loading up. Failing to elicit any reply from them for their conduct, I upbraided them severely for their laziness, and told them that if the only thing they wanted was to remain where they were and not come along with us any more, to do so by all means, but that Malcolm, Shahzad Mir, and myself, whatever they might choose to do, intended marching. Thereupon they replied sullenly that they would go no further, and hurriedly taking up their belongings from amongst a heap of baggage, they moved off in a body in a southerly direction, and were soon hidden from sight by the rising ground.

All this happened in a very short space of time, and fortunately, at the moment of the dispute, Esau and Lassoo were a little way off, busy with our things, or they too would have joined the deserters, as they one day afterwards told us. As it was, when we began to collect the mules again to try and load them, Lassoo was very uncertain in his mind as to which party he should throw his lot in with. Had he gone off with the muleteers, our difficulties would have been doubled, for none of us had had much experience in loading mules, and, even with it, loading a mule properly is no easy matter, whereas Lassoo had been a muleteer, and was far handier and quicker at the work than any of our other men. This we had already noticed, as he often used to give them a helping hand.

It was some time before we could collect all the mules again. Some of them seemed to know there was something up, and there was every chance of their being deserters. One little black chap in fact was so clever at evading our united efforts to catch him, that we had to give him up as a bad job, and load eleven animals instead of twelve.

We were reduced to so small a party that Shahzad Mir had to carry the plane-table. Either Malcolm or myself, taking a mule by the head rope, would lead the way, leaving only three to drive the mules along and keep them together, and readjust the loads, which was frequently necessary owing to our inexperience.

On looking over our baggage we found we had made one great mistake; we had allowed the muleteers to go off with the twenty remaining pounds of flour. But we had no inclination to run after them; they might have led us a chase for days, by which time the flour would have been eaten. What we were most anxious to do was to let these men see that we were in a position to be independent of their help, for we surmised they would very likely be watching us from a distance.

We learnt afterwards that these muleteers had deserted in accordance with a preconcerted plan, formed even before leaving Shushal, on the Pangong Lake, when every man had sworn to follow Ghulam Russul, whatever he might choose to do, and they had agreed amongst themselves to leave us as soon as the rations ran short. Furthermore, Ghulam Russul, whom they well knew had been with Littledale on his last famous journey, had deluded them into the idea that he could show them the way into Lhassa. They had imagined that if they all left us, it would be impossible for us to load up and march without them, and that we should be compelled to remain where we were. At night-time they had planned to come and steal our mules and ride on them to the capital.

As we moved off, we felt somewhat anxious in our minds as to whether we should find water, grass, and droppings for our fire, for if we met with ill luck we thought it quite probable that Esau and Lassoo too would join the muleteers. This of course would have been suicidal to them, as we were some 300 miles from Lhassa, which, as far as we knew, was the nearest inhabited place, and the exact direction of it they could not possibly have known.

We made a long march, longer than we had made for many a day, till we came to a large salt lake, round which we had to skirt. Everywhere grassy nullahs sloped down to it, and during the afternoon we came to a secluded nook with a pool of fresh water, and all around were the dried droppings of yak; evidently the place was a favourite haunt of these animals. This was a perfect camping ground for us, and, to prove to our two men how favourable our kismet was, we decided to halt. We all set to work with the unloading and watering of the mules, pitching the two little tents, making fires, and the numerous other little jobs always connected with making a camp. It seemed peaceful and quiet after all the grumbling and bickering we had been accustomed to. We were close by the edge of the lake, completely concealed in a hollow by rising ground on all sides, and we were rather anxious that the mules should not stray too high up and disclose our whereabouts. We concluded that these muleteers would not have sufficient courage and determination to march straight away, and were prepared to see an attempt being made any moment at capturing some of the mules.

Towards sunset we made preparations to guard against a surprise by night. We fastened a rope to the ground, very securely, between the two tents, to which we could picket the mules. In one tent was Malcolm and myself, and in the other Shahzad Mir, with Esau and Lassoo. At dusk we fastened all the mules to this rope, and arranged for each of us to take turns in watching throughout the night. Another advantage gained by this plan was that the animals were ready for us to load the first thing in the morning. Had we allowed them to stray during the night our work would have been doubled; as it was, it took us an hour and a half to load up. We also decided to make one long march instead of two, for being so short handed, all our time would have been spent in catching the mules and loading them. Besides, as we could not let them graze by night, we should have to give them more time by day.

Soon after dark, when everything was in readiness for the night, rain began to fall; it rained, as the saying goes, cats and dogs, such as we had never seen it rain before. All five of us were snug, dry, and warm in our little tents, from which we could watch the mules, whilst the deserters must have spent a most miserable night without any shelter and food, and the hot tea which they all loved so much. We felt that they were being deservedly punished for their sins. Esau and Lassoo soon realized how much they had already gained by following us, and they swore to stick to us through thick and thin, and this for evermore they undoubtedly did.

It rained during the greater part of the night, so that the sodden condition of the ground put all idea of early marching out of our head.

In order to lessen our work, and to make the marching easier for the mules, we decided to load only ten of them, and let two always go spare. We made a pile of the things we should not require, such as the muleteers' big cooking pot, and their tent, etc., and left them at the camp. By thus lightening our loads we reckoned we should be able to march sixteen or eighteen miles a day, an astounding fact for the muleteers, who had imagined we could not move without their aid. We drew comparisons between the welfare of the men with us and that of the deserters. The latter were possessors of all the flour and most of the cooked meat and the tobacco, but no cooking pots, while the former had three days' rice and plenty of tea, cooking utensils, and shelter at night, an advantage they were already fully aware of.

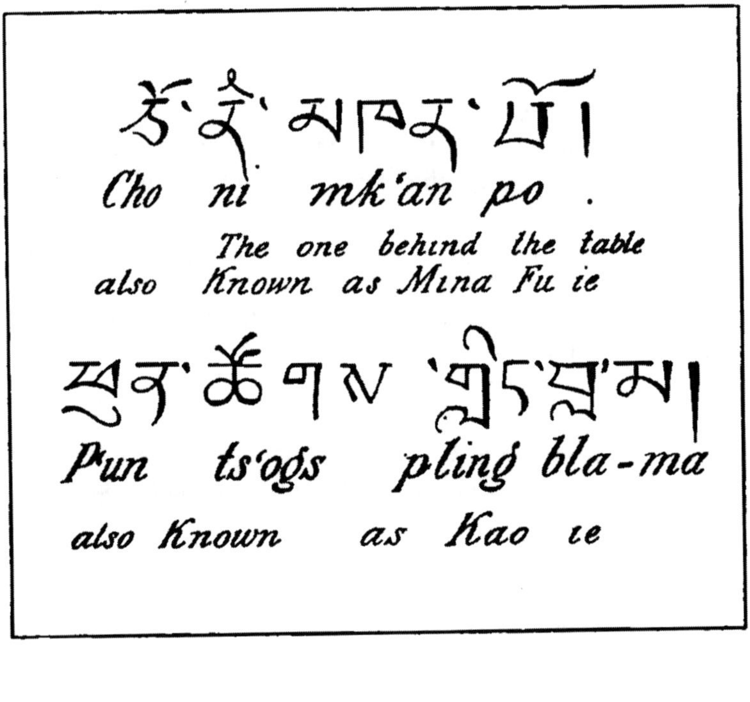

CHAPTER XIII.

RETURN OF THE DESERTERS—SHUKR ALI—LONG MARCHES—DEATH OF EIGHT MULES AND A PONY—A CHEERING REPAST.

On leaving Camp 74 on August 3rd, we had to cross an arm of the lake, or rather to make our way round it, for the rain had made the sand too soft to admit of our venturing on it. After marching for some considerable time, we therefore found ourselves just opposite our camp of the previous night, separated only by a narrow strip of treacherous ground. When we had gone thus far we noticed something or other moving on the crest of the high ground above our old camp, and on closer examination, by means of our field glasses, discovered that these moving objects were no other than the reappearance of the deserters. Soon afterwards another one came into sight, and then another. It struck us as highly probable that there had been some disagreement in the party, and that they were already beginning to taste the fruits of their crime.

We pretended to take no notice of them whatever, but rather increased the rate of our marching, keeping the animals close and compact, so that they might see for themselves how easy it was for us to manage without them. We could see them steering for our last night's encampment, where they no doubt stopped to regale themselves over a meal with the flour they had taken away, and to inspect and take whatever they fancied of the things we had left behind.

In order to save ourselves the trouble of searching for roots for our fire and vegetables on arrival at camp, we used each of us to pick up whatever we could during the march, putting the droppings of wild animals and roots into one bag, and the vegetables into another, which were hung on the back of one of the spare mules.

During our march of sixteen miles we saw nothing more of the deserters. We came to the conclusion that they must either have spent a considerable time over cooking their flour, and would catch us up again afterwards, or else we thought it just possible that having seen us marching along apparently without any difficulty, and having found their big cooking pot at the camp, they had concluded that it would be a hopeless task to pursue us any further, and had decided to steer a course of their own for Lhassa.

After passing over undulating grassy country, we halted on the south side of a salt-water lake, Camp 75, hidden in a secluded nook amidst the hills which rose from the water's edge. On the north side, some four or five miles off, ran a range of hills topped with snow peaks.

We found, by choosing a spot like this, that the muleteers could not have discovered our whereabouts from any high ground they would cross, and that to do so they would have to come right up to us. Our march had taken us over seven hours, so that as soon as camp had been pitched and water brought, it was time to collect and picket the mules for the night between our two tents, and begin our night watches.

During these lonely night watches, the absolute silence that reigned in this uninhabited country can never be described. The slightest movement of man or beast was so easily heard that it would have been impossible for a stranger to approach unnoticed. One's thoughts on these solitary occasions would wander far, far back, to others who slept peacefully amidst a scene of luxury and comfort. In order to keep ourselves awake and warm, we used to keep a pot of water in the red-hot ashes of our fire, and brew ourselves a cup of cocoa. I remember every step I took, or anything I laid hold of, seemed to make such a noise, that every moment I expected every one to awake, forgetting that sleep was sounder then than at other times.

The night passed off quietly, and at 4 o'clock we were all five of us busily engaged packing and loading up for another long march. So intent were we upon our work that at first we failed to notice that the deserters had actually reappeared, and were standing in doleful plight some little way off, without venturing to come up to us. Thereupon Malcolm and I approached them, chiefly with the object of searching the bundles they were carrying, to see whether they had any flour left, or anything else that would be useful to us. Strange to say, one of them, and the greediest, Mahomed Rahim, had brought on his shoulder the huge cooking pot in which the tea and soup used to be cooked for all the men. It was evident that he, at any rate, had hopes of our taking them into our service again, in which case he must have thought of the praise he would get from the other men for having thus exerted himself.

It was far from our intentions to take them on again as our servants, and how could we have been expected to? Had we felt that they would have served us faithfully, we should have unhesitatingly forgotten and forgiven their folly, but we instinctively felt that the only chance we had of accomplishing our journey without mishap was to throw off for good and for all these most ungrateful, unreliable men, who were bringing their own destruction upon themselves.

We made a single exception, in taking again into our service one man, by name Shukr Ali. We had a liking for him, and knew he was blessed with a family. He came under the condition that if he worked well and honestly, he would be entirely forgiven his misconduct, and would receive his entire wages, like the two men who had remained faithful. From what Shukr Ali told our two men, it was quite certain that our decision with regard to the remainder was not ill-judged.

After the delay we moved off steadily again, and for the first time found wild rhubarb growing. Besides this, we had found a moth and a beetle. All this encouraged us in the belief that we must be drawing nearer to more genial climes, and possibly, too, to some habitations of men.

Whilst making these long marches of sixteen or eighteen miles a day, which would take us eight or nine hours, we used to call a halt about half-time for a few minutes, when we found a place where extra good grass was growing, that whilst the mules grazed, all might recoup themselves with a little rest, and satisfy in some slight degree the hunger from which we always suffered, by eating some cold meat and any vegetables we could find.

One afternoon, after pitching camp, I had gone to the top of some adjacent hills to collect onions, for they generally grew on the higher ground. Whilst so employed, I chanced, as one was wont to do, to look round the surrounding country, and saw in the distance some men coming along in the same direction that we ourselves had come. Of course, I knew it must be another reappearance of the deserters. Not wishing to speak to them any more, nor that they should speak to our two men for fear they might contaminate them, I shouted to Shahzad Mir to take his gun and meet them, and forbid them to follow us any further. Until we felt certain that they had ceased to track us, the watching over our mules was a constant anxiety for all.

As a matter of fact, the occasion when Shahzad Mir turned these men back was the last on which we saw them. The nights we spent afterwards watching over our little camp, in half expectation of their sudden reappearance, were, as it turned out to be, only a waste of rest and energy, for we never saw these men again, and whether they found their way to Lhassa is a doubtful question. Whatever fate befel these wretched men, it was brought on by their own deeds, and against our most earnest endeavours to do all in our power for them. Whatever was in store for them they most assuredly deserved. They had tried and hoped to leave us to fate in the midst of solitude, and had curiously enough served themselves out with this very same punishment.

After this event all went smoothly and cheerily; all worked equally and with a will as one man. The mules, too, grew stronger on the excellent grass we had come to, and wild onions and rhubarb were abundant everywhere. Afterwards grass became scarce again, and one day we had to march twenty miles before a spot suitable to camp in could be found. Here lay a small lake, which, to our disappointment, was of brackish water, resulting in our having to resort to our original plan of digging. The night by this lake, Camp 78, was warm, the temperature not falling below forty degrees Fahr. Ahead of us the land appeared to be studded with lakes, and we decided to steer along the north side of them.

As rain had fallen during the early morning the tents were heavy, but the level marching in some degree compensated for this misfortune. That which we had surmised to be a number of lakes proved to be one salt one, which alone relieved the barren country we had quite unexpectedly marched into. The prospect, too, of shooting any game was disheartening, nor did there seem any chance of the mules getting any more grass. Yet once again, when our fortune was at a very low ebb, providential and unaccountable help was at hand, for suddenly there appeared in this desert country a solitary antelope. Our only reason for his being there was that he had lost his way. He was astonishingly tame, and easily shot. Even more wonderful still was our finding, in the middle of this expanse of sand, salt and gravel, a kind of oasis, consisting of about an acre of rising ground, covered with beautiful grass, and when we began to dig we found good water just below the surface. Instead of reading about some fairy tale, we were really acting one.

Soon after pitching our camp in this garden of plenty rain fell heavily. We thought of the deserters, and wondered what shelter or food they had providentially found. During the night the rain ceased, and a hard frost set in. When we began to load up, we found our tent was just like a sheet of thin iron, and the only way of folding it up was to bend the ends over and then stand on them.

We crossed some hills, and then descended into a valley of sandy soil. There was also rich grass, and several small streams flowed across the valley, taking their rise from the snow peaks north of us. Here we saw immense herds of antelope, all females and young ones. They were so timid that it was impossible to get nearer than 600 or 700 yards to them. Far away in the hills, too, we saw numbers of yak. We concluded that as thousands and thousands of wild antelope had chosen this pasture-land to live in, surely it must be a befitting place also for nomads and their flocks. We wondered why there was nobody living there, and still more that we could find no signs that anybody ever had done so. In this valley we even found a wild orchid. On arrival—we had marched sixteen miles in six hours—all the twelve animals were in fit and strong condition.

During the next day's march we again saw thousands of antelope, and the country was everywhere well watered, with abundance of good grass, rhubarb, and onions. All day long we had been gradually mounting, and just before halting, at a spot which we considered to be the top of our pass, we saw in a nullah close by a wild animal resembling a prodigious cat. Coming to close quarters, I killed her with my shot-gun; and on proceeding a little further up the nullah I found the remains of a young antelope, and, crouching under a rock near to the carcass, two small thickly-coated animals, no doubt the young ones of the mother I had just slain. They were strong little fellows, with large powerful paws, and difficult to hold; one in fact was as much as a man could manage. The dead mother we skinned, and brought her skin and skull back to India. We also made arrangements for keeping the two young ones, in hopes of bringing them back alive. We put each in a separate nosebag, tied up in such a way that the head remained outside. They were then hung, one on each side, on the back of a spare mule, and thus carried with impunity.

Our route took us along the edge of a fresh-water lake, on the banks of which was very fine vegetation. We discovered we had made a mistake the previous evening in imagining we had reached the summit of the pass, for after leaving the lake we had twelve more miles of uphill marching over a good deal of heavy ground and most barren country, the only vegetation being rhubarb. Several nullahs, too, had to be crossed. As we drew near the top three of our animals became completely knocked up, necessitating a rearrangement of the loads, and all the others were showing signs that they would suffer the same plight, had we insisted on continuing our march.

After climbing uphill all day long, we were thus compelled to halt for the night in one of the most unsuitable places conceivable. We were right on the summit of the pass, and ahead of us we could see nothing but absolutely barren land; therefore, to have gone any further would have only increased our difficulties, for more animals would certainly have succumbed after a very short distance.

We calculated that by giving the mules a night's rest and some of our very limited store of grain, they would recover sufficiently by the morning to enable us to descend again until we found some more grass.

After unloading, we all sallied forth in different directions in search of roots for making a fire, but none of us were

THE LAST CAMP OF OUR TWELVE MULES.

successful; all we could discover anywhere was the rhubarb and other hardy plants that will exist in these desolate high-lying places. Ever since the desertion of our muleteers we had carried along with us the poles of the tents we had discarded, so as to be prepared for a crisis of this description, so although our search was in vain, we were able to make sufficient fire to make tea with.

During our hunt for the firewood heavy clouds had been

gathering, and occasional showers had made themselves unpleasant. As soon as we had all returned a steady rainfall set in. Our mules had been picketed close to our little tent, for fear of their straying after grass during the night. Altogether our encampment at the top of this desolate pass, some 17,000 feet high, presented a very forlorn picture. Everything was wet or damp, and the poor mules stood with drooping, dripping heads. Still we had hopes of a frost setting in and the ground becoming hard for marching over in the morning. Our two little cats even seemed to feel our deplorable condition, for nothing would induce them to eat any of the raw meat we were able to spare them.

Soon after sunset intense darkness came over everything, and trusting for better fortune the following day, we soon fell asleep. During the night Malcolm happened to go outside the tent, and then returned to rouse me, saying that he thought some of the mules were dead. At first I could scarcely realize or grasp his meaning; a disaster of this description seemed to me incredible. I came out with him, and found six of the twelve lying down as though they were dead. Although it had ceased to rain, there were no stars visible, and the night was still and damp. We roused the men, who brought the candle lantern, and we discovered the astounding truth. Four of them lay stiff and dead—poor brutes! they had done yeoman service for us. Two others were very nearly dead; but even with the united efforts of all six of us we could get neither of them to stand up for a single minute, and they soon followed the fate of the other four.

A drizzling rain now set in, as by the light of the lantern we set about dragging the carcasses aside and removing their blankets to place on the survivors. Beyond this, we could do nothing more but wait for daylight. Then more disaster was added to our sad plight, for another mule died, and we doubted whether there would be any to survive this black night. We concluded that they must have eaten some poisonous plant, for their bellies became distended, they lost all power in their legs, and their groans were pitiable to hear. Our survivors consisted of four mules and one pony, and we now had to set about reducing our baggage to five loads. All that we could possibly do without had to be abandoned—in fact, we only kept one little tent, our bedding, guns, ammunition, and instruments. The two little wild cats were left there to feed on the dead bodies, and should certainly have thrived well. It was 11 o'clock before we dared venture on a descent of the pass, for the ground had become very heavy and sodden.

As we moved off we left a sad scene behind us ; seven dead carcasses lay there, and all kinds of things scattered about everywhere. Although we selected the nullah that afforded the best road, still at each step the poor mules sank into the mud above their fetlocks, and sometimes they sank down altogether, when the load had to be taken off, the animal dragged out, and reloaded. We knew our march would have to be a short one, and resolved to halt the moment we reached any grass. But our misfortunes had not yet come to an end, for, after going a short distance, our last pony collapsed completely and died. Shortly afterwards, another mule was added to the list. Three mules alone remained, and we could not know but that they, too, at any moment might die.

After we had gone about four miles, but only with the greatest difficulty, we found a little, but good, grass growing on the bank close by the stream which flowed down the nullah we were following. We at once halted and unloaded the three survivors, who were soon revelling in it. We then sent back and fetched the things we had discarded on the way, and set about re-arranging the remainder of our baggage into three loads. We agreed, too, that all should carry a load strapped like a knapsack on our backs, as well as a rifle and some ammunition, although these latter we had been carrying the whole way. Luckily we found the droppings of wild yak on this patch of grass, so were able to make a fire.

Our little tent just admitted of our bedding being placed on the ground with a box between as a table, while the men rigged one up with some poles and shawls, and made themselves very snug. Rain again fell that afternoon, and continued to do so throughout the night, until a frost set in, and the rain was changed to snow. We dared hardly think of what was happening to the three mules which had been left free to graze, for there was nowhere else to wander to. At daylight we found the ground covered with four inches of snow, which made us fear the worst. On going outside we found, to our great joy, the three survivors had in no way suffered throughout the night. We made up our minds to husband their strength, and treat them with the greatest care. We were certainly better off as regards grain than we had ever been before, and, instead of driving the mules any more, it was arranged that we should each take turns in leading one. Thus we could pick out the firmer ground, and very often assist the mule where he would otherwise have gone blundering on.

As we left camp 83, a very reduced little party, but full of hope, we found the going even heavier than it had been the previous day, for the animals constantly collapsed in the soft soil on the banks of the nullah; and we came to the conclusion that we were taking too much strength out of them in comparison with the ground we were actually covering, and that, therefore, our wisest plan would be to halt on the first grassy ground we might come to, and there wait in hopes of the weather improving. We had hardly gone two miles when we called a halt. We had found some good grass, and plenty of onions. The sun, too, began to shine, and we trusted we had come to an end of the rain and snow, and that the ground would soon dry up and admit of an early start the following morning. We made a splendid fire with our old tent and bed-poles, and cheered every one up with a good meal of venison and fried onions.

Having thus well fortified ourselves, we shouldered our guns and sallied forth in search of game and to explore ahead for the morrow. We failed in finding anything to shoot, but collected a few more flowers. Our best plan appeared to be to follow the nullah alongside which we had encamped.

CHAPTER XIV.

A SERPENTINE RIVER—HUNGER—MARMOTS—A PLEASANT CAMPING.

As we loaded up the next morning everything was shrouded in a thick white mist, and the ground was white with frost. The going was still very heavy, and the stream, which took a winding course, had to be frequently crossed. It was about ten yards broad, a foot or more deep, swiftly flowing, and very cold.

As the mist lifted the day became warm, and the three mules sank deeper than ever in the sodden ground. In spite of all our efforts, we could only make seven miles' headway, but at the same time we had been steadily descending.

On the banks we found good grass and plenty of onions. I photographed our camp, now much reduced in size, and afterwards set out barefooted down the stream on a journey of exploration, and in the hopes of finding something to shoot.

After paddling on for a short distance I found another important looking stream join its forces with the one I was following. This stream was of equal volume, and flowed in from the north. It would have been impossible to travel in a northerly direction, for the country was very mountainous and barren, stretching eventually on to snow peaks. After a time, I climbed a hill from which I could see there was a third stream flowing into this one, coming from a south-westerly direction. As far as I could judge, the river after this flowed easterly between two ranges of hills. I thought that if we could only follow it we were sure to find game, and perhaps people. It struck me, too, that perhaps it was the Chu Ma, the very river we were after.

RUBY.

Although I failed to find anything to shoot, I returned to camp with my information, which we dilated upon and argued over, so as to keep up the spirits of our men, and as rain again set in, it was satisfactory that we had something to fill all with expectation.

A white mist again shrouded us as we continued down the stream. Twice in the first five minutes we had to cross this icy cold water, so snake-like was the course the river took. The banks were too steep for the mules to have marched along them. It was a trying time for them, indeed, to be frequently crossing and recrossing the same stream, whose water came over our knees. All the mules, too, at different times collapsed in mid-stream, when the loads had to be carried ashore by us. At such a crisis as this we had no time to think of our little dog Ruby, who would always follow bravely after us, and was sometimes nearly washed away by the strong current. By the end of our march everybody was wet and cold, and the baggage was soaked. Luckily, the sun put in an appearance, and we were able to dry all our belongings. The immense number of onions that grew on the banks helped in no slight degree to feed the party, for we had run out of meat. Malcolm and I, therefore, set out in opposite directions to try and shoot something. Although we saw some antelope, neither of us had any success.

At this point where we had encamped, the stream took a southern course, apparently bending east again afterwards. We reckoned that we should cut off a corner by travelling east, and meeting the stream again later on. When we did get a chance of bettering our route, we seldom let it escape us. We marched over an undulating, sandy, grassy plain, a range of mountains a mile or so off running parallel on our left. Suddenly we struck another nullah, furnished with a stream equal in size to the one we had been following. At the same moment the rain, which had been threatening, poured without pity. We argued that it was better to continue the march than to try and camp under such conditions. We saw many tracks of kyang, which was all the more tantalizing to our desire for meat. The only animal we saw was a wolf.

At length we reached a corner where our original stream joined the one we were marching along, and we found we should have to cross this formidable body of water. We could see a few hundred yards off on the other bank a high-lying sandy spot to camp on, close to some green banks. To reach this goal was no easy matter. The three mules were getting very tired, so that two of them collapsed in the middle of the stream. The sand, too, on the further side was treacherous for a considerable distance.

By the time we had rescued our mules and carried our baggage to a place of safety, the sun was again kind enough to have another look at us. He was evidently displeased, for his presence was replaced by a heavy downpour, which continued for a couple of hours. Personally I lit my pipe, and soon fell asleep, till, at 3 o'clock, the sun again invited us to go forth to try and shoot some animal for food. We were soon off on the prowl, but all I saw was a white-headed vulture, a fox, and some sand grouse, and Malcolm was equally without success. I saw, however, that the stream meandered on sometimes between precipitous banks, increasing in volume, and with this news we fortified our men.

At sunset the weather looked angry, nor did it fall short of its foreboding; a strong east wind set in, and heavy rain fell throughout the night. We managed to keep ourselves fairly dry, and slept in spite of the storm that raged.

On waking at daybreak the wind was still blowing hard, but the rain had ceased—a real boisterous morning, when the sea waves would have rolled in with a mighty roar, as though to sweep away the very rocks. The river had swollen considerably and flowed strong and deep, as though on some errand of weighty importance. The water was stained to a dull reddish colour. It was out of the question for us to think of making an early march, for the ground resembled a quagmire. We went to inspect the nullah, to see whether it was possible to march along it; but further on the river ran flush with the precipitous sides on either hand, and soon disabused us of that idea.

About 2 o'clock we took a circuitous route over and round some hills, hitting off the river again lower down. Yet we still had to keep on the higher ground, crossing other troublesome nullahs and numerous hills, following generally its course. We had got to that stage of hunger when a little bird we saw became a victim to our guns. All at once a hare sprang up, but the indefatigable Ruby was after her, and thus did us out of a valuable supply. We struggled on with our loads on our backs, straggling one behind the other, instead of maintaining a compact little body as was our wont.

Still we were for ever on the look-out, when suddenly Esau, who was blessed with a splendid eyesight, spotted away in the grassy hills a moving black object, which we at once concluded must be a yak. While Malcolm went off to slay this meat for our suppers, followed by two of the men ready to bring in the food, I and the other two set about pitching camp.

All were instilled with fresh hope, and we collected a heap of roots to make a good fire to cook the meat over. But alas! we were all doomed to disappointment, for this moving object proved to be a black bear, which made off before Malcolm could even get near enough to fire at it. We could do nothing more than reason that the sight of a bear indicated that we must be nearer people. Besides, we had seen and shot little birds, and even the common house fly had paid us a visit. Each day, too, we had been gradually descending. With such arguments we believed that help was close at hand, and were buoyed up in hopes of it.

The next morning, the 17th August, was dull and gloomy; and the men were in the same state. They were probably feeling weak through want of meat, for the last three days they had lived on nothing but tea, while we had been regaled with Liebig and suchlike; still, in this we were most parsimonious, for we feared we might even get to worse straits. So careful were we that some of this was actually brought through China, and handed over to a missionary. As I marched on ahead I came to some sandy mounds, where I shot a very tiny hare, but in the grassy hills on our right hand I spotted a kyang, which Malcolm went after, but failed to get. Around and about were droppings both of yak and kyang, and we decided to camp here until we had shot something.

It was amusing, indeed, to see the four men making a square meal off the mite of a hare I had shot. Malcolm and I, leaving them to enjoy their repast and repose, set out in different directions in search of game, both breasting the steep range of hills which ran down to the river, and at the foot of which we had encamped. I carried a gun, a rifle, a knife, and some rope, and was lightly clad, so I was able to climb the highest peaks and spy into the most likely places. Yet I could find no game, though there were many tracks and many droppings.

I happened for a few moments to be taking shelter under a rock from a storm of sleet, when I saw, sitting up below me, some huge marmots. They were of an enormous size, as large as men. I could resist watching them no longer, for even a marmot is good food when one is hungry. On making my way to them some fine hares got up, and, thinking that the game in sight was better than the marmots out of sight down below, I killed a couple of them. This fusillade must have driven the monstrous marmots home, for they never showed themselves again. The holes down which they must have hidden were so large that I could have crawled down them myself. The two hares I strung together, and began to make my way homewards. On the way a third hare was added to my bag, and I rejoiced to think how glad the men would be when they saw me coming, laden with three fat hares, no light burden. Luckily, my way over the hills was all downhill, still I was very glad when our little camp came into sight, but was surprised that I could see nobody moving about, for I thought they would have been on the look-out, and would have been watching for my coming.

Good news was in store for me, and I soon learnt that Malcolm had been even more successful, for he had shot a kyang. Two of the men had gone off to bring in some of the meat, while the other two were making preparations for a big fire and a big feast. In order to give the men a chance of recovering themselves, we decided not to march the following day until 1 o'clock. Luckily the night turned out bright and clear, and we were able to take observations for latitude. Consequently, by the time I lay down for the night the hour was late. As I found myself falling asleep, I heard the mingled and indistinct murmuring of the men's voices, merry amidst their frying and their stewing. They must have presented a very different plight compared to their demeanour of the last few evenings. They had been changed from a sad and despondent crew into the happiest supper party in the world, only by means of a little wild donkey's flesh.

Now, of course, their religious scruples as to whether the animal had been hallaled or not, probably never entered their heads. Real hunger or thirst will make men do a great many things which nothing else on earth can. During all this time the three mules were gaining strength by the rest and the excellent pasture land.

We were up the next morning at 7 o'clock with a strong west wind blowing. We set about collecting onions for our breakfast, for one has no inclination to lie long in bed which is represented by mother earth. The morning was spent in feasting by the men, and in mapping by ourselves.

We calculated we had just crossed the ninety-second degree of longitude, and found our latitude to be 35° 11′. We discovered that if we wished to follow the river any further, we should have to cross to the other bank, for it was impossible, with the precipitous hills, to march any longer along the right bank on which we were.

The river flowed thigh deep with a swift current, and was thirty yards broad. Nevertheless, by carefully choosing the easiest crossing, and by loading the three mules lightly, with only half the baggage at a time, we managed, by making the double journey, to get the mules, ourselves, and our baggage over without any mishap. This was rather a long business, but once all on the other bank, we had soon loaded up the three mules again, and continued the descent, still following the river, all in good spirits. Towards evening we halted close to where another stream from the north joined the river we were following, and knew it would be in store for us to cross the next morning. We were struck by the appearance of the splendid green grass that grew on the hillsides, and the whole country in general seemed to be improving for the better. It looked as though we had completely come to the end of bleak regions and salt lakes, and that each day, as we should continue our gradual descent, even a more pleasing country was in store for us.

CHAPTER XV.

SHOOTING—A TROUBLESOME MULE—A YAK CEMETERY—I CHASE A KYANG — TENDER HEARTS—INSCRIBED STONES—LASSOO AND SHUKR ALI SICK—AN ARDUOUS CROSSING.

AFTER a frosty night, a still morning with a cloudless sky favoured us as we started forth to cross the stream that barred our way. It was no easy undertaking, for the sand was deep and treacherous, and the stream was filled with great lumps of floating ice. Some time was spent in these aquatic operations, for the mules sank deep into the water and had to be unloaded. Two fine gulls flew overhead, affording an easy shot for our guns and food for the party.

We made a double march to-day, and in the afternoon pursued our course along the sandy bed of the river, congratulating ourselves upon the firm level going. Presently, the river made a bend, so that if we wanted to stick to the bed, it became necessary to recross it. On sounding the bottom for this purpose we found it far too treacherous to dream of doing so. On first inspection of the banks of the river it seemed as though we should have to retrace our steps, for they looked too steep for climbing up. Still, we found that, owing to the soft nature of the sand, we were able to reach the top by marching in a slanting direction. By taking our time we at length reached the grassy plains above, and decided for the future to stick to them, instead of the uncertain bed of the river.

On the 20th August we found we were again running

out of meat, and decided whenever we saw anything to shoot that one of us should go after it, and if successful, that the caravan should at once halt. The country was favourable for game, so we had but little doubt that we should soon supply our wants. Such proved to be the case, for Malcolm shot a kyang, and we were all soon making a square meal.

We were ready for a second march in the afternoon, but were caught in a violent storm. We could see no distance ahead of us. We could not have halted and pitched our camp; we could not have found any shelter. To have halted would have meant frozen limbs. There was nothing to do but to face the storm and make what headway we could. As soon as the weather had abated, we found our way down to the river, and halted in a nook sheltered by the steep banks.

We all felt convinced that with so much grass and water people must be at hand. It was therefore arranged that Malcolm and Esau should go on ahead with knapsacks, rifles, and a good supply of meat, while I should follow on as quickly as I could with the other three men and the three mules, and still keep up the surveying. All set to work to make a big fire for cooking a large supply of wild donkey flesh to take on their journey. We were all busy with the preparations, and full of hopes for the venture of the morrow. It was arranged that the two adventurers should have a substantial breakfast before starting. Disappointment on this occasion was in store for us. Rain and sleet greeted us at dawn, and fell incessantly till midday. At that hour we fastened on the two knapsacks, and Malcolm and Esau set forth in search of people. We had arranged that both parties should keep on the north side of the river, so that there could be no danger of our losing one another.

As soon as these two had gone, I and the remainder

struck camp, and made preparations to march too. Again rain began to fall even heavier than before, and to add to our troubles, one of the three mules refused to be caught and loaded. Two whole hours did we waste in this soaking rain in our endeavours to catch this most obstinate, aggravating, yet clever mule. Then I felt that, as the day was drawing to a close, our wisest plan was to leave the animal victorious, and own ourselves beaten. I therefore gave orders to unload and pitch the camp again. Every one and everything was wet through, and just as we had fixed up our little shelter, Malcolm and Esau returned. The weather was altogether too intolerant, and they, like ourselves, had on this day to give in to the inevitable. We both agreed that the day was not quite good enough to start on. All we could do was to lie down and endeavour to keep warm, an impossibility, for everything was damp. We reaped some comfort in conjuring up thoughts of other snug places where all was warmth and sunshine.

After dark, as the rain had nearly ceased, we both went to the men's tent, where they had managed to keep themselves warmer than we had by means of a fire. Certainly the smoke was blinding, but what did that matter? We brought with us our store of brandy, and were soon cheerful under its influence with hot water. We talked to the men of boats and trains, of towns and other countries, so that they might know what sights were awaiting them as soon we had crossed this uninhabited land.

A dull, quiet morning succeeded this stormy weather. The two men again set forth, while I followed with the rest. As we proceeded we discovered we had marched into a *cul de sac*. On our right hand our road was blocked by the river, now increased to double its size. In front of us stretched a fine fresh-water lake, while on our left an arm of this lake lay, covering a distance of some miles to our rear. There was, under these circumstances, no alternative left.

I should either have to cross this arm or march back all the way round it. The first plan I attempted, but to no purpose, for the soil of the lake was too soft. I had, therefore, to begin a retrograde march. I felt lucky that the mules had not been lost altogether in the arm of the lake, as seemed probable at one time, so was less bitter against having to march in a westerly direction. Everywhere on the banks of this lake grew magnificent green grass, and there were signs of many yak. By the edges of this shallow fresh-water lay innumerable bones and scores of very fine heads and skeletons of dead yak. It seemed as though they all came to die by the shore of this wonderful lake.

I halted the little party in a garden of vegetables, and having made a meal off the last piece of the wild donkey, set out in search of game, but only bagged a couple of fat hares. About here I noticed large carrion birds, generally a sign that people are living in the neighbourhood. Enjoying the lake, too, were a multitude of various white birds, mostly in the middle of it.

It was my wish to start early, but the ground was white with snow at daybreak. In consequence, as we marched along the edge of the lake, the going was of the heaviest. A kyang came trotting up to see what we were after. Unfortunately, I only broke his foreleg, for, although I chased him for a very long way, he was still able to evade my shots and escape. It was satisfactory to find oneself marching east again. I at length pitched camp close to the water's edge, opposite my camp of the day before, on the other side of the arm.

As soon as the storm which had broken over us had passed off, I climbed the grassy hills that bordered the north shore of the lake, to shoot some food. I crept close up to two yak and wounded one of them, and chased him till the approaching darkness and a violent storm warned me it was time to return. I cared not how it rained, for I was angry and vexed with myself at having in one day wounded two harmless animals, and at the same time at having provided no food for the party.

As I made my way homewards along and down the steep grassy slopes, I saw another kyang, and, to fill up the cup of anguish, I wounded him, even with my last round of ammunition. Although in this condition he could not travel fast, still he could evade my getting near him. By exerting myself to the utmost, I found I could not only keep him in sight, but could drive him in the direction I wanted. It flashed across my mind, what if I could actually drive the poor kyang as far as the camp, where he would be caught, and oceans of meat would be provided for all, without the trouble of having to fetch it? Then on looking round I knew that darkness would end the chase, for camp was some miles off. As I pursued the kyang, or rather drove him, he entered a steepish nullah, down which a stream flowed, and by the side of this he succumbed. I rushed up with mixed feelings of joy and pity, and before he could struggle to his feet I had plunged my knife into him. At the same moment a deafening storm of thunder and lightning broke over me, and darkness followed.

For fear of losing my way I kept to the nullah, which finally emerged by the edge of the lake, along whose banks I trudged till, eventually, a dim light from the men's tent showed me where the camp was. Shortly after my arrival the storm passed off and the moon shone out. The men were hungry, and when I narrated my adventures, two of them, arming themselves with knives and a sack, set out under the lucid instructions I gave them to find the kyang and bring in some of the flesh. I had slept soundly before I was aroused again by the arrival of the hissing frying pan into my tent, alive with fresh meat and wild onions.

The morning after these storms was still, as though the elements had exhausted themselves. The lake resembled a large sheet of the smoothest glass, partially hidden by some light clouds that rested on it, awaiting a breath of wind or the sun's rays before they could be lifted. As I walked along the edge of the water I shot four hares, for in some of the rocky places they were plentiful enough.

Although I had hit off a well-defined track frequented by wild animals, still the sandy soil was so laden with moisture that the mules sank deep at almost every step. The lake, by reason of its sandy and rocky shore, reminded me more of an inlet sea than anything else. Then grassy slopes with flowers and vegetables eventually rose into high hills, which again were backed by snow-capped peaks. On the south side of the lake a vast plain extended to distant mountains. In whatever direction I chanced to look numbers of wild yak and kyang could be seen grazing, while on the lake itself many water-fowl had found a home. It was a veritable sportsman's or artist's paradise.

As soon as the mules were tired, I halted and went off to shoot a yak. A yak was always preferable to a kyang, for there was more fat to be got from the body. I soon found one above camp and had but little difficulty in shooting him. Having loaded myself with a sack of meat I descended again to camp. On arrival, to my surprise, Malcolm and Esau had returned. They had had, in fact, enough of trying to find people in stormy weather, when they had not even been able to light a fire. They, however, gave good reports of the road ahead, which they said would still bring us to abundance of grass teeming with yak, at the same time gradually descending.

This afternoon the three mules unfortunately strayed, and we turned into bed without even knowing where they had gone to. It seemed as though they were tired of carrying heavy loads over sodden ground and were bent upon a little pleasure of their own. One of the three mules invariably used to give us a deal of trouble in catching him for loading up. We found the only way of securing the rascal was for two of us to hold a long rope at both ends, allowing it to lie flat on the ground. Then the rest of us would drive the mule towards the rope, which was tightened as he reached it. Then those who held the two ends would run round in opposite directions, and thus encircle the animal in the coils. This plan, however, took up so much time and energy that eventually we used to fasten the mule with a long rope to one of the other two, when there was no difficulty in catching him. Of course, when his load was on, he made no attempt at escaping, but rather the reverse, for he would thrust himself forward as much as to say, "Just take off these things, please, and let's be off." He was a wonderfully clever mule, and the most useful one we had. Although small, he used to carry 400 pounds weight of baggage, about the equal of what the other two carried together.

After we had tracked the three wandering mules, who had selected a cosy nook, well concealed from view, we continued our march along the edge of the lake. Hares, terns, and gulls fell to our guns, and at night-time we camped by a garden of onions and rhubarb. Although this wonderful lake was a charming and delightful spot, with a genial climate, still we were not sorry on the 26th August to reach the eastern corner of it. Here we found sandy, hillocky ground, with good grass, a favourite haunt of the kyang.

A short distance from the lake we were lucky enough to strike another small stream, that took its rise from some of the neighbouring hills. This stream flowed away in an easterly direction, sometimes sluggish, at others fairly fast. The water was clear with sandy bottom, a few yards across, and only about a foot deep. In some places we could see numbers of tiny fish, which always made off at our approach. The banks of this little stream were sandy and grassy. All were delighted at having hit upon this sign of civilization. We decided, whatever happened, to follow it. By so doing we knew we must be descending the whole time, and what was more important still, we knew we should never suffer from scarcity of water. There would be, as well, always more chance of finding game and grass. We made a double and pleasant march along the stream, which all the time was increasing in volume, but at night-time we were almost beaten down by a heavy thunder-storm.

The next day we left the river, hitting it off again before halting. During the night the mules once more strayed, and prevented us from marching the following morning. Perhaps they had been taking shelter from another storm that had visited us. As the morning was fine we were not in the best frame of mind at having to wait till they were found. Yet we had plenty to do in writing, and mapping, and cleaning all our guns, etc. As we marched off in the afternoon, I was ahead carrying my shot-gun, and suddenly came close upon a goa. Although he was stung with No. 2 shot, he unfortunately managed to escape into the grassy hills. That evening another storm broke over us, just as we were flattering ourselves that we had escaped.

A yak probably carries his heart very low, for most of those which were shot received the bullet just behind the shoulder, yet on opening the dead body, we never found any wound inflicted on the heart itself. We were glad that the yak was provided with such internal arrangements, for the heart was the tit-bit of the animal. It was so tender that it could always be eaten directly after death. The kidneys were excellent, the liver was fair, and the tongue as tough and as hard as wood, according to our way of curing it. The probability is that, with proper means, the tongue would have been the most toothsome bit of any. The flesh itself was, as a rule, tough, even after several days' keeping, and was never as tender as the flesh of the kyang, but although close-grained, it was very sound, nutritious meat.

The choicest part of the wild donkey was its heart. I fancy the flesh of this animal, when we had stored it up for several days, had more flavour to it, a flavour, too, which was peculiar to the animal itself. As for antelope and goa,

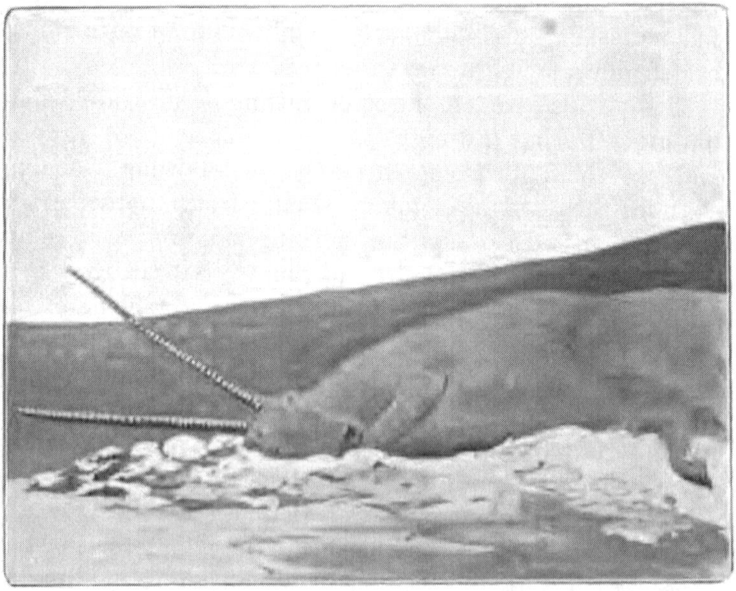

A DEAD ANTELOPE.

every particle of flesh was juicy and tender, and was always eagerly devoured by us all.

On the 29th August, when we vowed our three mules were worth their weight in gold, for with heavy loads they plodded most pluckily through the sodden soil, and over nasty, deep, stony nullahs, I happened to be walking on higher ground along the side of hills. I had my shot-gun and was after hares, for we were all very fond of them. Quite by chance I came upon the first sign of man's work.

I had found a mānė. A mānė is a heap of stones, consisting of only a few or of thousands, upon which are inscribed sacred sayings. They are common all over the country, wherever Tibetans live. This particular mānė consisted of three stones placed edgeways in the ground, and forming three sides of a square. Resting on these was a fourth stone, and they all bore inscriptions. This was a great find, and I shouted and waved to Malcolm and the men below, two of whom were soon eagerly making their way towards me to learn the news.

All were buoyed up with hope of soon meeting people, and when we halted after our first march, all were full of suggestions and expectations, and looked forward to once more getting some flour, mutton, salt, sugar, and butter. In two days at the most we calculated nomads would be found.

On one green hill we could see hundreds upon hundreds of yak grazing; there was, I believe, more yak visible than hill. We were particularly partial to these animals, for the reason already given on a previous page. The fat of the yak was so precious to us that we used to boil down every ounce of it, and put it into our old cocoa tins. These cakes of yak's fat were very much appreciated by all. We used to knock off bits of it and eat it as if it were Everton toffy.

We found that to cross the river would have been hazardous, but we discovered that, after winding round to the left, it made a sharp bend to the right again, and at this point rose up precipitous cliffs, forming the basis of high hills. We should, therefore, either have to go round or over these hills. The former would have taken days, and probably have led us out of our depth altogether. In such a situation we had no choice, and commenced to climb them.

In the midst of our difficulty, another of those violent

storms fell on us, accompanied with hail, that was blown painfully against man and beast. It was impossible to struggle on against such adversity—a stiff ascent and a blinding storm. Even this came to an end, when we slowly breasted the hill again. By nightfall we had come out victorious; we had descended again the other side, and had encamped close to the river. We knew, though, that we were not sufficiently strong to overcome many more obstacles such as we had just surmounted. A wet morning of mist and rain followed this event. When we were able, we marched off again along the banks of the river till we found it was joined by another river coming from the north. This we had to cross with care.

On the other side, some distance off, I saw a yak, and set out ahead to shoot it. I wounded him grievously, and feeling certain that he would not go very far, I waited for the caravan to arrive, so that a man could come after me to bring along some meat. He gave me a longer chase than I had anticipated, but the last bullet told, when he rolled over on his back and kicked violently with all fours in his final struggles. He was a very fine fellow, as the man with me remarked, "*Pahar ke muafic*" (like a mountain), and his horns were over three feet long.

Laden with meat, I walked on in search of our camp, and was beginning to get a little uneasy at not having seen any signs of which way they had gone, for the sun was setting, when two very faint shots announced their whereabouts. That night we fared sumptuously, for Malcolm too had slain a yak near camp, as he thought it quite possible that the one I had gone after might have escaped altogether, which would have meant no supper.

We were aroused early by moans from Lassoo. We found him lying on his back and groaning, and argued that he must have been suffering from indigestion. We had been anxious to make an early start, but Lassoo's sickness and a thick, wetting mist quickly dispelled this wish. By midday Lassoo was relieved by administering warm flannel and Cockle's pills, and the mist, too, by the cheering sun. On the march I shot a goa with my shot-gun. He was very tame, never attempting to run away more than twenty yards from me. Later on two yak came charging down

AN ENORMOUS YAK.

upon our caravan, within fifteen yards. Had they come much nearer we should have had to shoot them in self defence; yet we had no wish to, for we had abundance of meat for the time being, as much as we could manage to carry.

Although Colonel Prjevalsky writes that "wild yak shooting is as dangerous as it is exciting, for a wounded beast, especially an old bull, will often attack the pursuer," yet, personally speaking, I never found a yak attempt to charge, wounded or not, and consider there to be absolutely no more danger in shooting a yak than an antelope.

Towards evening, when we were thinking of calling a halt, we found another important river running in from the north, and which we should have to cross. We elected to do so that same evening, for we doubted being able to get the men to face the icy water the first thing in the morning. Both Lassoo and Shukr Ali were sick, so we only had Shahzad Mir and Esau to help us.

In first attempting to find a crossing, the current carried me off my legs, for the water was waist deep at this spot. By making more trials we found we could manage higher up the river, by crossing in a diagonal direction with the current. Here the river was twenty-five yards across, with the water up to the thighs, and the bed was uneven with big boulders.

These operations took some time, for, fearing accidents, we had to make double journeys. Worst of all was the cold north wind, that blew without pity. It was chilly work, to say the least of it, and when all had reached the green turf on the other bank, we all felt we could never have crossed that river again, not even for a sack of sovereigns!

CHAPTER XVI.

ANOTHER CHULA—MOUNTAINS—A QUEER ILLUSION—STRANGE VOICES—WE FIND WE ARE DESCENDING—A TIBETAN CAMP —ESAU SENT AS AN AMBASSADOR—AN INVITATION.

THE 1st of September was a dull morning with a very biting east wind, but our two invalids had been cured by means of Cockle's, and all of us felt relieved when we woke up to find we were on the right side of the river. I am afraid that our two sick men would not have recovered, had we delayed the crossing of the torrent the evening before. During our morning's march we kept close to the river's edge, which now flowed by majestically. In the latter half of the day the travelling was bad and toilsome, over a white, stony soil, abounding in unexpected quagmires, and enticing us further on to spongy, sloping ground, sliced up by innumerable nasty ragged nullahs. Even in this inhospitable stretch of land Lassoo found a hope of further good tidings in the shape of a chula, or mountain fireplace, apparently a month or two old.

Close to the river we quite unexpectedly hit upon a beautifully grassy spot, sheltered by some green hillocks from the incessant wind. It promised at sunset to turn out a bright, clear night, so as to afford us a chance of taking some latitudes, but clouds again began to gather around and eventually obscured every star, and produced a dim yet penetrating rain. This at daybreak was replaced by snow. Still we loaded up, and struggled along against the storm of snow and sleet that blew against our faces and impeded our progress. Later on the sun forced a way through the unkindly clouds, and the snow was quickly melted into the soil. All our labour in drying our baggage was wasted, for everything was soaked with rain again as soon as we began our second march, over a country alternating with patches of grass and white stones. It was an impossibility to see for any distance, but we steered by the noise from the swollen river, till, just before dusk, all became clear again. Then we learnt the cause of the icy wind that had been persecuting us. There rose up north and north-east of us, forty or fifty miles away, some lofty, snow-capped mountains, a truly magnificent picture to gaze upon. A sunny morning was an agreeable change for us, and, added to the fine sight of the snows, compensated for the sterile and monotonous plains of white stones over which we continued our march.

The only life we saw was a large gathering of sand-grouse. So confident were we of shooting a sumptuous meal, that as we drew near to these birds we began to reckon how many of them our four barrels would account for. They, too, must have had their share of reckoning, for without giving us a chance, they with one accord took to wing and flew high and far away, irritating us with their well-known notes.

After proceeding for about four miles we came to a large heap of stones, conspicuous in this flat, open plain. It was an indication of man's presence at some time or other. There was no writing on any of the stones. From here we descended to a lower level in the bed of the river. On one of the adjacent hills I had noticed, through my glasses, actually a man with a little dog. Look as often as we might, still there was no mistaking their identity, yet we could scarcely realise the fact.

Whilst the meat was being prepared for breakfast, I went off to interview the stranger. The nearer I came the more was I convinced that there really stood a man and his dog. Suddenly they disappeared from view, and fearing their escape I hastened my step, which soon brought me to within an easily recognisable distance, when, on the man with his little dog again showing themselves, I learnt that they were no other than two marmots.

After breakfast we heard what sounded like men shouting from the other side of the river. We all turned our eyes in the direction from whence it came, and, in spite of getting a good view, nothing was visible. We speculated as to what could possibly be the cause of the noise, for all had heard it, and, as is usual on these occasions, were none the wiser in the end. The only result was that there was considerable excitement amongst our little party. I have read of travellers hearing strange voices when traversing some of the deserts of Turkistan. Perhaps some of these phantoms who emitted those remarkable noises had wandered over into Tibet.

The monotonous plain we marched over in the afternoon seemed interminable, making the men wearier than the animals, for the going was firm and level. As soon as we had pitched our camp, clouds gathered around us from every quarter, and at length burst open with a violent thunderstorm. At such times we could do nothing more than lie down in our tent, and try to keep dry and look pleasant.

The day before yesterday the men had told us that they had meat left for five more days. We did not, therefore, trouble about shooting any of the kyang that happened to come and look at our camp, or to stalk any of the antelope we saw. After the storm had abated, they came to inform us that the meat was finished, not an uncommon state of affairs with us. It shows how difficult it was to provide for such unreasonable men, worthy as they were in most other respects.

We were beginning to think that, as we had marched so long and so far without seeing any living being, we must be the only people in existence. To any one who is anxious to avoid the police authorities, I can strongly recommend the Chang.

On the 4th of September we learnt from our own observations that we were actually at a lower altitude than Niagzu is, where we had last seen brushwood. We had unmistakably been descending ever since the great disaster befell our animals. After we had made our midday meal off the scrapings of a yak's tail we had carried for some days, and the carcass of a hare, we moved on again, still traversing the same kind of country.

Towards evening we found an old chula close by the river side, and, at no great distance from here, the ground whereon only a few months previously there must have been a fairly large encampment of nomads or merchants. From traces we found round and about, it was evident the caravan had consisted of camels and ponies; there were even the remains of a dead pony close by. We found the single horn of an antelope stuck into the ground, which was a convincing proof that the owners had possessed fire-arms. We saw also some pieces of string and odds and ends, which our men, of course, picked up. The caravan had evidently marched along the river we were following, for further on we found more camel droppings, but as to who they were and whence they had come from and where they were going, it was impossible to say. They benefited our little party by putting every one in the most hopeful and cheery frame of mind. Here were we at inhabitable altitudes, and we had seen unmistakable signs that told us that other people, too, had travelled in this part of the land.

There was much rain during the night. After loading up, Malcolm and I, separating, went ahead to do our best to shoot some meat. Malcolm luckily wounded a kyang, and drove the animal to the spot where we had halted. His heart was soon cut out and hissing with the onions in the frying pan, and all fared sumptuously. We carried away sufficient donkey flesh to last our party three days, and proceeded over the same monotonous plain, which later on was relieved by some sandy hillocks. The men's spirits were kept from falling through the discovery of some more chulas. This encouraged them to weather the storm that enveloped us.

During the night at Camp 107 our mules had strayed, so that on the morning of the 6th of September all idea of making a double march had to be abandoned, especially as there was a steady downfall of rain. It was, in fact, 11 o'clock before we were able to make a start, and at that hour a cold wind was blowing from the northern snows, and the day was altogether dull, heavy, and depressing; it awakened us to the realisation of our actual feelings. We became aware that we needed some little luxury, such as flour and salt. We seemed to be having rather a surfeit of our fids of wild donkey's flesh.

More than four months had elapsed since we had gaily cantered out of Leh post-haste. We longed to find somebody, and we would willingly have given a large sum for a loaf of bread. We wondered how it was that while our four men had of late been always nagging and quarrelling with one another over every little trifle, we ourselves had never disagreed for a minute. Our only solution was that there was nothing at all we could have argued about, for both our minds were bent heart and soul on the same object, namely, the accomplishment of what we had undertaken to do.

As we had seen signs of mankind, we began to talk over plans. We decided that when we reached a locality abounding in game, to leav three men and one mule there, and ourselves, with the other man and two mules, lightly loaded, to make enormous marches, and find people and bring back assistance with the greatest possible expedition. Thus, filled with these thoughts, both of the past and of the future, we continued our march in silence, so gloomy was the day. The daily practice of exploring on ahead had made the work of always keeping a sharp look out in front, to right and left of our route, habitual to us all.

Suddenly, in the dull light, I noticed far down the river, on the stretch of pasture lands that extended to the hills on the other side, something of whitish appearance. This at first, by means of our glasses, we made out to be a number of stone houses. Yet the idea seemed so ridiculous to us that we declared it was only some irregularities of the ground, such as we had often seen before, and conjured up into no end of impossible resemblances.

The dull, gloomy day had doubtless made us less sanguine of help than we usually were. Nevertheless, we still kept our eyes on the thing, and halted every three or four hundred yards to inspect again with our glasses, but only to repeat once more, "Merely irregularities of the ground." At length we reached a piece of rising ground, where another inspection produced the words, "Merely irregularities," and, "Stop a moment! Some one else have a look," I called, as I held out my glasses for the nearest man to take, stating, "I think it must be something else than 'merely irregularities of the ground.'"

The first man gazed intently, removed the glasses from his eyes, and passed them to another, still keeping his eyes fixed on these "irregularities of the ground." Thus we all looked and gazed, and all were astounded, for some could even discern smoke rising from the spot. We moved on quickly another few hundred yards, full of excitement, and suggesting a thousand problems in a very short time. Once more we halted and repeated our observations. Now the smoke was as clear as a pike-staff, and, what was still more astounding, we could actually solve the question of the "irregularities of the ground." These, indeed, we made out to be tents, and if there was a doubt it was soon dispelled by our noticing a short distance from the tents an immense number of animals, which we conjectured to be yak. We put two and two together and agreed with ourselves that the tents formed a large encampment, and the animals dotted about were the transport.

But our next question was, "By whom could they be inhabited?" The tents were certainly white, and we knew the tents of ordinary nomads were black. Was it an encampment of the Golok, or other robber tribes? Surely, we said, they have black tents too? Was it a Russian caravan travelling from Turkistan? Could it by any possible chance be some other travellers' camp, like ourselves, but on a much larger scale? Were they a body of Turkistan merchants? Then, again, we reflected that their tents would probably be black. We could not help thinking there must be some European dwelling in them. Whatever they might turn out to be, we decided to waste no more time in useless speculation, but to resort to action.

We decided on the following plan:—We sent Esau, because he could speak Tibetan well, with Shukr Ali, because he was of least use to us, armed with rifles, to cross the river and reconnoitre the camp, find out who they might be, and, if possible, bring back food and help. We ourselves, with Shahzad Mir and Lassoo, continued the march along the river till opposite the encampment, which lay a mile or so back from it. We then selected a hollow, surrounded by high rocks, and with good grass around, to pitch our camp on, completely out of sight of those on the other side of the river.

Thus we were thoroughly prepared for any emergency

that might occur. From our position we could take note of their every movement without being seen ourselves. While each of us watched in turn from the summit of the rocks, which we called our battlements, the rest were busy with the usual duties connected with pitching a camp or bivouac. We saw that our two men had safely crossed the river, and watched them getting nearer and nearer to the camp, till darkness hid them from our view.

As the night was dark and our two men had been explicitly told where they would find us, and as it was highly probable that the strangers opposite had no idea at all of our existence, we saw no reason why we should keep watch throughout the night. We certainly kept awake a later hour than usual, chiefly, I think, in the expectation of Esau turning up with a loaf of bread or some other food—for Esau is a shrewd, cunning fellow—whilst our conversation consisted merely of repeating our conjectures as to who these people might be, and what might be happening to our two men. With a gnawing feeling at the pit of our stomachs, which we thought might have been satisfied, we fell asleep.

Snow was on the ground when we anxiously rose the next morning, glasses in hand, to mount the battlements and watch. We found the previous day that with glasses we could just distinguish and count the tents, and with difficulty make out men. At first I could distinguish nothing of the strange camp, and merely put this down to the fact that it was not yet full daylight. Still I kept on straining and straining my eyes as the day grew brighter, yet I could see nothing.

So remarkable did it seem to me that I called Malcolm. Neither could he distinguish any signs of the camp up or down the river. We stood astounded, and somewhat crestfallen. What could have happened to the tents, and where were our two men, we asked over and over again? All our hopes, raised so high, of seeing people once again, and of getting food, were all of a sudden cruelly shattered. Yet surely, we argued, if there had been no tents, and our certainty, after all, was only an illusion, what could have happened to our two men? Had they been swept away in trying to recross the river, or were they lying ill behind some rock? It was impossible for us to know, and we resolved to wait and watch for them the whole day, and then, if there were no signs of them, to continue our march down the river bank, for we could not say how many more or how few days we might hold out without getting any help.

We were more surprised than ever to see two men, about 10 o'clock, trudging along up stream on the same side of the river as ourselves, and before very long were glad to recognise them. To judge from the way they were walking, we guessed they had good news for us, and such proved to be the case. We were all soon eagerly listening to their adventures.

Esau related how this encampment proved to be a joint one of Tibetan merchants on their way from Lhassa to China, and how he had been taken to the tent of the head merchant, where he had received hospitality, and slept the night. Esau had been primed with a story to tell that we were a merchant and a doctor on our way to China. The merchant had at once recognised Esau as coming from Ladakh, and, on hearing his story, he remarked they must be either English or Russians, for, he said, men of no other nations could accomplish such a journey. Then Esau related the whole truth, detailing how matters stood with us. At the mention of rupees the merchant pricked up his ears, and expressed his desire to see us and do a little business by selling us food. In order to gain his friendship Esau had told him we had nothing else but bags of rupees, while as a matter of fact we had only something like four hundred. Esau also accounted for the miraculous vanishing of the entire encampment. He said that before daybreak they had marched off along the river, which they had crossed lower down, and thence were going to travel on to Barong and Tankar on the Chinese border. The merchant had sent his salaam, and advised us to follow in his tracks and catch up his caravan, for he said he was most anxious to make our acquaintance. This plan suited us admirably, for we, like the merchant, were steering for Barong and Tankar. We pictured to ourselves the friendship and hospitality that awaited us, and anticipated overtaking the caravan that same evening, and the enjoyment of a cosy tent and a good supper, for Esau had told us he carried all kinds of supplies.

CHAPTER XVII.

WE CATCH UP THE MERCHANT'S CAMP—TIBETAN HOSPITALITY—WE FIND THAT WE HAVE DISCOVERED THE SOURCE OF THE CHU MA—BARGAINING.

It can well be imagined that we were not long in loading up our three mules, and were soon marching faster than was our wont down the banks of the river. Still, as we covered mile after mile, we were growing disappointed at finding no tracks of the caravan, especially, too, as from any high mounds that afforded a far-stretching view, we could see no signs of any camp at all. We began to lose heart and to fear the whole affair was a myth. We wondered whether the merchant had been deceiving Esau. Just then, as our doubts had become really serious, we reached the place where the caravan had crossed the river.

The merchant had certainly given good advice, and easy to follow, in telling us to overtake him by means of his tracks. They were clearly seen and numberless in the soft sandy soil; it seemed as though a whole army had swept along. By the water's edge was a mud pile two feet high, decorated with a stick on top. We were convinced that it was a landmark to point out to merchants where to cross in safety. Here we had to leave the river, which we had been following for nearly twelve days from its very source. We kept to the tracks of the merchant, expecting every moment to come upon the encampment. Our three mules were beginning to show signs of fatigue, and as sunset was close at hand we were reluctantly compelled to halt for the night without the fulfilment of our hopes. We were a little anxious and disappointed, for we argued that if the merchant always marched like this, we should never be able to catch him up.

The next morning, the 8th September, we tried hard to come in sight of the merchant. The tracks took us over a steep pass of deep sand and a descent down to a fine grassy valley, fed with a stream of clear bright water. Close to this we found they had encamped the night before. Here was the first good grass we had seen since leaving the river, so it was clear the merchant had declined to halt until he had reached a really good camping-ground, and we reckoned that the chances were that the next march would only be a short one.

We found the fires that had been lit were still burning, the dried droppings or argols were still red-hot, and various marks denoted where the different tents had been pitched, and the yak and ponies picketed. Such preparations as fire and water at hand induced us to halt for breakfast, and after despatching this frugal meal, Malcolm, Esau and myself, loaded with some rupees, which we had not set eyes on for months, set out in front, determined to catch up the merchants that very night, no matter how far they might have gone. We could no longer stand this vanishing like a will-o'-the-wisp. The other three men and three mules were to follow on in their own time, making as long a march as they could manage.

There was no difficulty in following the tracks, for we could sometimes see miles away a broad black-looking line over damp grassy or deep sandy ground showing the route that had been taken. We had a long though pleasant tramp before us, mostly through grassy valleys, bounded on either hand by fine ranges of hills. The sun had set, yet we were able easily to distinguish the tracks, and finally, after turning the corner of a valley, we saw lights burning some way off in some low-lying land, well sheltered by neighbouring hills from the bitterly cold wind that was blowing.

As long as we continued on the move we did not suffer, but a halt of a few minutes soon became unpleasant. After an eighteen-mile walk we were within half a mile of the tents, so we sent Esau on ahead, armed with one of our Chinese visiting cards, to announce to the merchant that we were outside, and were anxious to pay our respects to him, and, if possible, do a little business in the shape of food and hiring transport.

As soon as Esau had left us we quickly grew cold and impatient, for we had expected he would have at once come himself, or sent some one else, to bring us to the presence of the merchant. We could stand it no longer; we were famished with cold and hunger, and there lay the tents. We had done our share of being polite by sending our servant on in front. Why should we not go ourselves and enter the merchant's tent without more formality? As we drew near to the tents, the loud fierce barking of the big dogs gave tidings of our approach. Hunger and cold made us indifferent to these monsters, and had it not been for the kindness and intelligence of a small boy, who saw us, we might have had a very unpleasant time of it. With his aid we at length found our way to the head merchant's tent, where a dangerously fine-looking dog, luckily chained up to the pole, by his angry growls soon brought the merchant's servant from within. He must by this time have heard all about our arrival, for without more ado he beckoned to us to come inside the tent. We wanted no second invitation to escape from the icy-cold north wind that seemed to penetrate our very bones. We smiled with unfeigned pleasure and delight as we entered this cosy warm abode. On either side of the tent was a thick mattress, covered with dull red cloth, and on the end of each of them sat a Tibetan merchant, clothed in dark red robes. At the end of the tent was burning a gentle light, displaying his religious articles of silver and other precious metals that lay on a table—a light that was quite in accordance with the surroundings of comfort and snugness. In the middle of the tent was a fire of red-hot argols, glowing particularly bright on this cold night, supporting a shining copper kettle filled with tea.

At the end of one of the beds sat Esau, busily engaged in filling his inner man; whilst able to satisfy his own wants he seemed to have lost his senses and forgotten all about his masters'. A few sharp words of reproof soon brought him to his feet, and we were introduced to the two chief Tibetans in the camp. They signed to us to be seated, and then handed us a basin each, which the servant filled with hot tea. Into this he dropped a large lump of butter, and then held before us a large red leather bag, filled with tsampa, or finely-ground barley meal. From this we took several large spoonfuls and mixed up with the tea, adding whatever salt we fancied. The merchant's servant then handed us some chopsticks, and we were soon at work shovelling the hot mixture into our mouths, rather greedily, I'm afraid, and if I were to relate the number of basins we emptied that night, it would never be credited.

As soon as we had somewhat satisfied the gnawings of our hunger, we opened negotiations about purchasing supplies. The prices far excelled our purses, and as everything was packed up for their early march the next morning, no business could be done in that line. The merchant informed us that he only intended making a six-mile march, and he consented to lend us two ponies for our baggage, that they might help our three mules in reaching the camp the next day. He said he would leave his servant with them, with instructions that if our three mules did not arrive before midday, he was to wait no longer, but come on without them.

After thanking the two merchants for their hospitality, we left the tent to go to the shelter where it had been arranged we were to spend the night. We found ourselves stumbling over picketing ropes and threading our way amidst hosts of yak, till we drew up before a huge pile of goods with a large awning stretched over them. We sat down in the darkness by this mass of merchandise. Here we found no shelter from the wind, and to have remained there for any length of time would have been impossible; such a bitterly cold wind we had never experienced before —besides, we did not feel we were being treated with the little respect we were entitled to. In our present condition we could certainly not expect much, but here were we, two Englishmen, chucked along with the baggage under an awning, absolutely no shelter on a night like this, while the two Tibetan merchants were sleeping peacefully in warmth and comfort. We could withstand it no longer, and rose to find our way back to the merchants' tent. They had both gone to bed, but we informed them that we, too, had come to sleep inside the tent, and at cnce began to make ourselves at home. The merchants, though surprised at our intrusion, still were not in a frame of mind to object to our company. Either they had some pity for us on this bitter night, or more probably, owing to the late hour we had kept them up eating and talking, they were too tired to resort to argument or resistance. A numnah was placed on the ground between the two beds for us to lie upon. As soon as various coverings had been spread over us, we were soon warm again and both sound asleep.

Before daybreak I was aroused by some energetic Tibetan, gifted with a voice like a bull, bellowing forth "Chou-chou, chou-chou, chou-chou-ou-ou-ou!" which, I am told, means, "Up and get ready!" I think I must have dozed again after this, for I next remembered finding myself in the open on the ground. It was just getting light, and masses of laden yak were moving past us. We were both struck with astonishment; nobody seemed to take any notice of us. There we lay; there was no noise—everybody seemed as though he was going to do his own work and look to nothing else. Batch after batch quietly disappeared—merchants, tents, yak, ponies, men, dogs, and all. All seemed to know

THE KUSHOK'S TAME YAK.

what was happening but ourselves; we could not grasp the situation, but cold made us rise and try to warm ourselves.

In spite of the wonderful disappearance of this wonderful camp, we were glad to find that the merchant had kept his word, for we found two very fat-looking ponies had been left behind for us in charge of his servant Nimbri, who was provided also with the large red bag of tsampa and the other ingredients for mixing it up with. We weren't long in having the kettle boiling, and Malcolm and I sat down along with Nimbri to breakfast.

Esau had gone back to hasten on the mules for fear they should not arrive before noon. Nimbri was fully aware of the position he held as master of the ceremonies, and for some time was stingy with his doling out of the food; but a present of a knife and a rupee, which at first he refused, made him more liberal, and although all our conversation was carried on by signs, we all laughed heartily and enjoyed the fun. After our remarkable breakfast Nimbri gave us two large coats, and wrapping ourselves in these, we separated and went to sleep in some sunny nook.

I was aroused by Malcolm some time afterwards to come and have some more breakfast, when Nimbri made signs to us that it was about noon, and that he could wait no longer. Just at that moment the mules came into sight round the corner, the baggage was quickly transferred to the ponies, and our men had soon finished the tea and tsampa, which they so well deserved. We now looked forward to reaching the merchants' camp before darkness and learning something about the management of it, its size and composition. Malcolm and I, who were in front, were soon surrounded by a number of Tibetans, who made friendly jokes amongst themselves and were evidently amused at our appearance.

As soon as our baggage arrived, we pitched our little tent and attempted to return the hospitality of the merchants by inviting them to tea, which was all we could give them. We were anxious, too, to make a bargain with them for hiring a yak or pony for our baggage. Just before darkness the two merchants came, for our tent was not more than a hundred yards off from their own. The hospitality and comfort of our tent was but a poor apology for that of their own, as we all four of us sat crowded up in an uncomfortable heat. Esau was close at hand as interpreter, but we failed to come to any agreement about hiring animals for the morrow. We were able, however, to purchase some supplies, flour at eight annas, and afterwards one rupee a pound, and ghi and salt at correspondingly high rates.

The following morning the whole merchants' camp had moved off before we had begun to load up. We had no trouble in finding their tracks, and after a pleasant march we noticed one of the mountain sides thickly dotted with the merchants' yak out grazing, so we knew the tents would be close at hand; everything was in full swing as if the camp had been there for months. As we approached we were told by Nimbri to pitch our tent near the head merchant's, into whose tent we were soon invited to drink tea.

As we sat sipping and chatting about the country and the people, to our great astonishment and delight he informed us that the name of the river where we had first seen his camp was no other than the Chu Ma, the very one we had been in search of. Without being aware of it at the time, we had actually discovered the source of the Chu Ma just after leaving the beautiful fresh-water lake abounding in wild yak. We had also followed its course for nearly twelve days, a distance of about 120 miles. This river is also known to the Tibetans as the Ma Chu, and to the Mongols as the Nap-chitai-ulen. He informed us that the intention of the Tibetans to oppose the entrance of foreigners into Lhassa was stronger than it had ever been before; and it was his firm belief that no one ever would reach Lhassa.

After we had made some purchases in the shape of cheese, dates, and a piece of meat, we took our departure. In the course of the visit we had presented the head merchant with a small tin of saffron, which all Tibetans value so highly. We hoped that by doing so, when he came to visit our tent in return, he would be more inclined to listen to a bargain for helping us with our baggage.

As soon as we were ready for the reception in our tent of the two merchants, we sent word to them. We had purposely got out our bottle of brandy, and hoped that, if they would take some, they would become more liberal-minded. They certainly warmed up and appreciated this valuable intoxicant, although they were most cautious in the amount they took. We produced more saffron and talked and argued for a long while in hopes of buying a pony at a reasonable price. At length they agreed to let us have an old but powerful and useful pony for Rs. 60, for which they had at first demanded Rs. 120. It was a great relief for us to be able to do something for our three mules, and having struck this bargain, we soon hinted to the merchants that it was time for bed.

Before telling further of our adventures, it will be worth while to devote a chapter in describing the merchants' camp.

CHAPTER XVIII.

MANAGEMENT OF THE TIBETAN CARAVAN—TEA WITH THE MERCHANT—SHUGATZA RIVER—FRICTION—AN ALARM.

The general management and internal economy of this wonderful caravan was sufficiently full of interest to merit a small space being devoted to its description. The head of the caravan was a very fine-looking Tibetan from Lhassa; he must have stood well over six feet and was exceedingly well-built, decidedly the biggest Tibetan I have ever seen. In the camp he was always known as the "Kushok," and all attempts to find out his real name resulted in failure; I very much doubt if more than one or two members of the caravan knew it, and they dared not disclose it. The title "Kushok" was originally applied only to living Buddhas, but latterly it has become merely a term of respect or affection, and no longer has any religious significance.

Next in importance to the Kushok came another big merchant, who lived and slept in the same tent with him; besides these two there were numerous small merchants, some of whom owned, perhaps, as few as half a dozen yak; and, lastly, a lama or priest. Altogether they made up an imposing caravan of close on 1,500 yak, as near as we could calculate. We were told that one herdsman was employed to look after every sixty yak, but I cannot help thinking that, in reality, there were rather more; every man in the party, merchants, herdsmen, as well as the cooks and servants, was mounted, so that, when on the march, they presented a striking contrast to our sadly reduced little party.

Their daily routine was somewhat as follows. About 4 A.M. the inferior of the two big merchants would wake up and call to the head cook that it was time to get up, the latter would then give a loud shout, which sounded like "Chou-chou, chou-chou, chou-chou-ou-ou!" and which was promptly echoed by men on guard all through the camp. In a few moments every one was astir, tents were being struck and yak being loaded; in an incredibly short space of time this work was completed and the ponies were being saddled, and in rather under an hour from the word to get up being given the vast caravan was on the move.

The 1,500 yak were divided into seven distinct companies and moved in column, each company superintended by the merchants to whom the animals belonged, and kept in order by the servants and herdsmen under them. These seven companies were again divided into two wings, one consisting of four, the other of the remaining three companies. Every day they marched in the same order, generally with a considerable distance between the two wings, one moving off some time before the other, but everything was managed without the slightest noise or confusion. From the time the watchmen aroused the sleeping camp till the moment of marching off scarcely a voice was heard; it might then be necessary for some one of the mounted men to scream at a refractory yak to make him fall into his proper place; but so little, even of this, was there that, after the first day or two, we slept peacefully on while our Tibetan friends passed close by our tent. I am sorry to say that we were never able to witness their arrival in camp, but we saw enough to convince us that everything must have been conducted in the same systematic manner as the morning start.

On arrival in a fresh camp each company drove in its

picketing pegs with ropes attached, so as to form a good large rectangle; in the centre of this the baggage belonging to the company was carefully piled. Every load was lifted off the yak, and left ready tied up, so that it had merely to be placed on the brute's back in the morning, for as each load was accurately balanced no further tying was necessary. Over the pile of baggage an awning was pitched, and the servants made themselves snug little shelters in the middle, where they spread their bedding. The saddles were removed from the yak, and placed near the baggage, and then the animals were sent out to graze, a certain proportion of the attendants being told off to look after them. Then, and not till then, food was prepared for the first time during the day, for to save time in the cool of the morning, when only yak can travel with any comfort, the start was always made on empty stomachs; but now the cooks had got their fires going, work was over, and the cravings of hunger could be attended to.

We had no opportunity for seeing what arrangements the lesser merchants made for rationing their own men, but they were, I imagine, the same as those made by the Kushok. His plan was as follows:—Each man was provided with a leathern bag, which held about forty pounds of tsamba, that is, twenty days' rations. On ration days this was filled up for him by the cook, and he was at liberty to eat as much or as little as he pleased. He also had butter in proportion, but whatever he chose to do with his food no more was issued till next ration day. The cook brewed tea for all the employés in a huge cauldron, and when ready he gave a peculiar cry, upon which every man came round the fire, bringing his own tsamba, butter, and perhaps a little cheese (chura), sugar, or other delicacy provided out of his own pocket. Bowls were then produced from the ample folds of the sheepskin gowns, filled up with tea by the cook, and the meal began. When satisfied, bowls were licked perfectly clean and replaced in the gowns, and pipes produced. This took place twice a day, usually about midday and again about half-past four in the afternoon. About dusk the yak and ponies were brought in from grazing, and this, too, was a sight well worth seeing. I was enabled one day to get a photograph with the kodak, but my space does not allow me to reproduce it here. Most interesting it was to watch how cleverly a very small number of men could control a vast herd of semi-wild animals. All the herdsmen were armed with long slings, with which they slung stones or clods of earth at any stragglers, and the accuracy and strength of the practice they made, up to about seventy yards, was astonishing. Once in camp, a very few minutes sufficed for saddles to be adjusted, and for every yak to be picketed in his proper place ready for a start in the early morning. If by any chance an animal was missing, his absence was promptly discovered and reported to the Kushok; but, while we were with them, the absentees were always brought in before nightfall.

If there was one thing more than another which aroused our wonder in connection with this caravan, it was the extraordinary knowledge the Kushok had of every little thing that went on within it. Outwardly he appeared to take scarcely any interest in anything. He rarely came outside his tent, and seemed to spend most of his time in drinking tea and praying. Nevertheless, nothing occurred without his knowledge, and he certainly had managed to inspire the lesser merchants and underlings with the greatest awe of, and respect for, himself. No doubt he was kept carefully posted in all camp details by his private servant, a regular little prying busybody; but, even allowing for that, the way he kept his subordinates in order, without appearing to know or care what went on, was very remarkable.

Another thing that surprised us considerably was the civility of everybody in the caravan. Few, if any, of them had seen a European before, but we were strangely exempt from any offensive curiosity. Later on, in China, we often wished that we could move about with the same freedom as we had done in the Kushok's camp, and I am sure that many a foreigner in England has experienced far greater annoyance from the inquisitiveness of our fellow-countrymen than did we among these rough Tibetans. Equally strange was their respect for our property. While we had been in the wilds we had got into the way of leaving a lot of baggage outside the tent, the space inside being very limited, and to our delight we found that we could still do so with perfect safety; for, although the whole *cortège* passed our tent every morning, our cartridges, ropes, saddles, tent pegs, etc., were every bit as safe lying outside as if they had been inside with us. Enough has been said of this particular caravan and of its management to show that years of experience have resulted in an almost perfect system, but a few words about these caravans in general may not be out of place here.

To begin with, on the Lhassa-Sining route there is no regularly defined road, but every year the caravans renew various old landmarks, and set up new ones on prominent features, especially in the vicinity of the camping grounds. It may sometimes occur that there is no one in a caravan who has done the journey for two or three years, and if these landmarks were not carefully kept up, great difficulty might be experienced in finding sufficient grass and water for the animals, on whom so much depends. As it is, they frequently have to make long marches from one camp to another, there being no grass between the two. The greatest distance they did while we were with them was eighteen miles, but they told us they often did twenty-five, and even more, miles in a day. One caravan only leaves from each end every year.* They usually start in May or the beginning

* The annual tribute from Lhassa to the Chinese Emperor does not travel by this road, but goes by Labrang.

of June, and arrive at their destination, whether it be Lhassa or China, in October, thus getting the warmest time of year to travel, when grass is fairly plentiful, the ice is melted, and water easily obtainable.* The loads are very light, rarely being over 120 pounds, and the marches are regulated entirely by the supply of grass and water. They make the yak travel a great pace, close on three and half miles an hour, so as to get in before the sun is very hot, as they say that travelling fast takes less out of them than travelling in the heat.

A caravan going from Lhassa into China brings the famous pulo cloth, and great quantities of dried dates (kasur). These come into Lhassa from Calcutta, so that by the time they reach China they are naturally very expensive, running, as they do, about fifteen for a rupee, in Chinese coinage thirty cash a-piece, or a penny each in English money. When with the caravan we bought a hundred of these dates for two rupees, and thought we had paid a most exorbitant price, but on arriving in China we learnt that we had really got them very cheap.

Caravans from China into Lhassa are mostly employed carrying tea, the main staple of food in Tibet, and a certain amount of tobacco. The reason why only one caravan goes each way in a year is, that all the merchants are very much afraid of encountering robbers on the road. They therefore prefer to wait for one another, and travel in one large body, to running the risk of being looted *en route*. Very often these large caravans are employed trading for the Talé Lama, or other high officials in Lhassa, but whether this is invariably the case, or whether it was so on this occasion, I am unable to say. In matters of business, as well as of geography, the Kushok and his servants were very reticent after the first day or two.

* When we first joined the caravan on September 8th, they said they had been two months and twenty-five days on the road. They were expected in Tankar soon after we left, which was on October 17th.

At Tankar, the frontier town of Kansu, there are four Tibetan officials appointed by the Talé Lama to look after the interests of Tibetan merchants, and to arrange any difficulties that may arise between them and the Chinese, in addition to which duty one of the four has to accompany the tribute to Pekin each year. They thus have plenty to do, as there are many Tibetans on the Chinese frontier and a big merchant, such as our acquaintance was, might stay three years or more trading in China before returning to Lhassa. During that time he is bound to come in contact with numerous officials, some of whom would undoubtedly pick quarrels with and extract undue squeezes from him, if he had no official to whom he could appeal.

On the 11th of September we found the merchants had made such a long march, that it would be wise for ourselves to make two. The day was bitterly cold, for it was the coldest march we had experienced, and during our first halt we felt the weather so severely that Malcolm and I walked on ahead, leaving the men to bring on the three mules and the pony, for the men now were quite happy and living on the fat of the land. As soon as we had reached the merchant's camp, we took shelter under one of the awnings, and beckoned to Nimbri to tell him we wanted to take tea with the merchant. Nimbri gave us to understand that if we wanted to have tea with the merchant, we must pay one rupee for the pleasure. Having produced this sum, we were soon inside the Kushok's cosy tent, warming our toes and fingers by the glowing fire as we sipped our hot tea. Our conversation without Esau was very limited; besides, as the two merchants were anxious to pray, we soon took the hint and departed.

During the days spent with the merchant, we used to pay

one of his servants to supply us daily with argols for our fire, although, while leading a nomad's life, we had always found an inducement and pleasure to go argol hunting. A well-dried argol was well worth finding, and we experienced the same delight as a mushroom gatherer in finding an unusually large one, or a stamp collector in discovering a rare issue.

While pursuing the caravan the next day, we noticed some yak grazing in a nullah, and only a couple of miles or so from the new camp, and I thought that if I could shoot one of these, we might induce the merchants to carry the trophy for us into China. These yak were so placed that I had no alternative left me but to walk openly up the valley they were grazing in. They took no notice of me till within 150 yards, when they began to move off, but a single shot from my carbine knocked over the largest one stone dead. I was somewhat surprised, for I considered my shot had been directed too far back. On cutting up the brute, I found I had destroyed his liver, which had been the cause of his death.

On arrival into camp, I found one of the Kushok's ponies, on which he placed a high price, was dying. In order to save the animal's life, he had bought a spoonful of brandy from Malcolm, for a pound of flour. In this transaction the merchant was certainly the loser.

We learnt that the Kushok intended to remain halted the next day. This was welcome news to us, for our three mules had not had an entire day's rest for over two months, and all our writing and mapping was behindhand. We wanted, too, to purchase more supplies, which operation with these people always took up a great deal of time. Above all things, we thought we should be able to take a number of pictures with our kodak, illustrative of typical scenes in the camp.

The day of rest was a glorious one of peace and sunshine. The smoke from the different fires curled straight up towards the heavens, and all seemed to be enjoying the quiet change. On the opposite side of the valley we could see all the hundreds of yak, resembling at that distance a large ants' nest. The morning was spent entirely in buying supplies. The prices had been raised, so that we tried to buy from some of the minor merchants. But the ever inquisitive Nimbri, on discovering this, informed his master, who, being all, powerful in the camp, forbade the selling of any supplies to us except by himself. He made himself unpleasant with regard to other small matters. We could see it was the Kushok's intention to bleed us, and we were so placed that we could not help ourselves, yet, during the morning, he sent us a special blend of tea. It was certainly first-rate, both a thick and sustaining drink. During the afternoon we managed to take some snap-shots before the members of the camp could grasp what our little game was, or, more correctly speaking, grew suspicious of our intentions.

We were all reinvigorated by the one day's halt, and at daybreak continued our descent, all the way down a magnificent gorge, the mountains on either side being very lofty and precipitous. Eventually the gorge became very narrow, before reaching a well-marked camping ground of short, green grass. We had come to a district abounding in scrub and thorn bush two or three feet high. Some of the sticks of these bushes were an inch in diameter, while the air was scented with the fragrant smell of herbs. To see vegetation, even of this barren description, was a pleasant sensation to us, for we had seen no kind of vegetation bigger than a wild onion, since leaving Niagzu, some four months ago.

After our breakfast we proceeded on our march, following the dry bed of a stream, which brought us to a river which we learnt was the Shugatza, or Shuga Gol. This, strange to say, was flowing in a nearly opposite direction to that in which we ourselves were going, and was soon lost to view, hidden by the hills in its north-west course. On the right bank of the river, to which we had to cross, was the Kushok's camp, with the yak wandering about in the plain,

SOME MEMBERS OF THE KUSHOK'S CAMP.

which was covered with splendid grass. On the left bank was a range of hills called the Tong Hills.

We made several attempts at crossing the water, which, although deep and some thirty yards across, presented the advantage of a firm, stony bottom. We thought the Kushok might have pointed out the place to cross by. This, we at length found, was only three feet deep. That night we had no transactions at all with the merchants, although, curiously enough, they came to our servants' apology for a tent and hobnobbed with them.

Our route onwards, which was up-stream of the Shugatza, took us over fine prairie land, teeming with immense herds of kyang, who, under the leadership of some chosen stallion, manœuvred round and about us, often within shooting distance. They seemed in no way to feel this exceptionally warm day. We were at a very little higher altitude than Leh itself, and were not sorry to find the merchants had only marched nine miles, half the distance of the previous day.

We discovered the camp pitched just at the foot of a range of hills, which protected them from any welcome breeze that might have sprung up. A small stream trickled from these hills, and formed a pond below. So still was the atmosphere that the smoke from the several fires was diffused neither to the right nor to the left, but curled very slowly upwards. The ponies and yak were either standing knee-deep in the water or lying about in the grass with no inclination for grazing, while the men who were not attending to the fires were either asleep in the tents or stretched out in the open. It was a scene of absolute quiet and perfect peace.

We soon pitched our little camp, and took our latitude from the midday sun. As there was no wind we had some trouble in making our fire burn, so sent a message to the Kushok to ask him kindly to lend us some bellows. We also inquired if he would allow us to photograph himself and his own tent, which was always conspicuous in the camp by reason of the flag that flapped from the end of the pole. To neither of these requests would he assent. We had half expected that this would be the case, for the merchants somehow or other wore an air of indifference to us now, and had given up the friendly turn they first showed towards us. It might have been the natural behaviour of these men, and perhaps we were wrong in our surmises, but we felt as though a screw was loose somewhere.

Later on in the day he sent his servant Nimbri to borrow our frying-pan, small as it was. We at once saw an opening of showing the merchants that we were not going to be entirely dependent on them, so sent him back word that unless he would lend us his bellows each day, we would not lend him our frying-pan. This had the desired effect, for the merchant came to see us, and the bargain was struck. Although at the time we considered this of much importance, it showed how childish both parties had grown.

Since the time when we had first become acquainted with these merchants, and learnt that they were going to Barong in the Tsaidam before reaching Tankar on the Chinese border, we saw the advantage of travelling in their company, for we were all bound for the same destination. Yet we could never get any definite or reliable answer as to how far off Barong was, either from the merchants or from any of the underlings. In fact, whenever we broached the question, we were always given to understand that Barong was further off than ever. They would neither tell us anything about the road or how to find our way there, excepting that they repeated the intricacies of the route and the impossibility of finding it by ourselves.

We knew quite well they were desirous that we should travel with them for two reasons; firstly, that they might bleed us of all our rupees, and secondly, that they might rely upon our protection against predatory tribes, such as the Golok, in the neighbourhood of whose country we should have to march. The Kushok was very fond of our rifles, and admired them, yet when we offered him one during our bargains, he explained that it was of no use to him unless we gave him two or three hundred rounds of ammunition as well, which of course we could not do.

On this day, the 15th of September, the Kushok declared that Barong was a journey of twenty days distant, but we calculated from our own observations that it would only take us about a week to get there if we could but find the way. We knew we were unable to buy food for us all for twenty more days at his starvation prices, and decided to buy from him four or five days' rations and then leave the merchants by shoving on ahead and making longer marches. Of course, our great difficulty was to know the right way to go, for very often there was absolutely no clue for miles; and if we once wandered off wrongly, it would mean much useless meandering over mountains, during which we should probably be lost altogether. We tried our utmost to gain information about the road from the servants. One man told one thing and the next something else directly contrary to what the former had said. A great many of them very likely really did not know, and those who did had been forbidden by the Kushok to tell us. An order from the Kushok was not one to be trifled with, for in this caravan he was omnipotent.

One circumstance that exercised the Kushok's mind was the plane-table surveying of Shahzad Mir. To ward off suspicion, we purposely marched in the wake of the merchants; but Shahzad Mir would always arrive in camp a few minutes after ourselves, carrying the plane-table, and this always puzzled the Kushok. "Why," he asked, "was Shahzad Mir always made to come in last carrying this square board? What offence had he committed to merit such a punishment as this?" He was alluding to the Chinese penalty for crime of carrying the wooden collar, which is commonly known to us as the "cangue."

As we had reached a fine grass country, the merchants were going to make the most of it by allowing their yak plenty of time to graze. On the 16th of September they only marched three miles, and furthermore gave us to understand that they would remain at rest at this encampment the following day. They had certainly chosen a very beautiful spot. The camp was pitched on the richest of pasture land, with hills on either side of it. There was also a spring of cold, clear water, supplying enough for all. The stream formed by this spring separated the Tibetans from ourselves.

As soon as we learnt that it was the intention of the merchants to remain so long in this place, we grew impatient at what we considered to be a quite unnecessary delay on their part. So annoyed were we, that we went to the Kushok's tent and demanded four or five days' supply of flour and butter, which, up to date, we had only been buying in quantity sufficient for the day. To our astonishment he flatly refused to sell us this amount; he would only sell us just enough for present use. We at once saw the game he was playing. As long as he denied us more food than we daily required, he felt sure we dare not have faced the inhospitable and uninhabited solitude of the mountains again without means of sustenance at hand. We retired after this piece of incivility to our side of the spring to debate together upon what course to pursue. We made up our minds that, rather than be in the power or under the yoke of these Tibetans, we would risk all and launch forth again into the vast unknown, and thereupon gave orders to our men to prepare for loading up and marching again that very day.

At this crisis, we became aware that in an instant the camp of the Tibetans, from a scene of peace and repose, had become one of excitement, turmoil, and confusion. What on earth had happened? Some men were scaling the hills; even the Kushok himself had made this the scene of his contribution to the general hubbub, while others were running about and fixing their rests in the ground for firing, and were loading and priming their matchlocks.

CHAPTER XIX.

WE LEAVE THE KUSHOK — A USELESS CLIMB — SIGNS OF A DISASTROUS JOURNEY — A HOUSE OF PRAYER — MALCOLM SHOOTS A BEAR—ANXIETY FOR FOOD.

As soon as the Kushok had reached the summit of the hill above our own camp, we saw that he was pointing with his hand at something or other which was causing this uproar, for men were now firing off their matchlocks at some distant rocks. Just then Nimbri came to us to borrow our glasses for the Kushok. He came with such an air of superiority that we declined to lend them, which enraged the Kushok in no slight degree.

Being bitten with curiosity to find out what they were all gazing and pointing at, we climbed the hill ourselves, and saw, a long way down the valley, on the other bank of the Shugatza, smoke ascending to the skies, and apparently coming from some camp or other, for close to the place where the smoke rose were a number of animals dotted about, but whether they were yak, mules, or ponies, even with our glasses we could not clearly make out. One thing we all felt certain of was that there was another large encampment, even larger than the Tibetan one, on the banks of the Shuga Gol. Whether it was that belonging to another body of merchants, or, what was considered more likely, a large camp of the Golok tribe, it was impossible to decide at that distance.

Without more ado we made up our minds as to what line

of action to take. We gave orders to our men to load up the three mules and the pony, and, going up to the Kushok, told him we were off to join the new encampment, telling him that if these strangers proved to be another body of merchants, we would, without a doubt, be able to get supplies from them, and that if, on the other hand, they proved to be some of the Golok, why, we had no fear of them, for we were well armed.

Such a turning of the tables brought the Kushok to his proper standard, and made him recognize the fact that Englishmen have more ways of shifting than one. He begged us to remain with his caravan and give him our assistance, but finding that our decision was not to be revoked, for the mules, too, were by this time being loaded, he made up his mind still to benefit as much as he could by selling us the flour, etc.; and we, on our side, deeming that four or five days' certain supply was preferable to risking the chance of finding other merchants who would sell, decided to purchase this amount from him. Having settled it, we lost no time in completing the loading and leaving in triumph the Kushok's camp, receiving a hostile salute from the fierce dogs at our departure.

Although we had misgivings about finding our way to Barong, in the Tsaidam, and blamed the merchants for their secretiveness in this respect, still, we parted with feelings of friendship, for we could not forget the great hospitality and help they had given us in our distress, in spite of our anything but winning appearance, and, after all is said and done, the hankering after the rupees is the natural bent not only of Tibetan merchants, but of almost all other merchants of every civilized or uncivilized country.

Thus, on the afternoon of the 16th September, we once more launched forth into the wilds, an independent little party. We marched till long after dark that evening, but could see no light to show us where this strange encampment was located.

The first thing the next morning I ascended a hill, and, remarkable to relate, became convinced that the baggage animals we had seen from the Kushok's camp grazing, were nothing else than immense numbers of wild yak and wild kyang, and, as to the smoke, we accounted for this by the natural phenomenon of mist arising from the river, for we could see no signs of any encampment at all. During the morning we had but little difficulty in finding our way, for the route was marked by previous encampments and old chulas. We unloaded for breakfast by a fresh spring at the foot of some red hills, the home of the chough, whilst many hares dwelt in the stones and grass below.

Soon after starting again we noticed a nullah turning up northwards to our left, marked in a very conspicuous way by a natural wall of earth at the mouth, on which had been placed, as well as on the neighbouring hills, several heaps of stones piled one on the other three or four feet high. We knew by our map we should have to leave the Shuga Gol and cross a range of mountains called the Burhan Bota before reaching the Tsaidam, and we thought that this must be the spot, and that it had been thus significantly ornamented, that no one travelling this route could go past without noticing the way.

We found on nearer approach there were two roads into the nullah, one by a narrow pathway over the wall, and the other, a broader one, by a small stream on the right side of the wall. As we followed the stream a few hundred yards up the mouth of the nullah we came to the source of this water. It was busily bubbling forth from the top of a rock between four and five feet high that stood midway in our path. The rock was stained a black and yellow colour, and the water itself was quite hot, but was tasteless.

Just inside the wall at the entrance, other lower and

smaller walls had been built, apparently to afford protection from the winds. Against these were several chulas, and lying everywhere were quantities of bones of animals. The hot spring was doubtless the cause of all these landmarks, which had not been stuck up as a signboard to show the road to the Tsaidam, as we had taken it to mean, and in consequence of our mistake, we had a long, useless climb right up the nullah, over stony mountains, and down another nullah back to our valley again, on the banks of the Shugatza, having made but little progress, and tired our transport to no purpose.

Our men were complaining that they must have a meal of tea and tsampa before starting the morning's march, as they could not walk for five hours without. It appeared that one of them had a watch, and told them they had been marching five hours, whereas they had not been going for three. When I explained to them that they had only marched for this length of time, they were quite themselves again, and the sour looks which had disfigured their faces were soon changed to one of laughter.

We found numbers of yak and kyang along the banks of the river, but they were too knowing to allow of our shooting them. By reason of this, we had been doubting whether the track we were following was that of wild animals or otherwise, until our minds were relieved by Lassoo finding some camel droppings. These assuring signs, added to the discovery of more chulas, and marks of previous encampments, cast all doubts aside, and at length brought us to the mouth of a broad, stony nullah, which ran in the direction of some white, rocky hills, which looked perfectly impenetrable.

We began to regret not having exchanged with the merchants all our remaining rupees for more tsampa. It was always a pleasure to see our faithful followers enjoy this simple feast. They would eat their fill in silence, or rather partial fill, their eyes disclosing their thoughts, which wandered far back to their homes in Ladakh, where tea and tsampa is their staple food.

We had now left the banks of the Shuga Gol, and were about to enter the narrow opening of a nullah, which we rightly conjectured would take us over the Shuga range of mountains. At this spot were many camel droppings and other signs, which made it manifest that those who attempted to cross these mountains camped here just before or just after the toilsome journey.

It was a rugged, rough, cold-looking pass, and, at the various bends, the wind blew with violent, cruel blasts. For nearly four hours we continued to mount up this stony gorge, till a small patch of grass and the pangs of hunger demanded a halt. This was accompanied with much cold and damp, for during most of the morning snow and sleet had been falling. As we continued the ascent, our anxiety increased as to the chances of having to spend the night in so high and cheerless a place. Our fears were doubled by our finding every mile three or four skeletons of dead yak—tame ones, easily recognized by the small size and thinness of their horns. The caravan that had last marched by this route must have made a terrible and disastrous journey. Amongst other signs of their misfortunes we picked up a keg of opium.

At length joy crowned our fears, for we reached a large pile of stones, denoting that the summit of the pass was here. We continued from this point to descend steadily, till after sunset, and pitched our little tent in an old encamping ground. We knew that such was the case, for, close at hand, stood out alone a small hill, on which were three piles of stones the size of men. It is probable that there is a spring somewhere near this hill, but none of us had inclination to go in search, when we could satisfy our wants with the snow that lay around.

After a bitterly cold night we descended gaily over grassy plains, for the morning was bright and the sun had polished up the snow peaks that surrounded us on all sides, so that they shone again. Kyang, antelope, and sand-grouse had selected these pastures, and afforded us sport and provender as we marched. The pleasure of the day was somewhat marred by our inability to find any water before nightfall. At that hour we came to a very noticeable hill, standing at the entrance of a nullah. On the top of this hill was a large heap of stones decorated with many sticks and red rags. We were all glad to see it, for we had learnt by now that this signified a camping ground. There lay a few skeletons of tame yak. A spring of beautifully clear water took its rise here, while lovely grass grew everywhere.

We afterwards learnt that this remarkable spot is named Dapsoga, and the hill Ser, and that from here there are two roads which lead over the Burhan Bota range of mountains into the Tsaidam. One of these roads, called the Burhan Bota Pass, takes a more westerly course, and is longer than the other, which is called the Namoran Dawan (Pass). This latter road, though shorter, is more difficult by reason of the thick brushwood and the river, which has frequently to be crossed. Merchants who go this way complain that they invariably lose some of their baggage animals in the undergrowth. Of course, at the time of our arrival, we knew nothing about any road at all, and quite unconsciously elected to take the Namoran Dawan.

We followed the stream whose source we had found, which flowed rapidly over a stony bottom, so that, although the water was only knee deep, it was difficult for us to keep our footing. The precipitous mountains, that sometimes ran clean down to the water's edge, compelled us, on each occasion, to cross the torrent. These hills were rugged and bare. At other times the nullah became broad, with a wider bed to the river. At such places there grew grass and thick brushwood, some of it eight feet high. At one of these delightful spots we made our midday halt, as other caravans had done, judging from the many chulas we found. Further on we found many traces along the path of people, sheep and ponies having journeyed this way.

We found our commissariat was at its lowest ebb, for although we had seen a hare and three snipe, we had shot nothing, and we reflected that unless we killed something the next day we should have to live on air and water. As we looked down stream it seemed as though it would soon issue out into open plains, where we anticipated finding people.

It was hard to make a start the next morning, for Esau and Lassoo had got silly fancies into their heads that the water was too cold to cross, and until we explained to them the impossibility of this fact we remained at a standstill. The truth of their statement, nevertheless, we inwardly agreed to, and afterwards outwardly felt the force of it. Without any sun, and a strong north-east wind blowing, our constant plunging into the torrent, ever increasing in force and volume, deprived our legs of all feeling. Fortunately a solitary kyang fell to Malcolm's rifle, and at noon we saw, on the other side of the river, thick brushwood, unmistakably an old camping ground. Once more we stumbled over the stony bottom of the river, and then, collecting a pile of the thickest brushwood, we made a huge fire to dry our clothes by and to cook our wild donkey for breakfast.

As we proceeded after this rest and repast, we came to more jungle, composed principally of wild raspberry and currant bushes, and other red berries, to all of which we did ample justice; even the little dog, Ruby, picked the berries from the bushes with her mouth, for she must have felt the want of other nourishment as much as we ourselves did.

Around and about the bushes were more marks of sheep having recently been grazing there. All were jubilant, for even if we did not find people that evening, we had a small supply of meat. Our men at last lost all control as, with shouts of joy, they tore along through the fruit bushes towards a stone building which had appeared in sight.

All thought our goal at last was reached. On drawing closer to this, we found it consisted of a small stone building, about twelve feet square and of the same height. Looking through the rails of the small wooden door, we found the whole space occupied by a large prayer-wheel, which for ever was being turned round by the force of the stream. Over the door, in a ledge, was a packet of prayers, which I appropriated. The prayers were written on paper and wrapped up in cloth. On looking around for more curiosities, I found prayers and rags were hanging from several of the bushes and trees; on one particular fruit tree was the longest prayer of all, written on white cloth and tied by ropes to it. The temptation to take this religious offering was too great for me, for I untied the knots, and pulling down the cloth with a feeling of sacrilege, overpowered by that of curiosity, I hastily rolled the thing up and hid it away, glancing round in case there might be some one looking on unobserved but close at hand. It would have been a bad beginning to strike up a friendship with strangers by being caught in the act of outraging their religion. We were not, however, destined to meet people just at present. Shortly after our excitement had worn off, we saw slowly moving along with measured pace, on the opposite bank of the river, a fine black bear. This was his last evening walk, for Malcolm soon bowled him over with a well-directed bullet through the head. This episode, and the misty rain that now enshrouded us, demanded a halt.

We had to bring the bear's skin and fat over the river, after cutting him up on the other side, yet this unpleasant work and the wet weather made no impression on the good spirits of the men. Our Duffadar was perhaps the most jubilant, for he fully expected the next day to swagger through a Mongol village with all the war-paint he could muster under the trying times.

As we marched down the gorge we found strings of prayers hung from tree to tree, written on pieces of red, blue, and white-coloured cloth. But after about three miles' tramp through the fruit bushes, we crossed over a highish ridge and then debouched into an arid, stony plain, and our river wended away to the south. This was a very bitter disappointment to all, for just at the moment when we had expected to view the homely comfort of a nomad's camp, or of a Mongol village, we could see nothing but a stretch of desert country to relieve the eye.

We reproached ourselves for having been so thoughtless about our supply of meat, for we had only with us a small portion of the last donkey slain, and some of the bear's grease. Our three mules, though thin, were fairly strong, and we determined not to dally and bemoan our fate, but rather to hasten on all the quicker and try and cross this desolate country. After about twelve miles we hit off our stream again, and found a spot to halt by a little undergrowth. Everywhere else was bare and arid; even the hills, which gradually died away into the plains we were crossing, were entirely devoid of vegetation. At our little camp we could see signs of former encampments, and there was a pile of stones on the other side of the river, inviting us to cross, with as much as to say, "This is the way, gentlemen."

CHAPTER XX.

FOLLOWING THE NAMORAN—WE SPLIT INTO THREE PARTIES—WE MEET SOME YOUNG MONGOLS—THEIR HOSPITALITY—LOBSAN—THE BANA TRIBES.

SINCE leaving the merchants, Barong in the Tsaidam had been our goal, but the very incomplete maps, and the small scale upon which they were drawn, gave us but scanty assistance.

At noon I took the latitude, and learnt that, according to Rockhill's map, we had already arrived just north of Barong, which lay to our east, and, according to our other map, we were just south of the town. Our inclination was, therefore, to accept the invitation of the pile of stones, and follow the narrow track over the sand; but our men were so averse to crossing the water again, that we reluctantly gave way to them. In order to cross this tract of wearisome country, and to save the mules from the sun's rays, we did not move on again till late in the afternoon, with the intention of continuing the march by moonlight.

Our plans, however, were destroyed by reason of the dark, misty evening that spread over us, so that we deemed it wiser to halt for the night. We could hear the rushing of the Namoran Gol on our right hand, so were able to get plenty of water.

From here we marched almost due north, still following the Namoran, which became split up into many small rivulets. The way was sandy, with loose stones, and the small bushes which we had reached were half covered on one side by the sand, which had been heaped up by the force of the wind. The morning was very hot, and a sore trial for our three veterans, who could only travel at a slow pace. Yet how could we halt in such a wilderness? At length we reached sandy hillocks, covered with a kind of waving furze bush, such as grows by the seaside, and growing in between was long, coarse, green grass, while the river became more than ever split up into little streams, most of which one could jump across. Most acceptable of all were the tracks we found of ponies and camels. Yet, tracks or no tracks, it was impossible for our three mules to proceed any further, and choosing the most shade-giving bush, sheltered from the wind by a large, sandy hillock, we called a halt, and let our mules loose to revel in the running water and the coarse grass.

We climbed up the highest mound in the neighbourhood, to reconnoitre the stretch of country below us. We could see a vast plain, covered to a great extent with bush, extending to a far-distant range of hills. And we fancied we could make out a river flowing at right angles to our own route, and reckoned quite rightly that this must be the Bayan Gol. Nevertheless, we could see no signs of people or villages. The sun by its brightness made the actual distinguishing of objects an uncertain undertaking. We were perplexed as to our further progress, for to have marched on aimlessly with our three mules, to their probable death, would have been a foolish decision.

We finally agreed to carry out the following plans. While Shahzad Mir and Shukr Ali remained encamped with the mules, Malcolm would take Lassoo, and I Esau, and set out in different directions with the intention of not returning till we had found people. Futhermore, in order that we might find the camp, the two men left behind were going to make huge bonfires every hour after dark. In bush country with no definite landmark, even those most skilled in the arts of a wanderer have a difficult job in returning to a spot they have once left.

Having divided the remnants of the donkey flesh amongst the three parties, we set out on our different errands. While Malcolm was to travel north, I took a line a little more easterly. Esau and I kept our eyes and ears open for any signs of mankind, and at first we saw camel and pony droppings, as we had seen previously that day, and afterwards chulas; then places where the streams had been dammed to divert their course. Then we saw several tracks running north by east. But I was not anxious to go further north, for I felt convinced we were leaving Barong on our right, and behind us.

Whilst Esau and I paused in our deliberations our doubts were removed by hearing the distant bark of a dog. We hastened on without more ado in the direction of the noise, now and again drawing up and listening in silence for a repetition of the barking to guide us. Each time we heard it more distinctly, and all the while the tracks we were following became more defined and more numerous. We were actually following the footsteps of a man! Then we both suddenly stopped, for we could hear the cheerful voice of a boy or girl singing. We both ran through the bush to learn who this was.

We could hardly credit the picture we caught a glimpse of through the thick bush. There was a fine flock of fat sheep being driven homewards, for it was now evening, by some young boys and girls riding barebacked their well-fed ponies. They were singing all the while from mere light-heartedness, ignorant of all trouble and the outside world, and that two strangers were hidden but a few yards behind. I watched in secret this scene of perfect worldly peace and happiness, before disturbing the partakers of it by a loud incongruous exclamation, "Hullo!" They turned round at once to meet this unheard-of sound, and though they received us without fear, their astonishment might well be pardoned. We walked along with them, unable to understand each other, till we found ourselves surrounded by several men, one or two amongst whom were able to understand Esau's Tibetan talk.

They were all nice-looking fellows, with pleasant, smiling faces, of stout build, with strong arms and deep chests. As for the women they were quite becoming, with their bronzed faces illuminated by a reddish tint on each cheek. The youngters all looked the picture of plump health and happiness. Amongst the people in this district I never saw any kind of illness or disfigurement. After the preliminary salutations of "Where are you going?" "Where do you come from?" "Who are you?" etc., we made a small wood fire on the ground, and squatting round it began to talk over matters, and perhaps the thought uppermost in our minds was to convince them of the fact that we were really very hungry.

It was quite evident that the people amongst whom we had fallen were of a hospitable and kindly disposition. They were the Tsokpo or Sokpor Mongols. It was finally arranged that Esau should return with two of them, all mounted, to our camp, and bring on the caravan to this place, while I was to stop with them and await its arrival. A bright moon had just risen, which made it an easy night for travelling.

As soon as Esau had departed they beckoned to me to follow them. We went at a fast walk, as we twisted in and out between the bushes, all looking strange by moonlight. After half an hour, they suddenly turned to their right, and there I saw a clear, circular piece of ground, surrounded and concealed by bushes. In the centre was a hole in the ground, with a fire burning inside it, and around were arranged some huge cooking-pots, which were boiling something or other. Around this were squatting men and women, evidently waiting for their supper to be cooked. On one side were a number of sacks piled up, which I guessed contained grain. I was terribly hungry, and could scarcely keep my eyes from the cooking-pots, which just fitted the holes made in the

TSOKPO MONGOLS LIVING IN THE BUSH.

ground, by means of which the contents were being boiled. I was made to sit down by the fire against the sacks, when my host, who had guided me here, and appeared to be chief of the party, opened one of the pots, and forthwith pulled out a well-boiled shoulder of mutton, which I took from his hands and was soon gnawing at; on its completion my host presented me with a leg and afterwards with a neck. Then I began to reflect within myself what a reputation for an Englishman's greed I was bringing amongst these people, so I stoutly refused his pressing invitations to accept more, and contented myself with several doses of hot soup and tea, to which was added butter and tsampa.

At the conclusion of this much appreciated repast, during which each member of the party selected from any of the pots whichever bit of mutton he fancied, alternating his or her diet with the tea and tsampa or soup, they began to examine my clothes and belongings. Everything created the greatest curiosity; the use of my compass, which I tried to explain, was full of interest to them, but the greatest astonishment was shown at the ticking of my watch, which passed round the hands of the entire circle.

After we had finished our smoking and the examination was exhausted, men and women dispersed to their own particular corners for sleep, while I, lying down between two of them, was covered up with warm sheepskins, and soon fell asleep too. I was aroused long before daylight to find that our little caravan had arrived, and shortly afterwards, about 3 A.M., Malcolm himself appeared, accompanied by a number of friendly Mongols—for he, too, had come across them, and had met with equal hospitality. We soon had a big fire burning, and the kettle boiling; and whilst our men sat chatting with the Mongols, in the thorough enjoyment of their tea, tsampa, and butter, and of meeting strangers once again, Malcolm and I wrapped ourselves up in our blankets to sleep till sunrise.

On awaking from a refreshing rest we found our men still busily engaged in mixing up the tea and tsampa, whilst around and about lay Mongols sleeping soundly; everywhere, too, there lay scattered all our belongings, an easy prey to anybody who might feel inclined to take them. From the moment we fell in with these trustful, hospitable nomads, we instinctively felt that our guns, our ammunition, in fact, all we possessed, were just as safe amongst them from robbery as we had found them to be when travelling with the Tibetan merchants. As for our three noble mules, they were now enjoying what must have been to them a paradise. Everywhere grew rich grass and fruit bushes, intersected by small streams, and there they wandered knee-deep, grazing to their heart's content, doubtless entirely forgetful of all the trying times they had carried us through. It was no small pleasure to ourselves either, to see them thus provided for, and we agreed never to place another load on their backs as long as they remained in our care, but to hire, by hook or crook, ponies from the Mongols, whilst they should march the last 300 miles to the Chinese border with ease and comfort.

As soon as all were awake, and whilst a breakfast of more mutton and tea was being discussed, it was arranged that we should move on a few miles, to a spot where we could better bargain for supplies of food and for ponies to take us to the Chinese border.

The chief of the Mongols amongst whom we were living was a man called Lobsan, and it was close to his home in the bush that we had taken our things. It was soon common news throughout the few miles of bush wherein these nomads were residing that two strangers had arrived who were anxious to purchase food. Lobsan was a man well known throughout the district, and being a man of superior energy and intellect, he carried no small weight amongst his neighbours; besides, he had travelled more than the majority of them—he had made the journey three times to China, and in addition to that he had resided some months in the capital, Lhassa, and had become initiated in the studies of the Buddhist religion; he was, in consequence, acquainted with the different routes to Lhassa. He explained to us how we had traversed the Namoran route instead of the Burhan Bota, which was the longer of the two; he pointed out, too, the exact position of the town of Barong Tsaidam, agreeing admirably with our own calculations; above all, he strengthened and confirmed our information with regard to our discovery of the source of the Chu Ma river, an upper tributary of the Yang-tse.

We made our encampment under the shade of a large fruit tree, where Lobsan's stout ponies had brought our goods, and as we sat there with Lobsan by our side, men and women flocked in from all quarters to try their fortune in this novel market. It was soon current that our ready rupees were the exchange; rupees they preferred to most other things we could suggest, such as knives, watches or saffron. The only article they really asked for in return was "sin," or needles, of which we hadn't a single one. Some of them brought tsampa, or tulshi (flour), or mar (butter), or chura (cheese), each bringing from a few pounds down to half a pound of any article, and, as we had to lay in at least a fortnight's supply, a great deal of bargaining had to be negotiated. All this was managed through Lobsan, who probably received some slight remuneration from each of the successful bargains. As a rule, we paid a rupee for four pounds of tsampa, or flour, and the same price for a pound of butter, while two sheep cost us three and a half and four and a half rupees respectively.

As each Mongol turned up he would say what the price of his bag of flour or skin of butter was, and of course more than what was right. Many others would be standing around, watching with interest the new scene that presented itself, and see us demur with surprise at the high price that was asked; yet, although the price was never mentioned, all knew well what it was. The bargaining was carried out under cover of the sleeve of their sheepskin cloaks. Lobsan, after interviewing the vendor in this manner, would take hold of my hand, concealed inside his own sleeve, and seize four of my fingers, signifying that four rupees was the price of the goods; whereupon,

MALCOLM ENGAGES ATTENTION OF MONGOLS WITH "CADBURY": THEY THINK IT IS SNUFF.

looking him in the face, I would seize three of his fingers, or three and a half to represent three and a half rupees, as the case might be, as my price, and this information would at once be transmitted to all onlookers in the same fashion. Although every bargain was carried out in secrecy, without speaking a word, still all knew just as well what was taking place as if the tongue, instead of hidden fingers, had been the medium adopted.

Our attempts at purchasing some of their ponies were unsuccessful, for with our finances in such a crippled state, we could not, had we been willing, have paid the price they demanded, namely, 50 to 120 rupees for an altogether worn-out and aged baggage pony.

It took very little to amuse thoroughly these good-natured, unsophisticated nomads; even our sponge, which we at length had leisure and opportunity to make use of, attracted their curiosity. Still even more astonishing to them was a half-filled tin of Cadbury's cocoa, which they would insist could be nothing else than snuff. As Malcolm thus engaged their attention, I took a snap-shot of the little group with my kodak. As soon as they discovered this in my hands all was wonderment again, yet so trustful and unsuspicious were these people that they were not at all averse to being photographed, with the exception of one lady mounted on horseback; yet even she unwittingly fell a victim, as may be seen on the following page.

At our revolvers, when we fired off six shots without reloading, they were thoroughly filled with bewilderment, and standing up a slab of caked mud some twenty paces off as a target, they signed for me to try my skill upon it. Six successful holes redoubled their astonishment, and proved to them how easy it was for us to travel through districts which were considered dangerous, although we were so few. One of the more influential Mongols, seizing my unloaded revolver in an agitated and warlike fashion, snapped off the trigger six times in different directions, each time shouting out the word "Bana!" while all around laughed and acquiesced in the meaning of this man's frantic gestures.

It appeared that in order to reach China we should have to pass through a district inhabited by the Bana tribes, who are noted for their predatory habits.

MONGOL LADIES ON THE BAYAN GOL.

They are represented on the map by the name "Bana-khasum," "sum," meaning three—that is to say, there are three of these Bana tribes, who live round and about the regions of the Koko Nor Lake. These three tribes are again subdivided into eighteen small tribes, each with a separate chief, the whole being under the Sining Amban or Tsongt'u. It is on account of these and other tribes that merchants are afraid to traverse the country singly, and the reason why these Tsokpo Mongols so seldom make the journey to the Chinese frontier. It was fear of these Bana tribes that caused us so much delay before we could induce them to fit us out with sufficient ponies and accompany us over our last few hundred miles. The Bana men have been known to come even as far as Barong itself on a raid, and being better armed and more numerous than the Tsokpo Mongols, these latter live in no slight dread of going near their warlike neighbours.

CHAPTER XXI.

WITH THE MONGOLS—A HOSPITABLE OLD LADY—ON THE WAY TO TANKAR—A POISONOUS STREAM—BANA TENTS—I ABSTRACT AN INSCRIBED BONE—OUR COLDEST NIGHT—A WONDERFUL PLACE—KANJUR RUNGYUM.

It was arranged that on the following morning we should move on a two days' journey to Lobsan's tents, which were situated on the banks of the River Bayan Gol, where plans could be better formed for completing this last portion of our journey. We almost wished we had gone off to Barong, which lay a few miles south of us. The Tibetan merchants had told us that we should be able to hire camels there; but then, again, the Mongols assured us that although we might be able to hire camels, it was quite certain that the owners would not venture across the Bana country with so small a party, and that we should have to await the arrival of the Tibetan merchants, which would cause two or three weeks' delay, and perhaps more, but that if we did not mind that we had better go to Barong. We decided that our best plan was to stick to our Mongols, who thus far had treated us so well, and who, we felt sure, would eventually agree to take us to China.

Our first day lay through a land of thick hermok bushes and grass, including a sandy plain, the whole party being mounted on stout ponies. Towards evening we halted by a spring in a small grassy plain. Here we found other

Mongols, and it was evident that this spot, called Ootoo, was a regular camping ground.

With the help of a bright moon, we found them before daybreak loading up the ponies again, and as we continued our journey through the bush and grass country we saw several hares, pheasants, and goa. After a couple of miles we saw Mongol tents for the first time. These tents, which were made of sticks and thick felt, were of circular shape, with conical top, and had a small opening for a door. Scattered around them were numbers of sheep, goats, cows, ponies, and big black long-haired dogs, whose bark and attitude, apparently dangerous, were in reality harmless, for they were generally put to rout by the little terrier Ruby.

After a five hours' ride we halted to graze the ponies on the banks of a stream called Shishi, which flowed in a southerly direction and at this time of the year was easily fordable. We were soon on the move again, for the Mongols were anxious to reach their tents before nightfall. As we wended our way through the hermok bushes, Malcolm and I loitered behind to devour some of their berries. So busily engaged were we that we forgot how far behind we were, and on resuming our ride found we had wandered off the track, and could see no signs of our little party.

Separating, and keeping one another in view, we rode on in what we considered would be the proper direction, riding up every piece of high ground we came to for a better view. From one of these eminences Malcolm saw some ponies grazing in the distance. On our reaching them, they proved to be ponies belonging to some Mongols living on the banks of a river. We found there many groups of tents, from whose owners we learnt that Lobsan lived further up the river, so knew we had reached the banks of the Bayan Gol. After passing several other tents with the usual amount of cattle, we discovered just after sunset that

Lobsan's tents were situated on the opposite bank. We found the river some three feet deep and twenty yards across, and though the water was fairly clear, and flowing fast, it was safer to cross the river as rapidly as possible, for otherwise one was liable to sink into the soft mud that lines the bottom in these parts.

Our little camp was already pitched a couple of hundred yards from Lobsan's tent, and he, good-hearted fellow, was soon by our side with a supply of good tea and milk, of which attention and refreshment we showed our approval by holding up our thumbs and repeating the word "Hoch! Hoch!"

We broke the Sabbath by buying more tsampa and mar. It was curious to see these people examining each rupee, those with a crown on the Queen's head being separated from those without one, the crownless ones being far more appreciated, for some reason or other we could not discover.

We spent three days by Lobsan's tents, and the better we became acquainted with these people the more we were able to testify to their kindly dispositions. Throughout the stay our camp formed a general place of gathering from morn till eve, all coming to sight-see, barter, and gossip, so that we were seldom left to ourselves. Their talk was principally about "gourmo," which means rupees. They formed picturesque groups with their beaming faces. All the men wore black knee-boots, and thick sheepskin cloaks tucked in at the waist to adjust them to a convenient length, so as to hang over their breeches of the same material. These cloaks are generally slipped half off on a warm day, leaving one arm and part of their body bare. A leather hat with a white fur rim, and a red or blue top with a red tassel, was kept in its place by means of a chin-strap. There were other hats of nondescript shape. Many of them smoked the long and small-bowled pipe.

Sometimes they would bring us some fresh article to buy, notably vermicelli or kuamien from China, and millet, called "turma" by Mongols and "churma" by Tibetans. They doubtless led a very happy life, and had but little to think about. Their wants, in the shape of mutton, milk, grain, and fruit, were provided with very little labour. Their ponies, camels, and fat-tailed sheep, both black, white, and brown, required but little looking after in this peaceful district. In accordance with the seasons, they move off with their flocks to the place where we first saw them, or to the good grazing on the banks of the Namoran Gol. Another home with stone walls is ready for them a few miles away, in the village of Kyrma.

One afternoon we accepted an invitation from Lobsan to tea in his family tent. We had to stoop to enter by the door, which was only four feet high, and made by inserting two stout beams in the ground, which supported a third one. The door was closed by letting down a thick piece of felt.

In the middle of the tent we found a large shallow saucepan, which was held up about a foot from the ground by three iron legs, underneath which was the fire to warm the tea, and directly above this was a hole in the conical top of the tent, to let out the smoke. The tent was about twelve feet in diameter, and the custom is to sit round the tea, which is brewed for the whole circle. We were soon seated with the rest of the family, and one old lady, as mistress of the ceremony, stirred up the boiling tea, and ladled it out into small bowls for each of us in turn. Together with our tea was also served a quantity of tsampa and ground cheese. During this sociable meal others came in to participate in it, or perhaps more probably to have a closer inspection of ourselves, while others left to make room. We, too, were equally interested in scrutinizing the old and young of both sexes in their own home.

After we had drunk as much tea as we could, and more than was good for us, the old lady produced a large vessel of curds, a special luxury in honour of ourselves, and I regret to say that we could not do the justice to it that was expected from us. After this we were glad to get outside into the fresh air, for the tent had become very stuffy, and we both remarked how impossible it would be for the coldest blast to penetrate so snug a home.

Few of these Mongols possessed more than one wife, though, can a man afford it, there is nothing against his having two. Our friend Lobsan was of the latter class. A man is considered rich if he possesses a thousand sheep and from ten to fifteen ponies. A marriage amongst them is arranged in the following manner. The would-be husband sends a friend with a piece of white muslin called a "k'artag" to the father of the lady, who may either retain it or return it. Should the former be the case it shows that his suit is accepted, and the lover at once sends the father presents of money, wine, etc., and forthwith takes away his bride, and after much festivity she becomes his wife.

Upon the death of a Mongol, the body is laid out in the open plain for a few days, and a piece of cloth is placed inside the mouth. During this time birds and dogs enjoy an unrighteous repast upon the decaying flesh. When the feast is considered to be completed, friends of the dead body visit the corpse, and whatever bones are still remaining they smash up into small pieces and scatter to all quarters, so that every morsel is carried away, and nothing remains in the open plains. This accounted for our never finding any dead man's bones, though we did come across one or two skulls in good preservation. Tibetans have three different ways of disposing of their dead, the most usual being to place the corpse in a squatting position on a hilltop, and then push it over the edge, so that it finds its own last resting-place, and becomes food for the birds. Occasionally burning is resorted to, and very rarely, in the case of rich people, burial.

Throughout our stay with these people we always found them cheery, pleasant, and though naturally curious, still inoffensive. They could not quite grasp what I was up to when using a sextant in the middle of the day to take our latitude, but when they were told that I was only doing prayers, they withdrew.

On our third and last day on the banks of the Bayan Gol, all our arrangements had been completed. Sheep and other supplies had been bought for a good fortnight, and we had struck a bargain for our transport. Lobsan was to let us have five riding ponies and five baggage ponies, to take us as far as the town of Sining, in the province of Kansu, a few miles across the border. For this journey of 300 miles we were to pay him twenty rupees a pony, but as we had not sufficient money with us, for we had spent it nearly all, we were trusted by Lobsan to pay up the remainder at Sining. We believed that at that town we should come across some missionaries.

Our Mongols spent most of the last day praying, and as their priest had foretold that this was a propitious day to start on, and the one they had chosen was not, Lobsan came to us, saying that since such was the case they would like some of our things to load up and march a few hundred yards up the river, and come back again, so that they might be able to say they had started on a propitious day.

Early on the morning of the 1st of October we were ready to start, but the Mongols caused so many unaccountable delays, that it was 1 o'clock before we had actually moved off. The delay was caused chiefly by the Mongol lama, who came and prayed earnestly with the men who were to accompany us, and in order that fortune might favour their venture, incense was burnt and carried round the homes of the Mongols, and the ponies that were picked out for the journey. Our caravan consisted of Lobsan himself and three of his men, all mounted on ponies, and armed with two matchlocks and a spear of the extraordinary length of twenty-five feet. They, in addition to our ten ponies already mentioned, our flock of ten sheep, with the terrier Ruby, and our three mules, who marched unloaded, composed the party.

In spite of all the preparations and prayers that had been held, we moved off quite quietly, without any kind of demonstration, and, when once the loads had settled down, we covered ground at the rate of over three miles an hour, a great improvement on our accustomed pace. They were all stout ponies, and very fat, from the splendid grazing they enjoy, for no grain is allowed them.

As soon as we had reached a spot called Kanoo, where we were to halt for the night, the ponies were set free to graze, before being tied up close to us for the night without any covering. They were always let loose again with the first streak of daylight, so that they should not start on the march with empty stomachs. The Mongols always took care of their ponies, never losing an opportunity of relieving them of their loads and feeding them. They also used to change about: one day a pony would be ridden and the next he might be carrying a load.

The marches had to be regulated according to the water obtainable. On the third day, after going some six miles, we hit off the main road that runs from Barong to the Chinese border-town of Tankar, and whither we were bound. This track brought us to a clear-flowing rivulet, reminding us of a trout-stream at home.

Here we made a midday two hours' halt. When it was time to start again, we were astonished at the rapidity with which the Mongols reloaded their ponies. They were wonderfully quick and handy, very different from our original lot of Argoons from Leh. Their ponies were very tractable, although ridden with only a snaffle or merely a headstall; and without ever being shod, they stood the long marches we made well enough. They were always marched in one long string. One end of the rope was held in the hand of one of the mounted men, who led the way, and the other end passed through the headstall of each of the ponies in turn. This answers all right, but the animals can pick up no living as they march. As soon as we had travelled beyond the neighbourhood of the Bayan Gol, Lobsan and his men began to show their fears of the Bana tribes, for he was always begging us to march with our guns ready, nor to go ahead of, or loiter behind, the party. They themselves, during the greater part of the day, were praying aloud as they marched, relieving themselves sometimes by startling us with a loud, hearty song.

After leaving the stream, we came to the entrance of a narrow gorge, where Lobsan said we must keep our guns ready, for the Bana men hid behind rocks and appeared unexpectedly. His fears were increased by the sight of some croaking ravens. He maintained that the noise they were making was a bad omen, and to counteract the effect one of the old muzzle-loaders was placed on its stand and fired at the birds, but of course with no fatal results, for the croaking was redoubled, and we continued our ascent of the gorge. We then crossed a small plateau, and before entering another gorge we came to a stream, whose water they never drink, for it is considered a deadly poison to both man and beast. Although the water was quite clear, it tasted as though there was soda in it. On account of this poisonous stream, we had to make a ten hours' march before reaching any other water. Towards sunset we emerged into an open plain, and riding on a few miles we came to a spring and fruit bushes, evidently a haunt of bears, for one fine black fellow quickly made away towards the hills on our approach.

Some distance off in this plain of Noring Hol lay a salt lake, on whose further banks were the remains of two villages. These had been till lately Mongol homes, but the owners had fled in fear and deserted them on the approach of the Mohammedan rebels of Kansu, some of whom fled this way into Turkistan, after they had been defeated by the Chinese.

In this neighbourhood we saw for the first time the crests of hills covered with pine trees. Sometimes encampments are made in the valleys, and articles are made from the wood.

On the seventh day of our march we came to the spot, on the banks of the Tuling Gol, where lately there must have been a very considerable encampment. The posts to which the owners had tethered their animals still remained. Various articles lay scattered about, and the number of large fireplaces that had been built, testified to the numbers of the encampers. Here we learnt a small Chinese army had halted, in their pursuit of the Mohammedans fleeing into Turkistan.

Two more miles beyond this we came to a miserable village, Tuling, or Selling Gompa. This was quite the dirtiest and most dilapidated collection of houses that either of us had ever seen, or want to see again. All the inhabitants were either blind or lame or diseased in some shape or form, and, clad in filthy rags, they lay about basking in the sun and dirt. The big black dogs, blear-eyed and mangy, that crawled about, were well suited to the place. It was an asylum for all lepers, cripples, and other sufferers of these districts. It was close to this village that the French traveller, De Trouille de Rhins, had met an untimely end.

At this point there are two roads to China, one branching off half right, and the other half left. The former passes through a district from which much salt is obtained; it is a shorter but rougher road, and according to our Mongols

MONGOL CAMP: ONE OF OUR HALTS.

a more dangerous one. They therefore elected to travel by the other. There was a green valley up which the shorter road led, where we could see numbers of black tents of the Bana tribes, and their immense flocks of sheep, their cattle, tame yak, and ponies.

With the exception of one white tent, all these Bana tents were as black as could be. The roofs of them were for the most part octagonal, with a hole in the middle to release the smoke. To each corner a rope is attached, which is fastened to a stick driven into the ground, and this again is kept secure by another rope attached to a peg.

Now that we had come well into the midst of the Bana tribes, the Mongols' fears were redoubled, and they kept watch throughout the night. Soon after sunset they made up a number of big fires, so that we might represent a large camp, and in order to accustom their ponies to the noise of an attack, they rehearsed one, pretending that imaginary enemies had fallen upon us. They fired off their old matchlocks, and rushed here and there, crying out, "Ho! Hi!" We sat by a large fire of argols warming our toes, as we watched the performance, unwilling to help them with our guns in the terrible battle they were engaged in. As soon as they had beaten off the foe, they, our men, and ourselves, formed the three points of a triangle, and picketing the ponies in our middle, slept soundly throughout the night, without further disturbance from real or imaginary enemies.

Some ten miles from this camp we found a wonderful rock, standing out conspicuous and alone in the grassy valley we were marching down. On one side of this rock a small open courtyard had been built from big blocks of white stone, some of which were a foot deep and broad, and two feet long. The walls were some twelve feet high, while the courtyard itself was about twelve yards long and eight yards broad. On many of the stones were Chinese, and a few Tibetan, inscriptions, and on the interstices between two of them we found a Chinese cash. Hanging across one wall was a piece of rope, and attached to this were any number of hairs from horses' tails and shoulder-bones with inscriptions on them. Just as I had managed to cut off one of these bones unobserved, the whole rope, with all its attachments, fell to the ground. The Mongols at that moment entered, and although I concealed my bone, it was still a question whether they suspected me of the deed; however, very little harm was done, for they replaced the rope in its former position. Having entered the courtyard, we found a large cave some thirty feet high, and of the same diameter, inside the rock. But even still more remarkable than the cave itself is the entrance here of a subterranean passage, running all the way to the salt lake of Koko Nor. This wonderful place and the courtyard is said to have been the work of some superhuman agency, for the stones of the wall itself are considered to be too big and heavy for any mortal man to have placed there. The place is called Kanjur Rungyum, which means "sacred writings, not built by men."

At midday we halted by a small stream at the foot of a pass, called the Nicotine Kontal, so that the ponies might rest an hour or two before making the ascent. Our Mongols, for ever thinking of their Bana enemies, determined to improve the hour by a little target practice. It was a slow process, loading with powder and an irregular-shaped piece of lead, which was shoved down with a wooden ramrod, then placing the powder at the touch-hole, preparing the fuse, and resting the gun on the wooden rail which they raised to sight the gun before finally applying the fuse. They made far better practice at the target, which was 150 yards off, than we had anticipated.

After crossing this easy pass we travelled through a country of grass, and on the ninth day of our march saw

THREE REMAINING MULES AT KOKO NOR.

in the distance the small hill, with its cairn called Hatuturgy on top, that lies at the western end of the large lake of Koko Nor. The following day we found the country inhabited by more Bana people living in their black tents; they were dotted about all over the land, with immense flocks of sheep and countless herds of tame yak.

That night was the coldest we experienced during our journey. There were twenty-seven degrees (Fahr.) of frost, but, although we were sleeping on the ground without any tent, our slumbers were sounder than they sometimes are in a bed of luxury.

We journeyed along the northern shore of this inland sea, for people in China, when visiting the Koko Nor, talk of spending a week at the sea. This salt lake is about 230 miles round, with a few small islands. By reason of its colour it is called the Blue Lake or Koko Nor.

As we marched along all day we overtook large herds of yak being driven to the Chinese markets, laden with salt or wool. At midday we made our halt by one of the several streams that run into the lake from the ranges of hills. At night-time it was impossible to find a spot which would be out of sight of these black tents. This induced our Mongols to take more precautions than ever for their safety.

Much to their dismay, we agreed that I should ride on ahead the following morning with Esau the last hundred miles or so to the Chinese border town of Tankar. We knew how well Rockhill had been received at the little inn there, and I hoped that I should come across Tibetans who would help us to arrange for our onward journey through China. I hoped to have all ready by the time Malcolm arrived with the Mongols.

CHAPTER XXII.

ESAU AND I SET OFF—RECEPTION FROM THE BANAS—WE ARRIVE AT TANKAR—A FRIENDLY GUIDE—AN ABSURD TIP—DR. RIJNHART—TEA WITH LHASSA OFFICIALS—ARRIVAL OF MALCOLM AND THE MONGOLS—CHEN-LAO-PAN—CHINESE ETIQUETTE.

At daybreak on the 12th October, Esau and I, after filling ourselves with tea and tsampa, mounted the strongest two of the Mongol ponies. Our saddlebags were filled with food such as we had eaten at breakfast and a supply of cold meat. We also carried some rugs, for it was probable that we should have to spend two more nights in the wilds before reaching Tankar.

After riding some ten miles quietly over the prairie land, we entered a large camp of Bana men, with whom were living several lamas, who came out to inquire who we might be and were friendly enough in their conversation; most of the Bana men were away tending their flocks.

We rode on again for a considerable distance before we could find the wherewithal to boil some tea. There were the remnants of a very old Mongol encampment, where we gathered together some argols and a few sticks, and close by was water in the shape of a patch of snow, which even then had not melted. Before leaving we made an erection of mud, into which we placed a stick with a note fastened to it. This was to let Malcolm know that we were getting along all right.

We rode on till late in the afternoon, when we came to

the foot of a pass which forms the watershed of the Koko Nor and the Sining Ho. Here were grass, water, and dried argols, and fearing darkness might be on us before we could cross the pass, we unsaddled and prepared to spend the night. A few miles south of us lay the small salt lake of Baga Nor, quite close to the Koko Nor; to the west of us there were large camps of the Bana men, who were ignorant of our existence, for we had encamped in a depression of the ground and our two ponies grazed in secrecy.

While Esau was busy preparing the tea I collected a large sack of argols, that we might keep up a fire throughout the night, for there was a bitterly cold wind which blew down upon us from the north-east.

We saddled our ponies early the next morning, and found we had a nine-mile ride before reaching the top of the pass. There were two passes some five or six miles apart, and here were living more Bana people, with immense flocks as usual. It was certainly a chilly abode at this time of the year. We experienced this to our discomfort, for we were caught in a heavy snowstorm. At the second pass we met a large party of Tibetan lamas dressed in gay garments of red and yellow, the colours standing out particularly bright against the falling snow.

As soon as we commenced the descent we followed a small stream, the Sining Ho, and after twenty-two miles stopped to make tea in a large grassy valley dotted with more black tents and flocks. Whilst busily engaged with our breakfast an old shepherd came to see us, from whom we inquired whether we could reach Tankar that same evening. "Yes," he replied, "if your ponies are good enough, you will get there this evening," which was certainly wisdom.

We journeyed on till after sunset with no signs of Tankar; we had still followed the Sining Ho, which flowed between precipitous hills, with only space enough for the narrow track on its right bank. We were just moving along looking for a suitable camp when we found a few more Bana tents in front of us. Our reception was anything but civil, and we had some anxiety that the nomads might steal our ponies during the night, for it was impossible for us to travel along in the dark. We chose a spot on the lower ground by the water's edge, out of sight, and met with no mishap. With the first streak of daylight we were drinking our tea, and were soon on the move again. After marching for one mile we had to cross the river, which, by reason of the recent storms, had swollen considerably, and a dry passage could not be made; the water rose up over our ponies' hips, and the bottom of the river was uneven and uncertain, with big boulders.

We then entered what is called the grass country, whither the inhabitants of Tankar send their flocks to fatten. After six miles we passed a compact little village planted on the other side of the river. The land here and all down the river had been cultivated, in fact, every inch of ground. Some of the crops grew close up by the walls of the village, while others grew on the hillsides and slopes, where it looked impossible for crops to grow. Most of them had been cut, and the villagers in their blue garments were busily engaged in gathering them in.

We still followed the stream, the pathway being uneven with rocks and boulders, whilst the hills on our side rose close from the water's edge. After a short while we came to a pretty rustic-looking bridge, which invited one over the river to a snug monastery that nestled amongst the trees and bushes. The name of this monastery is Gompa Soba, and had I followed my own inclination and visited the place, kindness and hospitality would alone have been exhibited, as we afterwards learnt.

From here the road to Tankar, such as it is, passes through a cultivated district with a continuation of straggling villages and tall poplars. Being very hungry, and over-anxious to reach Tankar, the road in consequence appeared to be interminable. Perhaps this is what made Rockhill state that the distance from Tankar to Gompa Soba was thirteen miles, whereas, in reality, it is not much more than half the distance.

As we proceeded, the number of passers-by increased, and they appeared to take as much interest in little Ruby as they did in Esau and myself.

I told Esau to address some of these people in the Tibetan language, to try and find out how much further Tankar was, and any other information about the place. Many were thus accosted, and many without success, till at length we met a nice-looking elderly Chinaman, who was a merchant. He told us, to our great delight and astonishment, that there were two white doctors, one a lady, living at Tankar. He also told us of the little inn where we could get some sort of accommodation.

It was noon when we at length entered the town by the western gate, a great relief to our weary ponies. We began to ride through the main street, busy, dirty, and narrow, with a large crowd of Chinese, and a sprinkling of Mongols and Tibetans too. As we wended our way, observed by all, I told Esau to shout out in the Tibetan tongue for somebody to show us the way to the inn. Without avail we traversed the whole length of Tankar, and then tried a new expediency. We retraced our steps as far as the busiest corner we had seen, and calling a halt there, Esau in a loud voice again and again repeated the question.

This proceeding of ours naturally attracted a large crowd, and so pressed were we on all sides, that I thought it wise to back out of it. As soon as we had almost got ourselves clear, we found a man alongside of us who replied in Tibetan, "I'll show you the way to the inn." I smiled and nodded in acknowledgment of his kindness, and we moved off, followed by a crowd filled with wonderment as to where we had sprung from, especially as we were unaccompanied by any following or baggage animals.

We very shortly entered the door of the inn, which we found consisted of a very dirty square yard surrounded on all sides by stables or tiny rooms void of any furniture. Having been so far successful in finding it, the next thing was to procure food for the ponies and then for ourselves. Curiously enough, I could discover no innkeeper, for I had hoped to find a hearty welcome from the same man who had helped Rockhill, but what I considered of more importance at that moment was the discovery of a small stack of green grass at the further end of the yard. I at once went for it and began pulling out some of the grass, but this operation did not last very long, for I was caught hold of from all sides and was given to understand that the grass was not for my use. Just then our Tibetan speaking friend returned, whom I sent with Esau carrying a rupee to try and buy some grass. Now that I was left alone with Ruby we both attracted much attention from the people, all of whom, in turn, felt my hat, my coat, and my pants, to see of what material they were made, whilst others still more inquisitive felt my knees, for a Chinaman imagines we are blessed with no knee-caps. Esau was not long away, but had been unsuccessful on his errand, for no one would change the rupee because there was a crown on the Queen's head. I therefore selected a crownless one, which was more suited to their taste. This very soon produced a bundle of hay and a handful of small brass coins called "cash." This was, indeed, a windfall, and we felt we already had a firmer footing in the land. As a matter of fact, the few rupees we had left were not sufficient to pay off our Mongols, so without assistance we should have fared badly. Our friend then volunteered to run off and tell the white man of my arrival.

He could not have lived very far away, for he was soon back again.

I then ordered Esau to reward the Chinaman for all the trouble he had taken for us, so Esau, straightway pulling forth his coins, offered him a single cash. To our surprise he declined it with a smile, while Esau and I remarked that these Chinese were by no means the money-loving race they were generally represented to be. The narration of our first experience in Chinese money matters caused many a laugh amongst the good missionaries we afterwards came across, for the man we had offered a single cash to was a merchant of Tankar of no small importance, whilst the value of a single cash is equal to about the thirtieth portion of a penny. One might as well have offered sixpence to a head keeper at home after a big shoot.

I was just about to sally forth to try and purchase some bread, for I had noticed some at the corner only a short distance from the inn, when some one hurriedly trotted in and at once dismounted from his pony. He was somewhat better dressed than the ordinary crowd around, and on seeing me he came straight towards me. I could hardly make up my mind whether he was a European or a Chinaman, and when he addressed me in a mixture of French and Chinese I was still more mystified, so to simplify matters I replied, "I'm an Englishman," and held my hand out to him. He eagerly seized it and gave me the heartiest shake I had received for many a long day, and I felt thankful that we had found a European and a friend anxious to help us in this out-of-the-way place.

Mr. Rijnhart, for that was his name, was a Dutch missionary, and had only taken up his abode in Tankar within the last three months. He said, "You must come at once and live with me and my wife." In thanking him, I replied that it was impossible for me to do that, for I had nothing but what was on my back. With genuine hospitality he remarked that if such was the case it was more imperative than ever that I should come and live in his house. In another moment we were trotting through the street in single file, chatting all the while, when, suddenly turning to the left, we very shortly afterwards drew up at Rijnhart's little house. One step up out of the narrow lane landed us in an open court-yard, where his kind-hearted wife, Dr. Rijnhart, was waiting to welcome us, as well as Mr. Hall, of the China Inland Mission, who had come over to Tankar from Sining, and had only just returned with the Rijnharts from making a trip to the sea of Koko Nor. So it was indeed fortunate not to have arrived in Tankar during their absence. The Rijnharts had a small house; there were rooms and stables all round the four sides of the yard. Great honour was shown to me in the eyes of the Chinese by allotting to my use the room that faced the entrance. The Rijnharts, when by themselves, lived in Chinese fashion, and were on the most friendly terms with all the Chinese and Tibetan officials in the town. Besides being engaged in the great aim of all missionaries, these two good people administered bodily medicine as well; in fact, their sole means of existence arose from the small sums and kind they received in return. They were, indeed, leading a hard, unselfish life, yet they were a very happy couple, for they knew they were doing good.

The fact of their receiving payment for their doctoring may meet with censure from some people, but the results should be looked at. At Tankar the Rijnharts had entirely won over the hearts of the Chinese, and in consequence of this, we ourselves were treated with courtesy and civility by the officials. The customary hatred of foreigners by the Chinese had disappeared from Tankar.

During the afternoon some Lhassa officials dropped in for a chat and a cup of tea, or, more correctly speaking, a small bowl of tea. They were pleasant fellows with nice faces, and had been stationed at Tankar to see that justice was done to all Tibetans passing through this frontier town. There were four officials altogether, the most influential being called Sherchichaba, and the fourth Lusam Kindum. They took great interest in our journey, and were evidently pleased to meet me.

When they had departed, a very stout and hearty Chinaman stepped in. He was Chen-Lao-Pan, an agent for Forbes & Co., the wool merchants. He could only speak a few words of English, but as he laughed so frequently and so heartily, there was no feeling of awkwardness when with him. That night the many little homely comforts attended to by Dr. Rijnhart herself were highly appreciated by me, and I slept soundly.

The next morning we had leisure to look round before the arrival of Malcolm with the Mongols. Tankar is a busy little town of some 10,000 inhabitants, and owes its importance, not to its being a market centre, but to the fact that it is the first and last Chinese town passed by caravans journeying to and from Lhassa and Mongolia. It is a kind of depôt, for the merchandise is taken further in to the larger towns. We walked through the main street, and peeped into all the shops, most of which contained nick-nacks and a great deal of rubbish. We then mounted the walls on the western side, and noticed that great heaps of stones had been collected there for the people to throw down on to the heads of the Mohammedan rebels. Several mud houses had also been erected, where the soldiers had to sleep and keep watch in turn. From these walls a fine view of the surrounding country is gained. Tankar appears to be situated in a kind of hollow, with rising ground and hills on all sides. One of the principal hills lies north-west, and is called Ho La, or Ta Sand, and another hill lying south-east is called Ts'ai T'a by Tartars and Wupu by Tibetans. From the summit of one of the south-eastern hills, where a single tree has been planted, the town of Sining can be seen, a distance of ninety li. This tree is a useful landmark for travellers, as it can be seen for a long distance along the road. We could see, too, the river, which is here called the Ta Ho by the Chinese, and Ch'enkook by Mongols of the Tsaidam, running merrily through a land of cultivation, the most plentiful crops being wheat, barley, oats, millet, pease, and a little linseed and opium.

We had no sooner returned to Rijnhart's little house when Malcolm and the Mongols arrived, so our party was once more reunited. Since leaving Leh we had travelled over 1,983 miles, and for between three and four months had been at a height of about 1,600 feet above the sea level. In spite of the pressing invitations of our hosts, we decided to remain only one day at Tankar. It was now the middle of October, and before very long the severe winter of these parts would be upon us; furthermore, we were already due back in India some six weeks ago. We agreed to make the most of our short stay, so in the afternoon we visited the Yamen, in order to pay our respects to the "ting," or mayor, of Tankar. We spent some minutes in the first outer court-yard, which was decorated with some huge imitation stone lions, while our visiting card was being taken to this chief official. The people, as usual, took advantage of the delay to feel and inspect our clothes, and the state they were in would alone have warranted this scrutiny, let alone the curiosity these people exhibited with regard to the texture of the cloth. We were glad at length to escape and be ushered into the presence of the "ting," where all respect and attention was shown to us. We were given the great seat of honour, and provided with some delightful tea. We apologised for the dilapidated state we were in, but the "ting" replied that he had carefully read our passport, and knew we were great military officials from India, and quite understood our present circumstances; in fact, he wondered we had arrived with anything at all. Whilst chatting away, we inquired how many soldiers were in the town. None now, he replied, for all had been disbanded since the rebellion had been quelled. When our visit had lasted as long as was polite, we rose to depart, and the "ting," in order to show his great respect for us, accompanied us as far as the big gates, walking at a slow rate. These had been thrown open wide, as a still further sign of respect, where, amidst much bowing and raising of the hands to the head, we eventually got off.

We then made our way to the house of the Hsieht'ai, or Colonel, and why there should be a Colonel with no soldiers seemed ridiculous. However, this was no business of ours, but as he was the next important official in Tankar, it was our duty to visit him. He was a rather enfeebled, elderly gentleman, but very kind to us, and that very evening we received presents from him, consisting of a sheep for ourselves, and grass and liou or pease for our ponies. He asked many questions with regard to the Indian revenue, its army, etc., and asked how many men we ourselves commanded, and, in order to do ourselves justice, we calculated a single Englishman was equal to a great number of Chinamen, which he evidently did not.

Our third visit was to Chen-Lao-Pan, who lived in luxury and comfort and on the fat of the land. He sent us forth rejoicing with a bottle of Chinese wine and a packet of tobacco from Lancheo, the capital of Kansu, so famous for its tobacco grown and manufactured there.

At afternoon tea it is polite manners for the host to take some bread or cake from the guest's plate and place it on the table before him, and before drinking tea to raise the cup in both hands and nod to one's friends, who return the salutation in the same manner. It is also considered polite for a guest, when offered the seat of honour, to refuse it, when the host will at once try and put his guest into it. A show of resistance is at once made in return. The consequence is, that before the seat is eventually occupied by the guest, as it always is, a struggle of a few minutes duration is carried out against its occupation.

CHAPTER XXIII.

A VISIT TO CHEN-LAO-PAN—COLONEL YANG—THE DAUGHTER OF PRINCE KOKO NOR—A VISIT TO THE MONASTERY OF KUMBUM.

THE following morning we visited the Lhassa officials, but unfortunately found only one of them at home, Lusam Kindum, who was very friendly, and at once plied us with tea. He said that he himself was shortly going to Pekin with the big triennial tribute to the Emperor, consisting of pulo cloth, saffron, and incense. He showed us a rifle of German make which he had bought from one of the soldiers during the rebellion for eighteen taels, or £3 12*s*.

We made Lusam Kindum a small present of a knife, and he in return presented Malcolm with a beautifully embroidered golden cap such as he himself wore, and to me gave a "scarf of blessing," or k'artag, under which it was given, and I in return held this up to my forehead with a gentle nod. He, too, came down from the "k'ang" and accompanied us as far as the gates, which were opened in our honour.

We again visited Chen-Lao-Pan, where the "ting" and the Colonel turned up, so that the conversation and laughter waxed strong and loud, while the tea, the cakes, and pipes were liberally distributed. All knew that Chen-Lao-Pan possessed the best of everything, and was liberal with it withal. To add to the gathering, the Colonel's two little daughters, both well dressed, were trotted in to pay their respects. They must have been very young, for they were very little, and could scarcely walk, yet they made their curtseys all round in the most polite fashion, showing at what an early age the better educated Chinese are taught to a nicety the correct manners of society. As soon as the mayor and the Colonel, whose name was Yang, and his two little daughters had departed, we set about business, and the

BUDDHIST PRAYER-WHEEL, WITH SCARF OF BLESSING.

object of our second visit. This was the loan of some money to help us across China. Nothing could have delighted more the heart of this good-natured Chinaman than his freely lending us sixty taels, as well as giving us letters of credit to other agents throughout the country. Nor could we thank him sufficiently for the kind help he had given us. The lack of money at this time was our greatest difficulty. How could we cross China when we were penniless?

During the afternoon the Rijnharts were visited by the daughter of the Prince of Koko Nor. She was so splendidly dressed that I could not resist taking a snap-shot of her whilst being engaged in conversation with Dr. Rijnhart. We were sorry at having to leave Tankar on the morrow, especially as Rijnhart himself was coming with us and

DR. RIJNHART. DAUGHTER OF THE PRINCE OF KOKO NOR.

we were leaving his good wife to live alone; but we were thankful to know that in this busy little town the greatest officials were her staunchest friends.

TANKAR—SINING.

A Visit to the Monastery of Kumbum.

About 1 P.M. on October 17th, after having said "Good-bye" to Dr. Rijnhart, our hospitable hostess of the last few days, and having sent off our baggage by the direct road to Sining, we started for the famous monastery of Kumbum, which lies about seventy li south-east of Tankar. Our party consisted of Mr. Peter Rijnhart, our two selves, and Lassoo, the cook. We rode our Mongol ponies, on which we fastened our saddlebags, with all that we were likely to require.

Very lucky we were to be able to pay this visit under the guidance of Mr. Rijnhart, for not only has he a more intimate knowledge of the monastery than any other living man, but having made his home for two years in Lusar, ten months of which were spent in the monastery itself, he has made friends with a very large number of its inmates, more especially with Mina Fu-yeh, one of the greatest incarnate saints in the place,* in whose house we were to spend the night. Just outside the east gate of Tankar we passed a party of Tibetans, in the midst of whom was a big living Buddha, who had recently been appointed abbot of the monastery of Ta Koe Ri by the Talé Lama. On his way from Lhassa he had been attacked by a party of Mohammedans. All his attendants had been killed, and he alone had escaped to the mountains, where he wandered about for twenty-three days without food, till at last he found his way to Tankar. He was now on his way to take up his appointment, having recovered from the effects of his privations.

For the first fifteen li our road lay along the left bank of the Hsi Ho, till we crossed it by a bridge close to the village of Hsang Ho Ri (Sounding River). On the way we overtook strings of camels laden with the yearly tribute of pulo and incense from the Talé Lama to the Emperor. We noticed several caves in the cliffs inhabited by men—fortunate beings, for they had no rent to pay. At Hsang

* There are about seventy of these "incarnate saints" at Kumbum, among whom Mina Fu-yeh ranks sixth or seventh.

BRIDGE IN CHINA. FIVE MILES FROM TANKAR. MISSIONARY AND MULE ON BRIDGE.

Ho Ri is a small inn where flour and tea can be bought, and close by were some opium fields. This bridge was one of the many in Kansu which are built on the cantilever principle. They are plentiful throughout the Western Himalayas, but this was the first we had seen in China.

BRIDGE OF SHANG-HO-RI (SOUNDING RIVER) ON THE ROAD TO TANKAR.

We now had a stiffish climb to the top of a pass called the Wu La, whence we got a magnificent view over range after range of mountains, stretching away to the south. The descent was comparatively easy, and we were able to note the results of the recent Mohammedan rebellion. Every village that was not in ruins had loop-holed walls and fighting towers which had been specially erected. Our companion, Rijnhart, had spent some time in General Wei's* camp, he and his wife doctoring the wounded, thereby saving many a life, and earning the gratitude of their patients. He was, therefore, well qualified to point out various spots along our road where skirmishes or serious fighting had taken place. Many of the villages had been deserted, but the people were now returning, and beginning to again get their fields under cultivation. It will, however, be many a long day before grain and market produce regain their normal price. Rich and fertile though this little bit of Kansu is, it will be fully two years before it can recover from the trying times it passed through in 1895.

Once, just about sunset, we missed our way, and once one of the horses, while being led, slipped down a steep bank into a ravine, luckily without injuring himself or any one else. Otherwise our ride was devoid of incident, but the moon was high in the heavens by the time we arrived at our destination. We were quite unexpected, so it was some time before we could get any one to pay attention to our knocking at the stout wooden doors of the monastery; but at length it was opened by one of the great man's servants, who, as soon as he recognised Mr. Rijnhart, was all civility. The door we went in at was not the front door, as only the owner of the house was supposed to use that, and it would have been a great breach of etiquette on our part to have gone in by it. Our door led us into the stable yard, and while word was being taken to Mina Fu-yeh that Mr. Rijnhart, or Lin Hsien-shêng, as he was generally called, had arrived with two foreign friends, we busied ourselves looking after the horses, loosening girths, getting straw, etc. In a few moments we went upstairs, and, after passing through an open court ornamented in the middle with a flower bed, were ushered into the presence of one of the holiest men on the eastern border of Tibet.

* Wei Fou T'ai, sent from Hunan to quell the rebellion.

AUDIENCE ROOM OF THE KAMBO (ABBOT) OF KUMBUM.

The pictures around the room are representations of many idols embroidered or painted on silk scrolls. In the gilded cupboard to the right, behind each pane of glass, is a beautiful image of some Buddha. In front of the writing Buddha stands a copper prayer cylinder. Beside the Kambo, who sits behind the table, lies a stick on the end of which is an embroidered cylinder, suspended, which hangs over the left end of the table: this is used by him to touch the heads of worshippers who bow before him.—*This description, and the photograph from which the picture is taken, have been kindly supplied by Mr. Peter Rijnhart, the missionary at Tankar.*

Mina Fu-yeh* is a man twenty-seven years of age, or twenty-eight by Chinese calculation, and has been in the monastery since he was seven. Considerably below medium height, and of slight build, he has a very pleasant face,

MINA FU-YEH (BUDDHA).

especially when lit up by a happy smile, as it often is. It struck us both that the sedentary indoor life he is more or less bound to live was telling on his constitution, and that if he had spent more of his time in the open air, instead of in reading, writing, and meditation, his health would benefit greatly. However that may be, it did not interfere with

* Fu-yeh is the Chinese equivalent of Buddha.

his hospitality, for the moment we were seated he told us that food was being prepared, and that it would shortly be ready. He was living in a small room about twelve feet square, with massive stone walls, squatting on the "k'ang" or raised platform which occupied the greater portion of the room. On this "k'ang" was a low square table only a few inches high, holding a beautiful tea-cup made of stone, with a silver cover. On his right was a darkly-stained cupboard, wherein he kept his books, writing materials, and other nick-nacks. Hanging on the wall opposite him, and in no way harmonising with the other surroundings, was a coloured picture of the day illustrating some English boys and girls out of school. This had been given him by Mr. Rijnhart, who meanwhile told him all about us—who we were, where we had come from, and gave him a general outline of our journey, in all of which he took considerable interest, and, through Rijnhart, he asked us several questions, including the inevitable one, "Aren't you cold in those thin clothes?" No Chinaman or Tibetan seems able to grasp the European fashion of wearing tight clothing; to them our outer clothes appear to fit so closely that there can be no room for any underneath.

Mina Fu-yeh speaks Chinese, Mongolian, and Tibetan with equal ease and fluency, so that any questions we wished to ask we put to Rijnhart, who translated them into Chinese, the answer being received the reverse way. In this manner we were able to get a reliable statement about the priests who live on the "Dragon Colt's Island," the island in the Koko Nor, mention of which has been made by so many travellers. While marching along the north shore of the lake, we had just been able to make out the island away towards the south side, but no two men gave the same account of its inhabitants. Mina Fu-yeh said that there are twelve or thirteen priests living there, that they keep sheep and goats, and that, being free from depredations of wolves, their flocks thrive well. In winter, when the lake is frozen over, they cross to the mainland and lay in stores for the following summer. He himself, he added, was thinking of building a house there and getting a boat of some sort, so that he would be able to go backwards and forwards at any time of year. I don't suppose this idea of his will ever come to anything.

One was naturally diffident about asking a perfect stranger a great deal about his religious tenets, for although our host was a very liberal-minded man and far more ready to converse than most Tibetans, there was always the feeling that one might touch on some delicate subject and quite unintentionally annoy him. We therefore contented ourselves with asking Rijnhart privately what he had told him on other occasions. His explanation of how he came to be recognised as the reincarnation of the previous Mina Fu-yeh shows how convincing the proofs of identity are to one who has been brought up to accept and believe in the theory. He relates how, when very small, various articles were laid out from which he was to select those which had been his own in his previous life-time. Among these was a number of rosaries from which he had no difficulty in choosing his own, "For," he says, "I had used it daily for years; how is it possible that I should not know it from among all these others? Of course I knew it." So on with other articles; his identity was established without a doubt, and he became the heir to the accumulated property of fifteen former lifetimes.* He talks freely of his last lifetime, pointing out the site of the house in which he lived, and which was burnt down about two years before his death; it was, he says, a far finer house than the one he now occupies.

* Mina Fu-yeh is now in either his sixteenth or twenty-second lifetime; I am not sure which, so have given the lesser number in the text. This is, of course, only since he became an incarnate saint; there are no records of his previous lives. Sakya Muni had altogether 551 lives, 510 of which were prior to his becoming a saint.

In the course of conversation, he told us that he had spent some time in studies at Pekin, and that he had also been on a journey to the Eastern Mongols, where he read the sacred books to all who wished it. He selected them as they were more pious and more wealthy than the Tibetans or Western Mongols. While in Pekin he had had some dealings with foreigners, buying things in the stores, and was full of admiration for their honesty. He was much amused when we told him we were sorry we could not say the same for the Chinese. Most of his own people, those for whose spiritual welfare he is chiefly responsible, come from round Kuei-Tê, where he himself was born ; he has also a certain number of Tibetans and Mongols from the Koko Nor and Tsaidam. He was till recently Ta K'anpo or abbot of the monastery, a position of great dignity, being in fact the principal official.

All officials are elected for a period of three years, and the abbot during that time has a very peculiar privilege. He is allowed to send out eight parties of priests in different directions for three months carrying with them Ts.2,000 worth of merchandise. This they trade for sheep, cattle, horses, etc., which are sold at considerable profit on their return. All this profit goes into the pocket of the abbot, who runs no risk beyond the Ts.2,000 originally invested. All other expenses are defrayed out of the monastery funds.

Mina Fu-yeh had been most unfortunate in his business matters while abbot, for in 1894 he had sold a great proportion of his horses, etc., to Mohammedans. They, in accordance with the universal Chinese custom, deferred payment till New Year's Day, by which time the rebellion had broken out, some of his debtors had been killed, and others had left the country, so that he only collected a tithe of what was due to him ; in 1895 no party was sent out, owing to the disturbed state of the country, and in 1896 he had only sent out Ts.1,000 worth of stuff. With this he had done extremely well, but only made sufficient profit to cover his losses of 1894.*

While we had been conversing thus, our food, tea and large quantities of boiled mutton, was being prepared and was now brought in, a large dishful for the three of us, and a separate smaller dish for our host, as is only fitting for one who lives in such an odour of sanctity as he does.

We were very hungry after our ride, and in a few moments we were busy eating Tibetan fashion, *i.e.*, pocket-knives and fingers, each one selecting from the joint whatever morsel took his fancy; to do the thing properly each bone should be scraped scrupulously clean, but, though we did our best, our host could give us points at this. The ease and rapidity with which he cleaned up the most awkward-looking bones came as a revelation. As a matter of fact he had already had his evening meal, but etiquette compelled him to eat again to encourage us. We were waited upon by the treasurer of the establishment and by a jolly little boy, about twelve years old, a disciple of Mina Fu-yeh's, under whose tuition he was studying the sacred writings. In the intervals of

* Mina Fu-yeh's abbotship came to rather an abrupt termination owing to a quarrel with another influential Buddha called Shertoch Fu-yeh. At the time of the rebellion the priests were greatly exercised in their minds as to whether they should fight against the rebels or not. Most of the older men said that fighting was no part of a priest's duty, while the younger men were keen to be in the thick of it. Mina Fu-yeh, who was then abbot, said that they should not go out to fight, but that they should make every preparation, and if the monastery was attacked they should defend it to the last, otherwise they ought not to mix in worldly strife. This did not please the war party, who were headed by Shertoch Fu-yeh, and who made up their minds that fight they would. They went out on three separate occasions, and without doing any good; several were killed, a terrible thing for a devout Buddist, for he who dies a violent death is reincarnated in an animal, and must complete a cycle of sixty lifetimes before he can again become a man. This made the war party even more bitter against Mina Fu-yeh, as they realised how much wiser the course he had recommended would have been, and so inimical did they become that he had to resign his post and for some time was in fear of his life. Most of them speak rather disparagingly of his successor, who is, they said, an insignificant Buddha, only in his third or fourth lifetime.

filling up our bowls with tea and pressing food upon us, he amused himself and the company by teasing his teacher's dog, a very fat little Pekin pug, as it lay beside its master.

When we had eaten our fill we rose to say "Good-night," and apologised for having thrust ourselves in without due notice, having come, too, just when our host must have been about to go to bed. To this he replied that he was delighted that we had come, that he hoped that we would go all over the place, taking pictures if we wished to. The priests would be occupied in public reading in the big hall, but we should be free to go where we wished; he added that he was only writing extracts from the books when we came in, and that we had not disturbed him at all.

Of course we asked if we might see his writing, and when produced we were most unfeignedly astonished by it. Never have I seen more beautifully even writing, or better formed characters. Every here and there a word was written in red ink. On asking why this was we were told that it was the character for "Sum," or three, and stood for the Trinity of Buddha.

It was very late, so having again said "Good-night," we went to bed and slept soundly. The next morning we were up betimes, as we had a busy day before us. At daybreak we were awakened by hearing two short blasts from a long horn, followed by a louder blast which was dwelt upon till it gradually died away. This was the warning to the 4,000 priests at Kumbum to get ready for prayer; it was the commencement of a new day. But, early as we were, our host was before us, and when we left our room we found him making preparations for breakfast. He explained that his steward and several of his servants were away, so he had to do a great deal himself. It seemed strange to see an incarnate saint, who is held in the deepest reverence and worshipped by men, busying himself unlocking drawers, producing sugar and butter, and generally attending to the most trivial and mundane matters, chattering away all the time like an ordinary mortal.

Thanks, however, to these endeavours, our breakfast of tea and tsamba was soon ready. Rijnhart, of course, is an adept at mixing up the butter, meal, and sugar into the correct dough, but neither of us had acquired the art. For some time our host watched us in silence, smiling occasionally at our awkwardness, but at last he offered to do it for us, adding hastily to Rijnhart, "Please tell them my hands are quite clean." Breakfast over, we lost no time in starting, armed with the kodak, to visit the many temples and shrines which form the monastery.

When we arrived the previous evening, it was too dark to get any idea of how the monastery lay, but we were enabled to do so. Kumbum itself lies at the junction of two small valleys, one coming from the east, the other from the south, the buildings lying to the south of the former, while on the north is the "Precious Hill," which keeps off all evil influences. On the east side of the other valley are most of the private dwellings, while on the west are temples, chief among which is the famous "Gold-Tiled Temple" of Tsong K'aba. Lower down, below the junction of these two valleys, is the little town of Lusar. Altogether in Kumbum there are close on 4,000 priests, the vast majority of which, say seventy per cent., are Tibetans; of the rest about twenty per cent. are Mongols, and the remainder Chinese. Nearly all of them speak Chinese with a greater or less degree of fluency, but there are a few who speak only Mongol and Tibetan.

It has, I believe, been stated in print, though I have never seen it, that Kumbum is entirely Chinese in its government and organisation. That this is not the case needs no further proof than the fact that, in all things temporal, it is under the Tsong T'u, or Prince of the Koko Nor, a mandarin appointed by the Emperor to govern all his Tibetan dependencies in this direction ; he lives at Sining, and is known among Tibetans and Mongols as the " Seling Amban " ; on the other hand, if Kumbum were really Chinese, it would be subservient to the Fu of Sining, and would be governed by the Fu T'ai. There is, moreover, a distinct boundary line, separating the territory which comes under Fu T'ai from that which comes under the Tsong T'u, those living within the boundary paying taxes to the monastery, while those outside pay to Sining Fu.

CHAPTER XXIV.

THE STORY OF THE FIRST BUDDHA OF THE EMPIRE—THE SACRED TREE—THE GOLD-TILED TEMPLE—PARTING FROM MINA FU-YEH—THE GREEN GLAZED-TILE TEMPLE—THE FLOWER TEMPLE—SIGNS OF THE MOHAMMEDAN REBELLION—AT THE MISSION HOUSE.

WHEN we got outside Mina Fu-yeh's house, the first thing that caught our eyes was a row of eight small towers or chortens, like those one sees in Ladakh, from which, I believe, Kumbum gets its Chinese name of "T'ah Ri Ssi," the "Monastery of the Eight Towers." From these we crossed by a small bridge to the eastern side of the valley, where many of the private houses are, and got a good bird's-eye view of the whole place. Unfortunately it was a dull, cloudy day, unsuitable for taking photos with a kodak, so I did not get as many as I should have liked, but while we were standing looking across the valley, a number of priests came out from the public reading hall, and I managed to get a pretty fair picture of them.

Principal among the private dwellings is that of A-chia Fu-yeh, who belongs to Kumbum, and is the first Buddha of the Empire. The story is, that just before he died, the Emperor promised him that if, on his return to this world, he would repeat all the conversations they had had, in his then lifetime, he would make him the first Buddha in the Empire. In due time he was reincarnated, and of course had no difficulty in doing what was required, and the

Emperor fulfilled his promise. A-chia Fu-yeh now lives almost entirely in Pekin, in the presence of the Emperor, and rarely visits his distant home. A fire broke out in his house in 1895, which spoilt it a good deal, and it has not been restored yet.

All the private houses and temples at Kumbum are supposed to be whitewashed annually, but, like many other

CHORTENS OF KUMBUM.

things, this had been neglected owing to the rebellion. They were now due two coats of whitewash, and consequently did not look as clean and bright as they should have done. The method of whitewashing appears strange to us, for the custom is to mix the wash, then to ascend to the roof, and pour it down over the walls. The result is not quite satisfactory, as we should look at it, but customs like these cannot be altered.

We now recrossed the stream, and began our tour of the temples. The first place we visited was the kitchen, chiefly remarkable for its enormous iron cooking-pots. Of these there were three, fixed in a mud range, each big enough to hold a man with comfort, and each heated by a large furnace. Everything was perfectly clean, and one might have eaten one's food off the floor. From here we went to two small temples

KUMBUM.

of Sakya Muni, which stand on the right of the "Gold-Tiled Temple." In them there was nothing peculiar, merely the ordinary ornaments and lamps, which can be seen in any temple.

Just in this corner, however, is the original "Sacred Tree,"* which sprung, according to some, from Tsong K'aba's

* Mr. W. W. Rockhill states that he was informed by Mr. W. B. Hemsley that this tree is the "white sandal-wood." ("Diary of a Journey through Mongolia and Tibet," p. 68.)

hair, according to others, from his swaddling-clothes. However this may be, the main fact remains, that on its leaves a true believer can distinctly trace the figure of Sakya Muni, or his name in Tibetan characters. Some priests say that one thing is to be seen, some the other, but Mina Fu-yeh says that on some leaves the figure may be seen, on others the characters; as only firm believers can trace anything, the question is likely to remain in doubt, in spite of Huc's assertion that he detected images.

We now entered the "Gold-Tiled Temple," the chief feature of the place, and the pride of Eastern Tibet, the sacred shrine of Tsong K'aba, the restorer and purifier of the Buddhist religion. Born in the year 1360 A.D., he grew up to find the Buddhism of his day in a very corrupt and degenerate state; he devoted his life to rectifying this, and succeeded in re-establishing the old order of things in accordance with the original doctrines of the faith. He was the founder of what is known as the "Yellow Sect," who wore yellow garments in place of red, but nowadays they have reverted to the red cloak, except on rare occasions, though they always wear a big yellow hat when reading the sacred books.

Before the entrance to the shrine there were a few lamas busily kotowing, and the boards in front of the doorway have been worn away to a depth of three or four inches, and polished till they shine again by the hands of the devout, as they knock their heads before the image of the saint. Most of these lamas knew Mr. Rijnhart, and stopped a moment or two in their devotions to speak a word of welcome to us, and one of the door-keepers asked us why we did not knock our heads before entering? To this Rijnhart replied that this would be no sign of respect on our part, as our custom was to remove our hats on entering a sacred place, nor did we ever omit to do so.

On entering the door, the figure of Tsong K'aba, who is

in a sitting position, is considerably above one, and not easily seen in the dim, religious light. It is about eight feet high, I should say, and very richly gilt. Below and in front of him is the shrine, with the usual holy water vases and butter lamps, while on either side are handsome gold and silver lamps, and a fine pair of elephant tusks. We lit a few lamps, and then walked slowly round the building, carefully keeping everything on the right hand.

Next in interest to the golden image among the relics in this temple, comes the stone on which Tsong K'aba's mother sat when delivered of her saintly son. This is carefully kept just as it was when originally placed in the temple. We then went upstairs to the second story, where we would be on a level with the great image; at first, one of the guardians refused to allow us to ascend, but Rijnhart assured him that we meant no harm, and that we had Mina Fu-yeh's permission to go where we would. Somewhat reluctantly he gave way, but a small douceur on our departure made him look on foreigners with more favourable eyes. This story was entirely devoted to Tsong K'aba's figure, in front of which lamps were burning, while hundreds of "scarves of blessing" (k'artag) hung all round, placed there by the hands of the faithful. There was yet another story, from which we looked down on to the lower portion of the gilded roof. The priests say that there is a quarter of an inch of gold all over the roof, but even deducting a great deal from this, it must be of immense value, and one could not help wondering how it had escaped two Mohammedan rebellions in the last thirty years. One would have thought that they would have risked everything to secure such loot, and to deal such a blow to the rival religion as the sacking of this temple would be.

From the Gold-Tiled Temple we passed into a big courtyard, which lies in front of the temple or hall for public reading. This is merely a large hall, without relics or shrines. In the courtyard are two very big prayer wheels, which one turns with a handle. At each revolution a bell is rung mechanically, and, after ringing the bell, the turner is bound to complete another revolution, stopping just before it rings again.

From the public reading-hall we went into that for private reading—a fine room, with rows of low forms about six inches high, comfortably cushioned, and big enough to hold about 2,500 priests. In front of this is another courtyard, in which, we were told, it is no unusual sight to see 1,200 or 1,500 pairs of shoes, belonging to students inside. How any one can find his own when he comes out is a mystery.

In an upper room in this block of buildings is a collection of curios and other property belonging to the monastery, quantities of silver vases, lamps, and musical instruments, but by far the most interesting thing, and what we were most anxious to see, is a picture of Tsong K'aba, drawn by himself in his own blood. When he was at Lhassa he was anxious to send his mother news of his well-being, so he drew this picture and sent it to Amdo, where she was living. The moment it was delivered into her hands the picture spoke, telling her not to be anxious about her son, for he was in Lhassa, and in perfect health. This occurred over 400 years ago, but the picture is in wonderful preservation, and very fresh.

There is another interesting figure of one Mété Fu-yeh. This is made in mud, and, like the picture of Tsong K'aba, it is under glass. Some time after its completion, by some miraculous power, hair grew on the head of the saint. He must have been a holy man, indeed, to have been favoured with such a manifestation of divine power. Here, as elsewhere, we gave the caretakers a few cash and lit a few lamps, small civilities which never failed in securing us their goodwill, and in return for which they showed us any attention in their power.

As we were leaving this courtyard we met a very refined-looking and well-dressed priest. He was delighted to see Rijnhart, and inquired eagerly after his wife, how he liked living at Tankar, how long was he going to stay in Kumbum, and many other questions. This man and his elder brother are two of the richest priests in the monastery; the latter has bought the title of K'ombo, which ensures his returning

TWO SMALL SHRINES, WITH NUMBERS OF PRAYER WHEELS.

as a Buddha in his next lifetime, a distinction which, according to Mina Fu-yeh, is also in store for Mr. Rijnhart, as a reward for the good work he is now doing according to his lights. We now walked round the outside of the monastery, going up the hill at the back and descending on the other side close to the village of Lusar. On the way we passed two small shrines, chiefly remarkable for the number of prayer wheels or cylinders ranged outside them. All these we carefully set in motion, and then went on our way, feeling that the day had not been wasted. Round the outskirts were a few prayer stones like one sees in Ladakh, but they were nothing like so plentiful nor of such good workmanship as they are about Leh. It is a form of devotion which does not seem to have found great favour in Eastern Tibet. The next hour was pleasantly spent in the village buying curios, such as the yellow head dresses previously mentioned, Buddhist bells, and suchlike mementos of our visit; but there were two more small temples to be seen, food to be eaten, and a ride of fifty li to be made to Sining before sunset, so we could not afford to spend much time shopping.

Returning to the house we were stopping in, we gave orders for the horses to be fed and to be got ready to start as soon as we had had our midday meal. While this was being prepared we again went and sat with our host, who produced a small atlas given him by Rijnhart, on which we showed him our route, the road to India *viâ* Lhassa and Darjeeling, and the way to England by the Suez Canal. At present he is very full of a plan to accompany Rijnhart next time he goes home, and very likely to go on to America. Rijnhart has taught him the English names of many countries, and he took the greatest pride in pointing these out and repeating their names. But he has learnt a great deal more of Europeans than mere parrot-like repetition of a few names. In the course of conversation he has picked up a lot of our doctrines, and discusses them freely with Rijnhart, comparing them with his own, and expressing the profoundest admiration for the great Central Figure, which is to us what Tsong K'aba is to him, the ideal to live up to. In his own way he reconciles the two religions, saying that Tsong K'aba must have been a later incarnation of Jesus Christ, and that in reality he worships the same divinity that we do, but in a different way and with different details.

Before we left Mina Fu-yeh gave us each a photograph of himself, which had been taken and printed for him by Rijnhart; in return we promised to send ours, and when we asked if there was anything else he would like, he said, "Flower seeds! the queerer the shape and stranger the colour the better." These of course we promised. I hope he will be pleased when he gets them if he is still at Kumbum, for he was then thinking of making a journey either to the Eastern Mongols again or to Lhassa.* If only he could be persuaded to allow one to accompany him to the latter place what a chance it would be.

Food being now ready, we ate it as quickly as might be, for it was already close on two o'clock. It was no easy thing to get away, for, with true Tibetan hospitality, our host and his little disciple joined in pressing us to eat, the latter saying to Rijnhart with a great show of displeasure, "I know that when you're at home you always eat five basins of food, and here you only eat two." At last we were ready to start. Nothing delayed us except that a priest who had gone to get us a supply of sacred leaves had not yet returned; in a few moments he ran up with about a hundred of them, and received a suitable present in return. Mina Fu-yeh warned us never to put anything on top of them as they were very precious, and to do so would be sacrilege. He also assured us that they had wonderful medicinal powers, and that if ever we were ill we had only to make use of them and a prompt cure would result. Last good-byes were said, and then we left the house full of regrets that we had had to cut our stay so short.

There were still the two small temples to visit; they both lie close together, below the entrance to the big temples. The first of the two was called the Green Glazed-Tile Temple, to distinguish it from the others. One enters it by a gateway

* On former occasions he had stated to Rijnhart that he would not go to Lhassa this lifetime, having been there in his last.

underneath a stone arch. In front of the gateway about the centre of the courtyard is a large stone to which some cash were sticking.* Behind this are the two other sacred trees which have sprung from the original one mentioned above; unfortunately there was no caretaker in this temple when we went in, so we could not discover the history of this stone nor any reason for the cash being put there. However, not to leave anything undone, we left our own contribution with the rest.

Inside the temple is a large figure of Sakya Muni, and on either side of him, lining the walls to the right and left, are figures of the first eighteen missionaries to China, who carried the word from India to the Far East. It seems strange, looking at these figures, and thinking of those other devout Chinese pilgrims, who made the long journey to India, to try and get the original scriptures to take back to their native land, that Buddhism should have so totally disappeared from India, while flourishing in the country of its adoption.

We had now come to the last temple on the list, the Flower Temple, or Hua Miao. The courtyard of this temple was empty, but all round the walls are painted frescoes of horrible tortures. Inside there are a number of stuffed animals, terrible caricatures, many of them quite as grotesque as the tortured figures on the walls outside. Among them is a large tiger, which is always kept saddled and bridled, ready for the Spiritual Buddha to ride upon at any moment; it is occasionally used in ceremonies, the abbot of the monastery seating himself upon it.

During the recent rebellion, all arms destined to be used against the Mohammedans, either in defence of the monastery or otherwise, were brought to be blessed in this temple, and hither all men going out to fight brought their offerings.

* I cannot help thinking that this is the stone mentioned by Mr. W. W. Rockhill ("Diary of a Journey through Mongolia and Tibet," p. 69) as being in the north-east corner of the Gold-Tiled Temple. He does not appear to have been inside the latter building, and we certainly saw no stone there resembling his.

Our flying visit to Kumbum and its temples was now at an end, and the feeling uppermost in our minds was, without doubt, regret we could not afford to stay at least two or three days longer. We had seen a lot, but only enough to make us feel how much more there was to see and learn. The true Buddhist religion is one of deep interest, especially in these days of Theosophy and similar cults, and a man

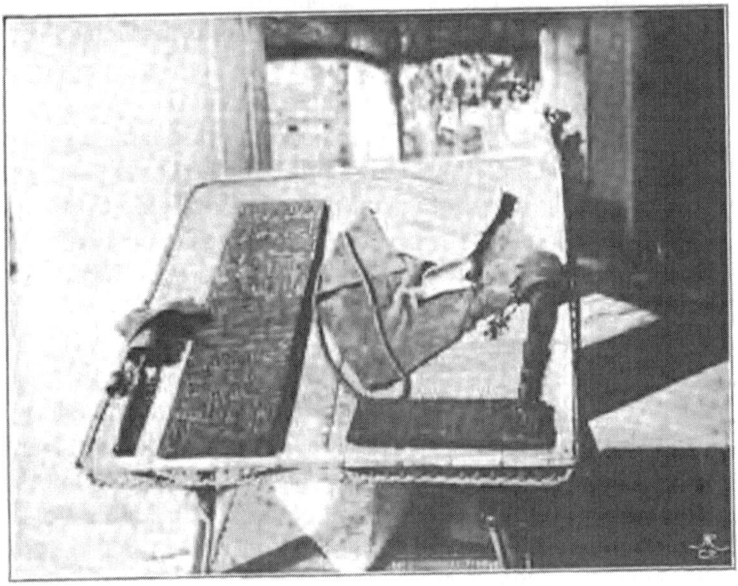

PRAYER WHEELS, BOARDS, ROSARY FROM LUSAR.

like Mina Fu-yeh, who is not only thoroughly well versed in all its tenets and scriptures, but is also sufficiently liberal minded to converse about them, is rare indeed.

Regrets, however, were vain. We had not a day to spare, and it was imperative that we should push on as rapidly as possible. So we made the best of it, and congratulated ourselves upon having seen as much as we had; for there is no gainsaying the fact, that, but for the friendly terms Rijnhart was on with the Buddhas and lamas of the place, we should never have gained entrance to the monastery, and by ourselves we should have seen nothing.

It was already late, and as the gates of every Chinese town are closed at sunset, we had to shove our animals along pretty smartly to get into Sining in time. From Lusar the road lies over an easy pass into the "Southern Valley," which it follows right up to the western gate of the town. On the way we passed a small temple of Pân Ku, who was, according to Chinese mythology, the only man on the sun. He knocked off bits which formed the moon, the stars and the planets, and then jumped off on to the earth, where his hair became grass, and his other features became corresponding ones on the earth's surface.

After riding hard for about fifteen li, we stopped at one of the little inns by the roadside, to refresh ourselves with bread and tea. As we proceeded we passed several water mills, and entered one for curiosity's sake. The mill was built over a stream, whose water was made to flow along a trough, thence on to the spokes of a wheel, which in consequence revolved. To the axis of this wheel a stout pole was fixed, which, penetrating the floor of the mill, supported a round, flat stone, which revolved also. Over this was another flat, round stone, hanging from the roof, through a hole in which grain was allowed to fall on to the lower stone, and thus be crushed. This particular mill was crushing mustard seed.

All the way to Sining signs of the rebellion were plentiful, just as they had been on the way from Tankar. The whole countryside had been devastated by the Mohammedans while they had had the upper hand, but at the city gate, which we passed through just at 6 P.M., the boot was on the other leg, for there, hanging in cages on the wall, were the heads of the ringleaders, who had been caught and executed by the orders of the Government, as soon as the soldiers had defeated the rebels. Among these heads was that of the Tibetan who had killed the French traveller, De Trouille

De Rhins, about two years previously. As we entered the city some soldiers passed out. Rijnhart told us, later on, that they called us "foreign devils," but as we did not understand a word of Chinese, we rode on in blissful ignorance of the insult.

A few minutes more riding brought us to the mission house, where we were most hospitably received by Mr. and Mrs. Ridley, and Mr. Hall, of the China Inland Mission, who have been working nobly for some years in this out-of-the-way corner of the globe.

I am afraid that the good missionaries at Sining were somewhat taken aback at our turning up on Sunday evening, but this in no wise detracted from the hospitality of our reception. I must frankly admit that both Malcolm and I had quite lost count of days of the week for months one day had been so like another. We were, therefore, quite ignorant of the fact that it was Sunday, till Mrs. Ridley happened to mention it.

Introductions were soon over, and we were taken into a most comfortably furnished drawing-room, the home-like appearance of which was greatly enhanced by an English stove. After washing our hands we went in to tea; we were hungry after our ride, and some first-rate home-made cakes proved altogether too great a temptation for us. I don't think either of us ever ate so much cake before, and I don't suppose we ever shall again.

In the course of conversation Hall told us that he had arranged for mules to start for Lancheo with our baggage the following day, but that it might be two or three days before we, ourselves, would be able to get on. This, however, did not much matter, as, by travelling fast, we should easily be able to overtake it.

We sat up late that night listening to Ridley's account of their experiences during the rebellion, and we were able to form some idea of the trying time they had passed through.

CHAPTER XXV.

THE MOHAMMEDAN REBELLION IN CHINA, 1895-6.

WHILE all Europe was busily engaged watching the progress of the war between China and Japan, and speculating as to what its ultimate result would be, the Province of Kansu was passing through a time of war and murder, fire and pillage, such as has rarely been known, and the severity of which can scarcely be realized, except by those who have visited the scene of it.

So scanty were the reports which appeared in the English or Indian papers, that Malcolm and I were little prepared for the scenes of devastation we passed through, or for the stories we heard from the missionaries, who spoke only from their own experiences.

The first signs of disturbance occurred in March, 1895, arising out of a quarrel between the two sects of Mohammedans—the "Salars" or "white-capped" sect, and the "black-capped" Mohammedans. The former came into China about 400 years ago. They are far more devout and far more fanatical than the "black caps," and to this day they preserve very many traces of their western origin. They live in eighteen villages, or "kung," on the south side of the Yellow River, and number nearly 20,000 souls.

The Tao T'ai of Sining, a high district official, went to Hsiun-Hua-Ting, about eighty miles from Sining, the scene of the disturbance, with a view to inquiring into and settling it. In a moment of indiscretion he seized and put to death an important Salar chief; this was the signal for an outbreak. The Salars rose *en masse*, the Tao T'ai was imprisoned, and the rebellion, which was to last for more than a year, had begun. Towards the end of March a body of soldiers, under a Major Uang, was treacherously attacked by Salars; twenty-four were killed and many wounded.

The outcome of this attack was a proclamation by the governor-general of the province of Kansu, to the effect that all Salars were to be killed without mercy. This was a hasty and ill-advised step, as its immediate result was to cause great excitement and disaffection among all Mohammedans of both sects—a very serious matter—comprising as they did about one quarter of the whole population of the province, while in wealth and enterprise they represented an even larger proportion. A second proclamation to the effect that there were good and bad Salars, and that only the latter were to be destroyed, did nothing to allay the feeling of uneasiness.

During April people from the villages crowded into Sining, bringing in what grain and family belongings they could carry. Meanwhile all available soldiers from Lancheo, the capital of the province, Liang-Cheo, and other towns to the east, were sent up to Sining; but they were sadly insufficient to cope with the work there was before them. A reward of Ts.10 for every living Salar, and Ts.5 for every dead one was offered, and Tibetan soldiers were induced to help the Chinese by promises of Salar territory.

By the end of April three Salar villages had been taken, but the Tao T'ai was still a prisoner, and the rising was undoubtedly on the increase. Luckily for Kansu, there was one man in Sining at this time who was thoroughly able to cope with the difficulties which arose. This was General Teng, the general in command at Sining. Throughout the rebellion he behaved in a truly heroic manner, and succeeded in winning the entire confidence and affection of the people, a bright contrast to most Chinese officials, whose only idea is self. He was also an able commander; his troops followed him as they followed no one else, with the natural result that when led by him they were almost invariably victorious.

General Teng left Sining for the disturbed district about the end of April, and was absent about two months, defeating the rebels in two battles, and taking the city of Hsiun-Hua-Ting. Soon after his return, however, disquieting rumours were heard of further risings at Ho-Cheo and other places.

Ho-Cheo is the principal Mohammedan city in Kansu. Their chief colleges are there, and it is one of the few places where Arabic is well known. An outbreak there was almost certain to ensure the rebellion becoming general, and no longer remaining confined to the "white-capped" sect.

Since the last rebellion, which ended some twenty-three years ago, no Mohammedans have been allowed to reside inside the cities, but have been compelled to reside in the suburbs, and seeing that in 1895 nearly every town of importance in Kansu had a Mohammedan suburb, the seriousness of a general outbreak can be imagined.

On the 11th July, General Teng again left Sining for the seat of war, and in a very few days he inflicted a severe defeat on the rebels, killing 700, with but slight loss to his own side; but the tide of rebellion was now too strong to be checked, and the death of a few hundreds made no appreciable difference. Sining was gradually being closed in, and was now almost shut off from the seat of war. To add to the trouble, a rumour got about that 10,000 Mohammedans in the east suburb of Sining itself were on the eve of rebelling, a danger which would be rendered even more serious by the absence of the general with every available soldier from the garrison.

Towards the end of July the enemy gradually closed in on the city, burning villages, and murdering men, women, and children; in Sin-Tien-Pu, a city to the west, about 2,000 people were killed. To-Pa, a walled town, was able to hold its own, but in most places the inhabitants were powerless to defend themselves, greatly owing to want of able and determined leaders. Sining itself was little better, but happily for all within the walls General Teng suddenly returned.

Shortly after his arrival it became known that certain influential people in the city had made a plot, which would, they hoped, result in his degradation, thereby removing the greatest obstacle in the way of Mohammedan success. A certain gentleman of the name of Chu, backed up by three other men of position, had drawn up a petition, which he had presented to the Taitai general, with a request that it might be forwarded to Lancheo. The petition was to the effect that after his last big fight, General Teng had ruthlessly butchered 700 harmless individuals, and that he ought to be disgraced. It seems incredible that even Chinamen could be so lost to any sense of patriotism, that they could accept Mohammedan silver as a reward for bringing about the downfall of the one man on whom the safety of their fellow-countrymen depended. The news of this plot soon spread among the people, and retribution swiftly followed. Mr. Chu was caught in the streets, and paid the penalty for his treachery with his life, while his three colleagues narrowly escaped. Their houses were wrecked, and every stick of property was destroyed by the infuriated mob.

The villages in the immediate vicinity of Sining were the next to suffer, and on the 26th July a large number of wounded people, mostly women and children, arrived in the city. The Temple of the God of Literature was turned into a temporary hospital, and the missionaries were begged to go and see what they could do for the sufferers. Needless to say, they lost not a moment in answering this appeal, and from that time on their hands were full, from early morning to late at night.

How some of the wounded ever managed to struggle as far as the city is more than the missionaries could tell us. One old woman, sixty-four years of age, had fourteen lance thrusts and a sword cut on her body, while a six-months-old child had three sword cuts on its face alone, and yet both these and many others in similar cases had travelled a distance of seventeen English miles before they could get any aid. So badly wounded were some of them, that they had taken three and four days on the road, and yet they had lived through it all.

All August the enemy ravaged the country, burning and pillaging, and a few small engagements took place. On the 16th August two rebels were caught and brought into the city. They said that there were 9,000 rebels in the valley to the north of Sining, that they were going to block the road from Lancheo, under Han-Uen-Sheo, the chief insurrectionary leader, and that Sining itself was to be surrounded on the 15th of the seventh moon—*i.e.*, on the 3rd September.

A curious story came in about this time from Sin Ch'en, whether true or not I cannot say; but the story goes that the rebels had succeeded in cutting the people off from the river, their only water supply. Death stared them in the face, for to surrender meant death without mercy; but Providence was on their side, for the rats in the town had worked a way to the river bed, and through this the water trickled into the city, slowly at first, but gradually increasing in volume until the supply was sufficient for man and beast.

At last the event which had been feared so long occurred; the rebels in the east suburb of Sining broke out on the 1st

September, and the inhabitants had to make up their minds to withstand a prolonged siege with all its attendant horrors. Several times the general had applied to Lancheo for reinforcements, but had been met with the reply that these Mohammedans were good people, and that there was no fear of their not remaining loyal. The Tao T'ai had also been of the same opinion, or said he was, with the result that they now had to pay dearly for their undue confidence. On the news of this fresh outbreak the city was thrown into a state of wild confusion. Common people and soldiers rushed promiscuously on to the walls, while those on guard hastened to the city gate. In the suburb the Mohammedans set fire to all the Chinese houses, and piled up furniture in the streets to act as a protection against an attack from the city, while above all the noise and confusion was the firing of guns and cannon from the city walls.

The 3rd September was a day of heavy fighting; a number of rebels came down from the north valley, and the men of the garrison went out to meet them. Fighting went on all day, decidedly in favour of the Chinese; but late in the day an attack on the suburb, made through a mistaken order, ended most disastrously, so that what should have been a very successful day ended as the reverse. Han-Uen-Sheo himself arrived in the suburb a few days later. Prices began to rise in Sining, oil being sold at three times its usual cost. Distrust of the officials was again excited by a statement being made that the Tao T'ai had received Ts.5,000 from the Mohammedans to promise that their submission would be accepted, should they wish it. This report was undoubtedly believed by many of the people, though on what grounds is hard to say.

The 21st September was another day of hard fighting, ending in favour of the Chinese, although the enemy managed to fire some temples and grain outside the city. The Chinese had a great advantage in arms, the horse soldiers being armed with European rifles, while the infantry and Tibetans all had guns of native manufacture; the rebels, on the other hand, having very few of any kind. Seventy of them were killed or wounded in this day's fighting.

Towards the end of this month the garrison was increased by 130 soldiers and 300 faithful Salars and Tibetans, a welcome addition, as they are both far bolder men than the average Chinaman. About the middle of October news reached the besieged city that eleven battalions had reached Ping-Chong-i, about sixty li only from Sining, but that the rebels were holding the narrow gorges of Siao Hsia in force, and blocking their further progress.

In one engagement, some rebels, disguised as Chinese soldiers, met these relieving battalions on the march. The latter took the rebels for troops from Sining, and were preparing to greet them, when suddenly the disguise was thrown off, and the Chinese, being caught at a disadvantage, suffered severely, over a hundred of them being killed, and a number of rifles with a large amount of ammunition being lost. Every day the Mohammedans gave proofs of their individual courage, showing that had they been anything like as well armed as the Chinese, they would in all probability have got into Sining.

In the same way another month passed, the wretched inhabitants of Sining anxiously awaiting news and relief from the east, while every few days fighting took place outside the walls. Diphtheria added to the trials of the defenders, and the missionaries were all more or less worn out with their labours. One can scarcely picture to oneself the horror of Mrs. Ridley's position at this time. She, the only white lady in the city, had to face the daily uncertainty as to whether the enemy would succeed in getting in or not, and the possibility (always present in China) of the populace turning against her as well, actuated by the wild idea that their troubles were all caused by the "foreign devils" in their midst.

On the 16th of November, a fresh rumour arrived to the effect that reinforcements had not yet reached Lancheo, but the resulting disappointment was somewhat alleviated by the arrival of two men who had been sent down to Niempe, a walled town, 120 li from Sining, to try and find out the truth about a supply of guns and ammunition reported to have arrived there. These men each brought back a specimen of the rifles, which proved to be Remingtons, and which so delighted the General that he sent off eighty men through the hills to bring back as many rifles and as much ammunition as they could manage. These men got safely through, and returned a week later with a number of Remingtons and some French repeating rifles and ammunition.

On the 30th November, the news arrived of another fight at Ping-Chong-i, resulting in a decisive victory for the rebels, who captured all the arms from the Chinese troops. A few days later 200 people were killed in the south valley, and rumours of relief were very conflicting. At one time the reliefs were expected in a few days, at another they had not yet left Lancheo; but at last what seemed to be reliable information was received that thirteen battalions of veteran soldiers had arrived at Ping Fang, 120 miles from Sining.

A day or two afterwards the besieged were further encouraged by the safe arrival of a large convoy with oil, grain, and other useful articles, including a large quantity of pipe-lighters.

Every one was greatly delighted, especially at the news of the reinforcement, coming, as it did, so close on the news of the defeat at Ping-Chong-i, and when all hope of relief for some time had apparently vanished. The escort with the convoy got into the city unmolested, but about a thousand men belonging to it made two unsuccessful attempts to leave, being driven back on both occasions. But the end was soon to come now, and the rebels seemed to have heard the news of the large bodies of men coming up to the relief of the beleaguered city, for numbers of them began to offer their submission, which, needless to say, was not accepted, partly through mistrust, and partly from a desire on the part of the Chinese to avenge the deaths of those who had fallen, and the destruction of their property.

On the 2nd of January, 1896, about twelve horse soldiers arrived and demanded admission to the city, saying that they had come from Lancheo, that General Li, Commander-in-Chief of the Kansu forces, was a few miles behind, and that a Colonel T'ang, from Lancheo, was also following. However, they had no official documents, and admission was refused until the Commander-in-Chief himself should arrive. Meanwhile the excitement in the city at the prospect of the siege shortly coming to an end was intense, an excitement which was increased by the non-arrival of the Commander-in-Chief, and by a very large body of men, apparently soldiers, being seen to pass into the rebel quarters in the suburb. Next day the excitement increased, if possible. Colonel T'ang arrived, and was admitted; but it was reported that General Li was afraid to come into the city, lest the people should attack him. However, the next day he arrived, the rebels apparently making no efforts to prevent his entry.

As soon as the Commander-in-Chief had been received officially by the city dignitaries, he was intercepted by a deputation of the gentry, who presented him with a memorandum they had prepared, showing the places which had been destroyed, and a list of the 40,000 people slain. The General then explained that the rebels had submitted to him at Ping-Chong-i, and that through want of ammunition, and having already suffered two defeats, he had been compelled to accept their submission, instead of being able to punish them.* The procession then wound its way to the principal yamen. The streets were crowded with people, all begging and beseeching the Commander-in-Chief on no account to make terms with the enemy, but to avenge the deaths of those they had lost. This must have been a most affecting sight, especially when one remembers that there can have been few, if any, in all that crowd, who had not lost a husband, a wife, a brother, a sister, or some other near relative, in those terrible months of civil war. But there were not yet sufficient troops in Sining to enable the Chinese to take the offensive.

On the 7th of January the first news of the outer world since the 24th of July reached the missionaries in Sining, as a small party of soldiers brought them up a quantity of letters from Lancheo. All danger was now at an end; there were plenty of troops near at hand, and communication with the east had been established. The final relief was effected on the 14th of the same month, when the first batch of troops, 2,000 in number, arrived amid general rejoicing, especially as their leader was General Ho, a native of the district, in whom the people had far greater confidence than they had in the Commander-in-Chief.

The work of retribution now began. The submission accepted by Commander-in-Chief Li was set aside, and the Chinese gave full play to their lust for vengeance. First the south suburb was absolutely wrecked, the rebels' houses were gutted, and their mosque razed to the ground. About thirty of them who were hiding in cupboards and other places were promptly killed. Some notices were put up in the city the same evening, saying that, as the people had submitted to the Commander-in-Chief their property was to be respected.

* This act on the part of the Commander-in-Chief was greatly resented by the people of Sining, for which reason, it was supposed, he was afraid to enter the city on the 2nd and 3rd. The officials of Sining flatly refused to acquiesce in the Commander-in-Chief's acceptation of submission.

The only answer from the infuriated mob was to tear down the notices, smash up the notice boards, and drag the responsible officials from their houses into the streets, where they were mercilessly beaten, and but for the prompt action of General Teng, to whom alone the people looked for orders, they would certainly have been killed. Had the Commander-in-Chief been in the city at the time he would have fared no better, and possibly worse.

For the next month Generals Ho and Teng were occupied driving the rebels out of the villages and strongholds they had captured, and restoring order in the district, the method employed being the somewhat drastic one of putting to death without question every Mohammedan who fell into their hands; thus at Shen-Chong, a village twenty miles up the south valley, 600 to 700 were slaughtered, while many set fire to their houses and were burnt to death.

This cleared the south valley and opened the road to T'ah-rï-sï, where the festival of the Chinese New Year was held as usual, on the 12th February. The north valley and the east suburb still had to be dealt with.

On the 15th February a number of Chinese went up the north valley to worship at the graves of their ancestors, some soldiers having preceded them the day before. While engaged in their devotions, and thinking little of danger, 200 rebels wearing Chinese uniforms suddenly swept down upon them from the west, and finding them defenceless, cut them down right and left; fortunately, some cavalry from the city came to the rescue promptly and so saved many lives, but fifty had already been killed and numbers wounded. One boy was brought into Sining with twenty-four wounds, another with seventeen, and a third with sixteen. How these ever recovered is a marvel, but recover they did, thanks to the missionaries. Can one wonder after this that the Chinese soldiers refused to spare any, even when ordered to do so by their officers.

Village after village now fell into the hands of the two generals, who, on the 19th February, were reinforced by ten battalions (5000 men) from the south, under General Uei-Kuang-Tao, commander-in-chief of the Hunan troops. These troops were quartered in the east suburb, and on their arrival Commander-in-Chief Li took the earliest opportunity to leave a city where he was so cordially disliked, and where his safety was very doubtful. With a view to getting away, he summoned those leaders who had tendered their submission at Ping Chong Island, handed them and their affairs over to General Teng, and left for Lancheo with thirty or forty followers.

Commander-in-Chief Li's departure was the signal for a general slaughter to commence, and the quicker we pass over this painful subject the better. Suffice it to say that the name of every rebel of any importance was extracted from these leaders, those in the suburb were called out, any refusing to come were killed on the spot, and the remainder murdered after a semblance of a trial; the only thing we can say is that torture, so common a feature of Chinese justice, was never resorted to—retribution was sure and swift. For many days this continued, as rebels were brought in from the villages to be dealt with in the city, the heads of important men being hung up in cages just inside the west gate.

Meanwhile the Hunan soldiers under General Uei were not distinguishing themselves; they were worsted in nearly every engagement, and Generals Ho and Teng constantly had to come to their assistance. One little incident rather tended to dim their fame in the eyes of those who had been so long besieged. Eight battalions went to retake a small village called Su-kia-pu. For four days they bombarded it steadily without a shot being fired in reply, but fearing some deep-laid plot, they dared not attempt an assault; on the fourth day General Ho came to their assistance.

Encouraged by these reinforcements, the Hunan troops rushed to take the stronghold by storm. They had just got to the gate when they were met by an old woman, who meekly inquired why they had been firing so long, for besides herself there were only two old women in the village; she herself was lame and the other two blind, for which reasons they had stayed when every one else had run away.

By the middle of March the last places in the north valley had been relieved, but the rebels still held the fortress of To-Pa, the honour of reducing which was left to General Uei, a task he and his soldiers (15,000) proved quite unable to accomplish. He was at length superseded by General Teng, who was ordered back to Sining from the district where he had been very successful. His return was followed by many of the worst of the rebels leaving the country, and by the fall of To-Pa, when the execution of ringleaders was recommenced, and went on without cessation for many days, about sixteen being brought in daily for justice.

After this, there was one more outbreak in the south-east; about 400 rebels were killed in a fight, the Chinese losing about a hundred. This was on the 10th of June, some fifteen months after the disturbance at Hsiun-Hua-Ting, and was the last of the regular fighting that occurred.

Law and order was gradually restored; business became brisk, but for a long time disease, especially diphtheria, was rampant, and the stench in the streets was appalling. By the time we passed through Sining, towards the end of October, all signs of the rebellion had passed away from within the city walls, but outside was ample testimony to the severity of the struggle, nor could it be otherwise when one reflects that 10,000 rebels were reported to have fled to the north-west, 10,000 more, chiefly old men, women, and children, to have died of cold and starvation on the mountains, and 18,000, almost entirely women and children, to have submitted. Excepting the 10,000 who got away to the north-west, all the able-bodied young men had been simply wiped out.

Such bloody disturbances affected the homes of other people as well, for the rebels who fled north-west over the districts in the neighbourhood of the Koko Nor, spread a feeling of the greatest consternation amongst the inhabitants through whose land they passed. The Mohammedans were fleeing for their lives, and being without the necessaries of life hesitated at no deeds of plunder whenever a chance occurred. On the other hand, the poor Mongols, being of a more peaceful nature, and possessing but inferior arms, had no resource left but abandoning their homes to seek safety in flight until the hungry wave had rolled on.

These cruel acts of devastation naturally caused some anxiety to the Chinese officials residing in Chinese Turkistan, so much so, that they deemed it expedient to make appeals to the Russians for help in case it might be required. It must not be lost sight of that the Mohammedans of Chinese Turkistan might have become contaminated and followed the example of their co-religionists in the east. Had that been the case, the results might have been extremely serious.

As soon as the rebellion had been completely quelled, there remained in the recently disturbed districts thousands of idle soldiers who had received their arms for the occasion. These men, although they had been marched up from Shantong and other provinces, were disbanded in Kansu, many hundreds of miles away from their homes, and, having spent all the pay they had received, they started a system of highway robbery, and in other ways became a source of danger to all. This was to some extent carried on with impunity, as there was a scarcity of men of the district, for in addition to the 40,000 Chinese who had been slain, there were some 5,000 more who had died from diseases contracted through the overcrowding and filthiness of the streets.

Before the soldiers had squandered their money, trade, in spite of the high prices demanded, was brisk.

The difference in the prices of food before and after the rebellion, will give some idea of the privations undergone by the poorer classes, more especially by the women and children :—

Before the Rebellion.			After.
Wheat, rose from	700 cash.	..	1700 cash.
Oats „ „	450 „	.	1250 „
Barley „ „	400 „	..	1000 „
Peas „ „	600 „	..	1250 „
Bran „ „	150 „	..	550
Salt „ „	1200 „	..	2500 „
Chickens, each	60 „	..	140 to 160 „
Pheasants „	80 „	..	125 to 150 „
Oil, per pound	43 „	.	110 „
Coals „	$2\frac{1}{2}$ „	.	$4\frac{1}{4}$ „
Pork „	80 „	..	140 „
Mutton „	35 „	..	60 „

Winter pears from 6 to 15 to 25 to 50 cash each ; vegetables in the same proportion.

Another unaccountable calamity befell these unfortunate people, in the shape of the sudden appearance of a mighty army of mice, which, just at the time when the grain was ready for reaping, devoured up the entire crops in the north and west valleys. From whence they sprung, or whither they disappeared, nobody knew. After such misfortunes, it is hard to realize how the people managed to exist at all.

It was rumoured that the Emperor had sent money to help them, but even if it reached them, it would have been useless in a place where there was no food to buy. All the grain captured from the rebels had been expended in feeding the soldiers.

It would appear that the severe and cruel treatment by both soldiers and the people displayed on the Mohammedans who remained, and the massacre of many hundreds of others who had submitted, notably at To-Pa, their chief stronghold, would merely have the effect of sowing the seeds of a future and more disastrous rebellion.

There is no doubt that the hatred between the Mohammedans and Chinese is more intense than ever. There are, I believe, still some thirty or forty thousand Mohammedans left in the north and south-east valleys. Were these to rise, there is the still more serious possibility of the Government Mohammedan soldiers casting in their lot with them. Were such a coalition to take place, very grievous trouble would be caused, and the north-west provinces would, before very long, be in the hands of the rebels.

It would be wise for the Chinese Government to enquire into the cause of the last rebellion, and by that means discover a remedy to prevent another one. Like the majority of wars, the cause was a religious one. It was, I am told, merely due to the interference of a Chinese official in a religious squabble between two Mohammedan sects called the white and black caps.

The judgment finally given was considered to be a one-sided decision, and ignited the first spark of the rebellion. Had the difference that had arisen between these two fanatical sects been entrusted to the arbitration of a few Mohammedan representatives chosen from each party, an amicable understanding might have been arrived at.

The hatred between the Chinese and the Mohammedans is so deeply rooted, that even if an impartial judgment is given, the Mohammedans, whose minds are so prejudiced, will scarcely credit the truth. There have been for years, and certainly will be for many more, internal squabbles in the homesteads and villages of the two sects, and, as long as these are judged by Chinese officials, there will always be the chance of another outbreak.

It seems remarkable that, although there have been two previous outbreaks during the present century, the last coming to an end only twenty years ago, no adequate means are taken to remove either the cause of another rebellion, or to cope with one which has risen.

First, the cause might be avoided by the appointment of certain Mohammedan officials, elected from amongst those who had remained loyal during the last rebellion, to manage all their internal affairs, and more especially those of a religious nature. Unless something of this kind is attempted it is utterly impossible for these two peoples, differing so vastly in their character and religious ideas, to live in harmony for any length of time. Secondly, the coping with the insurgents could more easily and speedily be accomplished, were powerful garrisons maintained at Ho Cheo and Lancheo, and other cities of importance and Mohammedan centres, properly trained, equipped, and kept in this state by efficient officers, existing in reality instead of merely on paper.

It seems incredible that the Chinese Government, with their previous experience, and their knowledge of the restless and fanatical dispositions of the Mohammedans, more especially of the black caps or Salar sect, and well aware of their greater enterprise and energy besides, should have been powerless at the time of the outbreak. The rebellion, in consequence, spread at an alarming rate, not to be suppressed before many thousands of men, women, and children had been killed or massacred. Even then the penalty was scarcely paid, for years of starvation and misery were lying in store for those who had escaped the calamity.

CHAPTER XXVI.

PARTING FROM LOBSAN—STARTING FOR LANCHEO—A RUINED SUBURB—GOOD DONE BY MISSIONARIES—WE TAKE LEAVE OF MR. RIDLEY—OUR FIRST CHINESE INN.

Next morning, the 19th of October, was decidedly a busy one; our throng of friends had to be settled up with, and our fresh mules had to be started off for Lancheo. In China, when travelling with pack mules, one's baggage is first tied on to arched wooden frames, which, when everything is ready, are simply lifted up and placed across the saddle, and, if necessary, a man can ride on top of his baggage. This is an excellent arrangement, as the mules are never kept standing with their loads on, and, on arriving at one's inn at the end of a day's journey, the frames are simply lifted off the saddles and carried, just as they are, straight into one's room. Those things that are required can then be undone, while the remainder are ready for loading again the following morning; the only drawback is that, as the frames ride entirely by balance, great care must be taken in making up the loads.

The weights these mules carried came rather as a revelation to us, the regulation being 240 Chinese pounds, which is equivalent to 320 English pounds, and if a man is to ride his weight is always reckoned as one hundred Chinese pounds. In India some of the mountain-battery mules carry loads as heavy, or even heavier, than these, but they are as a rule far bigger mules, and are much better looked after;

moreover they are very rarely, if ever, called upon to do the marches that a mule does in China, where the average stage is ninety li, or thirty miles, a day.

About 11 o'clock the baggage started in charge of our Duffadar, who also took Esau and Shukr Ali with him, to assist in looking after the muleteers; although neither of these men knew a word of Chinese, we had no more anxiety in sending them off by themselves in the province of Kansu, than we should have had in India; in many parts of the country it might have been a somewhat risky proceeding, but away in the north-west corner of the empire, the people are so much in the habit of mixing with Tibetans, Mongols, and others, that they take comparatively little notice of foreigners.

Meanwhile the Mongols had been getting the balance of pay due to them, and, as they had done us good service, we gave them some extra baksheesh, or "wine-money," as they call it, and also the old pony we had bought from the Tibetan merchant. This put them all in high good humour; they said that if we ever again came to their country they hoped that we would employ them, Lobsan adding that his real name, by which he could always be found, was "Dsun Choni Lama," * by this he was known to everybody, whereas Lobsan was only his nickname. As soon as they had got their pay they went off into the town, where, I have no doubt, they were very soon relieved of the greater part of it by the wily Chinese.

Our business indoors was now finished and we were able to accompany Ridley round the town. First of all we went to see about hiring animals to take us to Lancheo, but the replies we received were not encouraging. We were told that there were a large number of soldiers leaving Sining, and that it was very hard to procure carriage of any sort, in fact, although quite civil, the officials, who could have helped

* "Dsun" signifying the particular division of the Tsaidam from which he came, the remainder being really his name.

us had they wanted to, made it clear that they scarcely thought it worth while doing so; they contented themselves with taking a copy of our passport, a very lengthy and somewhat useless proceeding.

Another obstacle in the way of our departure was that the official intimation of our having left Tankar had not arrived, for it is the custom, whenever travellers of importance leave a Chinese town, with carriage supplied by the yamen, for intimation to be sent to the next place on their route, where this carriage will have to be changed. In the present case notice had certainly been sent off from Tankar, but had not reached Sining, at least, so we were told. After leaving the yamen we wended our way through the city towards the eastern suburb, meeting on our way numbers of mounted soldiers. They had escorted a high military official, who had left Sining that morning, and were now returning to the city. A very motley crew they were, mounted on miserable little rats of ponies, and carrying numbers of banners, the colour and device of which will, they believe, strike terror into the hearts of the enemy; even the Japanese war seems to have been powerless to disabuse them of this idea.

On our arrival at the eastern gate of the city we mounted the city walls, and looked down upon the suburb, which had once been the home of 10,000 Chinese Mohammedans. Not a roof was left; of a big mosque which used to stand between the city wall and the outskirts of the suburb scarcely a trace was visible—only a few pillars remained to mark the spot where all those followers of the Prophet used to assemble for worship. From looking down on this scene of desolation, one was able to imagine what would have occurred had the rebels got the upper hand, and been able to wreck the city. Had this happened, it is terrible to think what the fate of our fellow-countrymen within the walls would have been. It is just possible that, having remained neutral, their lives might have been spared, but in the awful confusion there would have been, this is more than doubtful.

We spent some time on the wall, while Ridley showed us all the different points of interest—the road by which the soldiers came in to relieve the city, the path by which reinforcements and supplies used to reach the rebels, the place where the defenders' only serviceable big gun was

RUINS OF THE E. SUBURB OF SINING.

mounted, and many spots where encounters had occurred. At one time there had been an order that every man entering Sining had to bring in a stone, and piles of these were lying on the ramparts, ready to be hurled down on the heads of the insurgents. There were some soldiers of the garrison lying about on the wall, where, also, their huts were. Some of these were indebted to the missionaries for medical treatment and nursing when wounded; they seemed glad to see Ridley, and to be grateful for the kindness they had received. On our way back to the mission-house, and on other occasions, we were able to ask Ridley how the work of the mission was progressing.

There has been a mission-station at Sining for about ten years, but, unfortunately, the work has not been continuous. On at least one occasion the station has been given up, and from time to time breaks have occurred. This has naturally militated very strongly against the success of the mission, and the result has been that the number of converts has been small, and, moreover, one or two of those who were looked upon as firm believers have fallen away.

Thus the missionaries have met with considerable disappointment, and it is no wonder that there should again be talk of giving up the station. Mr. and Mrs. Ridley, as well as Mr. Hall, who has had a very long experience of Sining, were, however, greatly opposed to this. During the rebellion they had been able to do a great deal of good among the townspeople. Numbers had been wounded, and knowing that they would find friends in need, they had come to the mission-house for treatment. In this, and in many other ways, they had been able to gain the confidence of the people in a way they had never been able to do before, and, as they all say, now, if ever, is the time we shall be able to do good. Mr. Ridley, in October, 1896, had just been offered a transfer to another station, where there was a church and a fairly large congregation of Christians, but it was not hard to see that his heart was set on staying at Sining, and I am glad to think that he got his wish. Some people may be inclined to ask whether it is worth while keeping up a mission-station when the results attained are so small, but it is scarcely fair to judge merely from the returns of converts and inquirers that are sent in annually. A great deal of good may be done which does not come to the surface, and, whatever one's private opinion and convictions may be, one cannot but admire the devotion of those who give up everything for the cause they consider to be right.

On our return to the mission-house we found that in our absence Hall and Rijnhart had been able to arrange for mules to take us to Lancheo on the following morning, and as Ridley had business to settle at the headquarters of the mission, he agreed to accompany us. We made every preparation for an early start; Ridley gave us each a "mantsi," or "priest's begging-bowl," as a memento of our visit, and Mrs. Ridley filled our saddle-bags with cakes and other luxuries.

In spite of all our forethought, it was late before we had said our last farewells to Mrs. Ridley and her children, and further delay was caused by a doubt as to whether the ferry near the north gate of the city was plying or not. No one was quite sure, so we decided to leave by the west gate, where we knew for certain that we should find boats to take us to the north bank of the Si Ho, along which runs the road, though by doing so we added about three miles to the day's journey. We had not gone far before a boy ran after us from the mission-house, bringing the little terrier "Ruby," who had followed us so far; she seemed to realize that there was more marching in store for her, and not to appreciate leaving the quarters where she had been so comfortable, for before long she again disappeared in the crowd. This time she was not so easily recovered; first one of the muleteers and then Hall went back to look for her. The former returned without any news, and I had just given up hope of ever seeing her again when Hall rode up with her in his arms, greatly to my delight I need scarcely say. Meanwhile Ridley and Malcolm had crossed by the ferry and were some distance on their way, so Rijnhart and I had to push on hard to overtake them.

Travelling on a road like this, any little landmarks mentioned by other travellers are eagerly looked for, and on

A SEDAN CHAIR.

this day's march there were two such landmarks, or more correctly speaking, there should have been two; the first, thirty li from Sining, a bridge over the Si Ho, mentioned by Mr. Littledale in his lecture before the Royal Geographical Society on his return from Pekin; the second, another thirty li on, was the "Peh Ma Ssï," or "White Horse Temple," mentioned by Mr. Rockhill in both his books.* Unfortunately, these are now things of the past; the bridge was swept away in a flood very soon after Mr. Littledale saw it, and the White Horse Temple was utterly wrecked by the fanatical Mohammedans.

Owing to our late start, we were only able to do eighty li, darkness having overtaken us before we got to the stage, the name of which was Chang Kia Tsai. This was our first experience of the Chinese inn, and we had certainly struck a very poor sample of the article; like everything in the neighbourhood, it had suffered heavily in the rebellion, and was only just beginning to recover itself. There was, however, stabling for the animals, and a room with four walls and parts of a roof for ourselves, containing, of course, a k'ang, or stove-bed, without which no Chinese room is complete. We were all ready for bed, and as we had a long day before us, we had a hasty supper and then turned in.

The next morning, the 21st October, we were up long before daylight, having made up our minds to get to Shang Tan (140 li) by night. We had left our two remaining mules with Hall, at Sining, and were now very glad that we had been able to do so, as looking after and feeding them on the road would have been a great nuisance, and the further we took them the less they would have been worth. Ridley and Rijnhart each rode sturdy little country ponies of their own, excellent, sure-footed hacks over the rough roads, but Malcolm and I were both rather uncomfortable, and

* A photograph of this temple, as it used to be, faces page 64 of Rockhill's "Diary of a Journey through Mongolia and Tibet."

decidedly insecure, perched up on top of our blankets, on pack saddles; Lassoo, on the other hand, seemed perfectly happy, and, like nearly all Asiatics, was quite content to sit all day on his mule, never dismounting unless told to do so, or unless it were to get something to eat.

All along the road we were able to buy most excellent bread, which is made in various shapes, with beautifully white flour; the kinds we appreciated most were the "Ko kuei," which is made in large round flat loaves, weighing about three pounds apiece, and the "Huei huei," or, Mohammedan bread, so called because only the Mohammedans make it in this shape, which resembles that of the ordinary cake; these loaves weigh about two pounds, and have a very nice crust. These larger loaves are sold by the weight; rolls and smaller loaves are sold at so many cash each. Bread was dear in 1896, costing thirty to forty cash a pound (1d. to 1¼d.); in ordinary years it will not be more than half that price.

Ninety li (thirty miles) from Chang Kia Tsai, we got to Lou Ya. From here there are two roads to Lancheo, the cart road going off to the left by Ping-Fang, while the mule track, which is the shorter, follows the river, and at this point enters the Ta Hsia, the "great gorges," so called in contradistinction to the "Hsiao Hsia," or "little gorges," which are about ten miles east of "Sining." The sun was setting as we entered these gorges, so we missed seeing some very beautiful scenery at its best; we could, however, realise how difficult, not to say dangerous, a journey Mrs. Ridley must have had along this track, when she had come through in a mule litter a few months previously, being too ill to travel any other way. For a man on foot, or for a pack animal, the road was easy enough, even in the dark, but getting a litter and two mules round some of the very sharp bends must have been a decidedly risky proceeding.

CHAPTER XXVII.

SHANG TAN—HO TSUI TSI—FIRST VIEW OF THE YELLOW RIVER—ON A RAFT—AT LANCHEO—A TELEGRAPH TROUBLE.

For forty li our road lay through these gorges, most of the way a considerable height above the river bed, and, owing to the darkness, our progress was slow, so that it was not till 11 P.M. that we got to our inn. Here we made inquiries for our baggage, but could get no information, though we subsequently found out that it and our two men were at another inn of the same village.

Shang Tan lies at the mouth of a river, the Ta T'ung, which we crossed by a ferry; the missionaries, and any people holding official positions in the country, are exempted from paying toll for these ferries, and when travelling, or sending any property about, they usually carry a flag, with name and title inscribed in Chinese characters. I had a flag with my name on it, which was made in Sining, just to show who the baggage belonged to, but, of course, we could not claim exemption from tolls. Round Shang Tan there is a great deal of melon cultivation, and the fields are covered with stones, which perform the two-fold duty of protecting the ground from the fierce rays of the sun and raising the fruit out of the water should it rain heavily.

Towards evening we got to Ho Tsui Tsi, the last place in this direction which was wrecked by the Mohammedans, and beyond this the difference was at once apparent. Our halting-place that night was Ma Huei Tsi, a very small village, consisting almost entirely of inns; in fact, its only *raison d'être* must have been as a convenience for travellers. Nevertheless, instead of coming to a ramshackle, tumble-down house, very likely without any front door, the inn was in good repair, and the roof intact, quite a change after the stricken district we had passed through.

Ten miles from Ma Huei Tsi the road passes over a spur of the hills, and one gets one's first view of the mighty Huang Ho (Yellow River). On the other side the road descends to the pretty little straggling town of Ho K'eo Tsi (the "mouth of the river") so called because at this point the Si Ho, which we had followed from some distance above Tankar, runs into the Yellow River. On both the ascending and descending sides of this spur, there are earthen pans dug in the soil, in which salt is collected from the brackish streams which abound.

Ten li further on the river has to be crossed by a ferry to a town called Sin Ch'eng. When we got there, the ferry boat was at the far side of the river and the ferrymen busy doing something else; for about two hours we sat on the bank shouting to them to come across to us, and every now and then one of them would shout back that they would be over presently. At last we got exasperated, and seeing our hopes of getting into Lancheo that night rapidly vanishing, we entered into negotiations with a man to take us the rest of the distance by raft. We had just agreed on the price to be paid, and the man had gone away to make a few necessary preparations, when our baggage, which we thought was still ahead of us, turned up, and at the same time the ferry boat started to come across from the other side.

Shahzad Mir, Esau, and Shukr Ali had had a very pleasant time; their muleteers had given no trouble, and the food they had got on the road, filled as it was with oil, suited their taste admirably. It was now agreed that Ridley and the baggage should cross by the ferry to Sin

Ch'eng and come on to Lancheo the next day with all the servants, while Rijnhart, Malcolm, and I went straight on on the raft, which was now ready. This raft was a strangely flimsy conveyance about eight feet by five feet; it was supported by six inflated deer skins, and over them was lashed a very light framework, on which we put our blankets. We were particularly cautioned when getting on board not to put our feet on the skins for fear of bursting them, and if possible to step where two cross pieces of the framework met.

In a few moments we were seated and waving adieux to Ridley, who almost simultaneously left the bank in the ferry boat. In addition to the three of us, there were two men to manage the raft, so we were pretty well crowded, and quite unable to shift our positions. When in smooth water we were some three inches clear and able to keep more or less dry, but in the rapids, which were of frequent occurrence, the water kept washing over the frame, thereby adding considerably to our discomfort. However, the novelty of the experience kept us amused, and there was plenty of variety. For a bit all would go smoothly, then in a few moments we would be in the middle of a rapid, and for the next minute or two the raft would dance madly round and round; it was like a panorama where the spectators revolved instead of the scenes. Now and then a new sensation would be added, when, going through a shallow, we suddenly heard the skins scraping along the bottom; but though amusing and more or less exciting, we had the satisfaction of knowing that there was no danger. Every now and then one of the men had to turn round to blow up a skin from which too much air had escaped; but in spite of this and their other duties, they found time to extract from some part of their clothes some singularly uninviting looking black bread, but before commencing to eat themselves they, with true Chinese politeness, offered it to us. We of course refused; however hungry we might have been, and however tempting the food might have looked, it would have been a great breach of etiquette to have availed ourselves of their offer.

Meanwhile the sun was rapidly setting, and we began to realise that our chances of getting into the city before the gates were closed were small. On starting we had been assured that we could get from Sin Ch'eng to Lancheo, a distance of seventy li by road, and about the same by water, in one Chinese hour, which is equal to two English hours, but we soon realised that this was an impossibility; double that time looked a great deal nearer the mark.

From Sin Ch'eng downwards we had kept passing numbers of huge water-wheels, which lift the water out of the river and irrigate the fields in the neighbourhood. Some of them must have been fully sixty feet in diameter, and being constructed entirely of wood are very curious. Sometimes they are single and sometimes in groups of four or five; at intervals, when not anxiously watching the setting sun, I kept thinking what interesting pictures these wheels would make, but the kodak was with the baggage and the opportunity lost.

Meanwhile, Rijnhart had been making inquiries as to what chance we had of getting a raft at Lancheo, on which to continue our journey down the Yellow River. All along the road reports had been most conflicting, some people telling us that rafts were constantly leaving with wool for various places down the river, others telling us that we should have to go some distance by land, and then get a boat or a raft below the gorges. All we knew for certain was that Mr. and Mrs. Littledale had managed to get on to a raft at Lancheo, and we did not see why we shouldn't do likewise. Now, however, we seemed to be within measurable distance of the truth, for the owner of our raft told us that he would take us to an inn in the suburbs where we would be able to get all the information we required. It was now too late for us to get into the city, so this arrangement suited us admirably.

Night came on as we entered the outskirts of the city, and by the time we disembarked it was quite dark. In single file we wended our way to the inn; one of the men, carrying the raft, brought up the rear. Arrived there, we got half a room, which was not made more agreeable by a Chinaman smoking opium heavily in the other half, and in a few moments the landlord brought us some tea. From him we learnt that a raft was leaving with wool the very next morning, and that we might be able to induce the owners to wait till the evening, or at all events until our baggage should come in; this was excellent news, and we went to sleep well contented and happy in the thought that on the morrow we should be able to telegraph home, and allay any fears that might have arisen with regard to our safety.

The first thing next morning we saw one of the owners of the raft, but all we got out of him was, that he must go and see his friends, and that he would let us know. Whatever his intentions were at the time, we never saw him again. We then went to the telegraph office and despatched our messages, a proceeding which took us very nearly an hour, as many different people had to be consulted on so unusual a proceeding, telegrams to India puzzling the officials terribly. We also sent a wire and prepaid the reply, asking when the Gulf of Pe Chili was likely to be frozen over. At last the matter was settled, as we thought, so we made our way to the mission house. We had sent up a note announcing our arrival and saying that we would follow ourselves a little later. There we found Mr. and Mrs. Botham, Mr. Hunter, and Mr. Mason, who received us very cordially in their comfortable home. As soon as introductions were over, Rijnhart left to make inquiries about a raft, and shortly afterwards Ridley turned up, having made a very early start from Sin Ch'eng.

In Lancheo there is a Roman Catholic mission, as well

as the China Inland Mission, but the two never mix, or associate in any way; for some reason, they find that the work does not admit of any intercourse between the two branches of the Church, so, by mutual consent apparently, they keep apart. From an outsider's point of view, this seems a pity, but no doubt experience has shown that it is the wiser plan. The China Inland Mission station has been established a good many years, and although they have not yet got a large enough number of converts and inquirers to have a church, they have been getting on slowly in the right direction. Being in the capital of Kansu, it is the principal station of that province, and the headquarters of the superintendent, to which post Mr. Botham has just been appointed, after spending many years in the Hsian plain.

We had not been long in our new quarters before Rijnhart came back, saying that several rafts had left that morning, and that no others would be leaving for several days; he had also ascertained that the best thing we could now do would be to take carts as far as a place called Chong Wei, and trust to get a boat there to take us on. This we decided to do, so Mr. Hunter and I went off to make the necessary arrangements, while Rijnhart and Malcolm went into the town to buy provisions for the road.

Just as they were leaving, the head telegraph official came round and said that he had despatched the telegram to Tien Tsin about the state of the Gulf of Pe Chili, but that he could not send off the others as he was unable to ascertain what the cost would be; moreover, he had just heard from Hsian Fu that the wire was broken beyond that place, and that our message would have to go by Yamen runners for three days. Very useful this, when we had hoped to get an answer in forty-eight hours at the latest. With regard to the English and Indian telegrams, we were able to surmount the difficulty by wiring to the headquarters of the China Inland Mission at Shanghai, in

Mr. Botham's name, asking them to send the messages for us, a request with which they very kindly complied, but, owing to our not touching Shanghai on our way to India, it was some months before we were able to repay them.

By the evening we had made all our necessary preparations for another start on the following morning, and Ridley added to the many kindnesses he had already done us by lending us some money for current expenses on the road. Moreover, Rijnhart now finally made up his mind to accompany us all the way to the coast; he had business to do there, and this seemed to him a favourable opportunity for going down to do it. We were both delighted at the prospect of his companionship through China, where his knowledge of the people and their language was bound to be invaluable to us, besides saving us from wholesale swindling. Many and many a time we had reason to thank our stars that he came to this decision.

SHOWING STAGES FROM SINING TO LANCHEO.

20th October.—Sining to	Chang-Kia-Tsai	80	li.
21st ,,	,, Niempe	80	,,
,, ,,	,, Shang Tan	90	,,
22nd ,,	,, Ma-Huei-Tsi	90	,,
23rd ,,	,, Sin-Ch'eng	50	,,
24th ,,	,, Lancheo	70	,,

LANCHEO (CAPITAL OF KANSU) TO CHONG WEI.

25th October.—Lancheo to	Shui-Peh-Ho	70	li.
26th ,,	,, Shan-Kia-Tong	60	,,
,, ,,	,, Lu-Tong-Tsi	30	,,
27th ,,	,, Chong-Chang-Tsi	50	,,
,, ,,	,, Ta-La-Pai	60	,,
28th ,,	,, Han-Shih-Pu	40	,,
,, ,,	,, Ih-Tiao-Shan	20	,,
29th ,,	,, ?	50	,,
,, ,,	,, ?	40	,,
30th ,,	,, K'an-T'ang-Tsi	60	,,
,, ,,	,, Ih-Uan-Chuen	40	,,
31st ,,	,, Sha-Poh-Tsi	70	,,
,, ,,	,, Chong Wei	40	,,

Chong Wei to Pao T'eo by boat, eight days' journey. Flat-bottomed wool-boat.

CHAPTER XXVIII.

WE PAY OFF SHUKR ALI—LANCHEO TO CHONG WEI—OFFICIAL INCIVILITY—LOSE RUBY—SHAHZAD MIR MISTAKEN FOR A REBEL.

Soon after daybreak on the 25th October we bade farewell to the missionaries, and, accompanied by Ridley and Rijnhart, made our way to the inn on the far side of the river, from which our carts were to start, and in which our men had slept the previous night. Our baggage was now of the most miscellaneous description, for in addition to the instruments, clothes, and flowers which we had brought with us, there were the curios we had bought, and last, but not least, provisions of bread, meat, vegetables, and butter for a seven days' journey across a sandy desert country, where little could be bought, the inns providing accommodation, but scarcely anything else.

We were determined not to starve any more, and made due preparations to guard against doing so. To carry these numerous articles, as well as ourselves and our men, we had engaged two carts, each drawn by a mule and a pony. As when hiring baggage mules, so again now a regular contract had to be drawn up and signed by the contracting parties. Our agreement was that each cart was to carry 500 Chinese pounds, equal to 666 English pounds, including passengers, and to land us in Chong Wei on the 31st October. There is also another and bigger sort of cart in this part of China, which carries 1,200 pounds, and is drawn by three animals, but it was not suited to our requirements.

THE ONLY WAY TO DRIVE IN NORTH CHINA.

As usual in making a start, the first day there was considerable delay, and even after everything was ready as far as we were concerned our carters flatly refused to start till another party, consisting of two officials—one military, the other customs-house—who were going to Ning-Shia-Fu, were also prepared to make a move, and this was not till just 11 A.M., some five hours after leaving the mission-house.

Our last care before starting was to pay off Shukr Ali, whom we were sending back to Ladakh *viâ* Yarkand. The inn which we were leaving for Chong Wei was also the inn from which the carts make their departure for Yarkand, so we arranged with the innkeeper that he was to keep Shukr Ali until a caravan should be starting, leaving him a sum of money for board and lodging, Ridley, moreover, very kindly promising to see that the innkeeper did not defraud him or delay his departure.

Some months later we heard that Shukr Ali had arrived in Kashgar, where he presented himself to the British Resident, Captain Macartney, and coolly stated that he had been defrauded of a portion of his just dues. He appears, however, to have omitted to mention the fact of his desertion with the remainder of our flour, or any of his many sins of omission and commission by which he had forfeited all claim to any consideration. We did, indeed, send him Rs. 40 in answer to the appeal of the Resident, but with a special request that he should be made to clearly understand that he was in no way entitled to it. I can only hope that this was done. Had it not been for the fact that his behaviour up to the 2nd August was infinitely better than that of the other men, we would certainly never have taken him back into our service.

The usual method of cart travelling in China is to make an early morning start, to halt a couple of hours about midday, and then to go on till sunset, or rather later; but as the animals travel at a walk the whole time, the amount of ground covered is not very great—in fact, if you manage to do forty miles in a day you may congratulate yourself on having done well. Our first day's journey was only seventy li, or about twenty-three miles, and then we halted for the night at Shui-Peh-Ho. The following day, during our mid-day halt, we made the acquaintance of some of our fellow-travellers, after which they generally used to come and converse with us while we were having our meals, and occasionally made themselves very entertaining. The road was dull and uninteresting in the extreme, very rough and very sandy, which made the work uncommonly hard for the animals; scarcely a sign of cultivation anywhere, except just round the small groups of houses occasionally to be seen, which seem to have no *raison d'être*, except to supply the wants of destitute travellers, should any come along the road. In some places things are so bad that the unfortunate people have to send several miles for their water, but somehow the advisability of shifting to a more favourable part of the country never seems to strike them.

One day the monotony of our journey was broken by a slight *fracas* between the carters and ourselves, they having made up their minds to stop for the day at 2 P.M., while we were equally determined that they should go on another fifty li. Halting so early made it quite impossible for them to land us in Chong Wei on the day they had agreed upon, but this did not appear to affect them in the least, and threats of taking them to the Yamen at Chong Wei were equally unavailing, so that I am bound to confess that they fairly beat us, and we remained stuck in a little village for the rest of the day.

On the 31st October, the day our cart journey should have ended, we were woken up at 2 A.M., the carters saying they were in a hurry to start. Nothing loth, we made a hasty breakfast, rolled up our blankets, and made every preparation for departure. Our fellow-travellers moved off, but there were no signs of our carts getting ready, so we went outside to inquire what had happened to them, and were informed that one pony had run away, and that the men had gone in search of it, so there was nothing to do but to return to the inn and await events. Soon tiring of this, I decided to stroll on ahead, never doubting that the others would soon follow me in the carts.

The men had already gone on, so, taking Ruby with me, I set off down the road, which soon developed into a succession of sand hills, with many cart ruts in several places nearly two feet deep—anything but pleasant walking in the dark. It did not take me long to catch up to the men, but by this time I had been deserted by Ruby, the faithful companion of so many days' travelling. This troubled me little at the time, as I quite made up my mind that, not relishing the keen morning air, she had returned to the inn to put in as much more sleep as possible.

After going about thirteen miles I came to a small village, where I tried to get some bread, but my endeavours being unsuccessful, whether owing to some flaw in my Chinese or not I cannot say, I decided to walk on to the next place. On I went, following the cart tracks, which formed an apology for a road, down the bed of a narrow stream, and between high cliffs, till I at length emerged on the banks of what was undcubtedly our old friend the Yellow River. I knew I could not be mistaken in this, as there is no other river in this part of China with anything like the same volume of water. The tracks led me along the left bank of the river, till they eventually stopped abruptly at the water's edge. High above me I could see a track across some forbidding-looking sand hills, but to reach it one had a difficult piece of ground to negotiate which was utterly impracticable for carts. I knew there was no other road by which the carts could go, and, as far as I could see, there was no possibility of their getting any further. It was now about midday. We were all very hungry, and quite at a loss what to do, so, in default of any better plan, I made up my mind to wait where I was till Rijnhart and Malcolm should arrive; so, choosing a shady spot, I lay down, and was soon fast asleep.

It was about 5 P.M. when I woke, refreshed by sleep, but still very hungry, and anxious for the arrival of the carts, which, however, were nowhere to be seen; but just as it was getting dusk, a boat came round a bend of the river, being dragged up the far side by sturdy Chinamen. They went a short distance further up the river than where I was, and then dropped across to my side. This was evidently a ferry-boat, and was in the habit of meeting carts and travellers at intervals during the day, so, feeling sure it was certain to take me somewhere, I got on board with the men, expecting to be ferried across to some village on the far side, which was hidden by the curve of the bank, but to my astonishment we went straight down the river, about half a mile. Here the boat stopped, and out we all got. The boatmen moored the boat for the night, and then started off across some fields. I followed in silence, wondering what the upshot of it all was likely to be. There I was, a stranger in a strange land, destitute of money and food, and quite unable to speak the language, or make myself understood except occasionally by signs. And in this Shahzad Mir, Esau, and Lassoo, were of no help; they were indeed only extra mouths to feed, and no money to do it with. After walking about half a mile we came to a small group of houses, and one of the boatmen, a good sort of fellow, made signs for us to follow him into one of them. Here we found an old lady, evidently his wife, and to our great delight our demands for "momo" (bread) and "tsa" (tea) were promptly complied with. We had indeed fallen upon our feet, for in addition to these luxuries the room was clean and comfortable, but all efforts to make our host and hostess understand that we would like some eggs availed us nothing. Even when we all four sat in a row, each

ON THE ROAD FROM LANCHEO, CHINA.

making the noise he imagined was most like a laying hen, our object never dawned upon them, and at last, when it became obvious that they thought this was only our way of enjoying ourselves, we gave up in despair and went to sleep.

Next morning, after more bread and tea, I went out and anxiously looked up the river for signs of the ferry-boat or the carts, but nothing occurred till about midday, when the carters arrived leading their animals, and now, for the first time I really grasped the meaning of the abruptly ending cart road, the steep track over the sand hills, and the ferry-boat. The carts are dragged down as far as possible by the animals, which are then unharnessed, led up the steep cliff and across the sand hills down to the village in which I had passed the night, and in the meanwhile the carts are shipped on to the ferry-boat and brought down until the road again becomes fit for wheeled traffic.

Soon after Rijnhart and Malcolm arrived with the carts in the boat, which this time came right down to the village, but, to my great sorrow, Ruby was not with them, nor had they seen her. It certainly seemed hard that, after travelling so many miles, she should be lost when comparatively near the goal. It appeared that the pony had not returned the previous morning till nearly seven, and that the carters had again struck work and insisted on stopping for the night at the village through which I had passed after my unsuccessful attempt to get bread. They had said that they could not possibly get to the ferry that night, and that, as they had no intention of sleeping in the open, they would go no further.

However, now that we were all united, our first care was to start off the men in the carts for Chong Wei, while we got a raft for ourselves to take us down the river. The whole party was in motion again by 2 P.M., and about half an hour before sunset we got down to our landing place, a sort of coal wharf about two miles from the city of Chong Wei.

We had previously agreed with our carters to go to a certain inn in the east suburb, so we made our way there as quickly as possible, expecting the carts to come in before night. In this, however, we were disappointed, but it was a matter of indifference to us, as our men had plenty of money and were perfectly safe. The innkeeper made us a capital supper of mutton and rice, and while we were discussing it, a Chinaman, who turned out to be an agent for one of the wool firms, with that easy familiarity characteristic of the race, came in and gave us all the news of the place; and from him we learnt that there was another foreigner living near the west gate of the city, so we made up our minds to visit him in the morning and find out the best way of getting on to Pao T'eo.

CHONG WEI.

Soon after daylight the next morning we started off to the wharf, where the wool boats lie while taking in cargo, in hopes that we might be able to get a passage in one as far as Ning-Shia-Fu or Shih-Tsui-Tsi, or, failing in that, that we might be able to hire a boat for ourselves. In this we failed, the prices asked being absolutely prohibitive, and we also learnt that another and hitherto unthought-of danger was staring us in the face, and that was that it was quite possible that the river would freeze below Shih-Tsui-Tsi in a very few days, in which case we should have to make a tedious camel journey through the Ordos country to Pao T'eo, by no means a pleasant look-out in the wintry weather that was now coming on; but as a set-off against this we heard that Messrs. Forbes & Co., the wool merchants, whose agent we had met at Tankar, had an office just opposite the inn in which we were lodging, and that very possibly they might be able to help us on our journey.

With this information to cheer us we rushed back to the town and into Forbes's office, where we found all the agents and principal men discussing a hearty breakfast, of which

STREET IN THE TONG KUAN (E. SUBURB), CHONG WEI, YELLOW RIVER.

they invited us to partake, but we refused, contenting ourselves with tea, without which no business or pleasure can be conducted in China. As soon as breakfast was over, the two senior agents turned their attention to our wants. After examining our credentials, consisting of the two letters from our old friend Chen-Lao-Pan, they told us that they would do all they could to help us, and that, as they had a boat starting on the next day but one, they would arrange for passages for ourselves, our men, and 500 pounds of baggage. In this we were to be taken to Shui-Tsui-Tsi, where we would find another of their agents, who would doubtless do his best to help us on, either by river or by land. In return we were to pay the sum of 12,000 cash, an exorbitant sounding sum, but one which represents in English money about £1 15*s*. As an alternative route we might have gone by carts as far as Ning-Shia-Fu, and thence by boat, camels, or other means to Pao T'eo; but after mature consideration we came to the conclusion that the water journey would be the more convenient, and probably the more speedy, so closed with their offer at once.

This was a good morning's work, and we crossed the street to breakfast in our inn, almost as hungry as we had been in Tibet. We were followed immediately into the yard by our carts and servants, so, to save any bother, we paid the former off at once, and, such is the cheek of the Chinese carter, they grumbled at not getting wine money in addition to the full amount of Ts.19, for which they should have landed us in Chong Wei two days sooner than they actually had. The altercation thus caused collected rather a crowd, who were far from being as civil as those we had hitherto met—in fact, Chong Wei was the only place in China where we experienced any inconvenience from the inquisitive objection to foreigners of which one hears so much; but had it not been for Rijnhart we might have got into serious trouble here, as will be seen later. One man among the crowd demanded to see our cards, stating that he was a messenger from the Yamen, and that he had been sent down officially. Rijnhart promptly demanded the big man's card as a proof of *bona fides*, knowing full well that no Chinese would ever send a messenger on an errand like this without this mark of respect. On his failure to produce it, Rijnhart refused to give up ours, and how right he was became evident when we found our friend to be nothing but a street loafer. Had we been in the hands of an ordinary interpreter, we might have acceded to this demand, and thus become an object of ridicule to all the bystanders. The crowd now saw that one at least of the party was well acquainted with Chinese customs, and mended their manners accordingly, their behaviour being still further improved on the arrival of one of Mr. Forbes's agents, who had a few remarks to make. Nevertheless, though no longer offensive, we had to place Shahzad Mir near the entrance to our apartment to prevent them crowding too close round while we were eating.

On some occasions our worthy guard was called away from his post for another purpose, when the inquisitive crowd would at once take advantage of his absence, and a mass of peering faces would obscure all the air and nearly all the light from the door of our little room. A toe over the threshold invited a rap from one of our sticks, but still we required more ventilation and adopted a plan and a surprise quite novel to the Chinaman. Seizing a tumbler full of water, either Malcolm or I would fling the contents on them, and at the same time laugh right merrily, and, although annoyed at the time we could not help doing this at the result. The crowd at once dispersed on every side; those who had been unfortunate in getting a wetting at first became enraged, but those who had escaped were only too glad to join us in our chaff against their fellow-countrymen. Had we put on a serious mien all would have united in abusing us and we should never have enjoyed a moment's breathing space. The only time we really found peace was at dusk, when the innkeeper closed the big gates of the yard, and only those living at the inn were allowed inside. We wished that dusk had reigned during the whole of our stay at Chong Wei.

Breakfast over, Rijnhart and I started to find out the foreigner of whom we had heard the previous night, and also to pay a visit at the Yamen, where I thought I might be able to get some further information about our journey to the coast. In this, however, I was unsuccessful, and a very few moments sufficed to show me that any incivility shown to foreigners would certainly not incur the disapproval of the Yamen. Our reception was very different from anything we had experienced at any of the other Yamens. My visiting card, a brilliant crimson piece of paper, with my name in black Chinese characters, was the same size as that used by generals and others of equal rank, *i.e.*, nearly a foot in length, and had hitherto always commanded respect, but was here treated with contempt, the doorkeeper refusing to take it in to the mandarin, while the crowd kept insolently jostling and shoving against us. Even my passport, elsewhere a regular "open sesame," in which I was referred to in the most flattering terms, was of little good; and even when we were finally admitted it was not into the presence of the big man himself, but only of his head clerk, who did not even offer us chairs, but adopted a tone of insolence such as only a Chinese jack-in-office can.

Rijnhart was equal to the occasion, and soon showed him that his arrogant tone did not impress us with a sense of his importance as he had doubtless hoped it would do; but seeing that nothing was to be gained by stopping there, we left as soon as we possibly could, and went in search of the foreigner. We had no difficulty in finding out his inn, and most highly surprised and delighted he appeared at seeing us. It was evident from his surroundings that he had been living a very solitary life and was practising the strictest asceticism; luxury there was none.

It soon turned out that he and Rijnhart were old acquaintances, having landed in China about the same time, and thus the ice was speedily broken, and I quickly learnt that our new friend's name was Mr. Lumberg, that he was a Swede, and belonged to that branch of the International Mission Alliance. He had been some months in Chong Wei trying to open a mission station, but so far, owing to the opposition of the Yamen, he had not been very successful. He was very anxious to hire a house, but, although many of the townspeople were willing to let, the Yamen people secretly but effectually stopped them doing so, at the same time assuring Mr. Lumberg that they were doing all they could to help him, even going so far as to put up notices in public places proclaiming his wants. The petty official of Chong Wei was thus able to gratify his personal spite against foreigners while guarding against the displeasure of his superior at Lancheo, a man well known to be favourably disposed towards them.

When we returned to our inn, Lumberg accompanied us, and eventually we persuaded him to send for his bedding and spend the night with us. It was now, for the first time, that we heard what a hornet's nest Mr. Littledale had raised by his remarks before the Royal Geographical Society, about sending unprotected Swedish girls to live in out-of-the-way parts of China. Well meant as these remarks undoubtedly were, the Swedes considered that his object was to strike a blow at their missionary enterprise, and when the matter was taken up by the Swedish Government, it roused a feeling of resentment that will not die out for some time, and which, in some cases, seemed to extend to the whole race of Englishmen. Although we were invariably treated with the greatest hospitality, one could not

OUR INN AT CHONG WEI.

help seeing that this feeling existed. From the accounts we heard, it certainly seemed as though these remarks were a little unnecessary, and certainly not one of those ladies of whom Mr. Littledale spoke with such sympathy has ever thanked him for it. We were assured that unmarried girls were never sent to out-stations alone, but were invariably sent to live with a married couple, and every precaution taken to guard them from any danger. At the same time, there is no doubt that Mr. Littledale's intention has been misunderstood, and could this misunderstanding be cleared up, I think it would be all for the better.

That evening, while walking in the streets, accompanied by Shahzad Mir, an incident occurred, which, but for Rijnhart's shrewdness and knowledge of the Chinese, might have landed us in a row. Shahzad Mir was dressed in semi-European clothes, and being an unmistakable Mohammedan, some of the people jumped to the conclusion that he was a "Salar" in disguise. No sooner had this idea been started than it spread rapidly. A crowd collected, and began following us, shouting excitedly. We quickened our pace slightly, and told Shahzad Mir not to get separated from us. The crowd and shouting gradually increased, and things were looking awkward, when, seizing his opportunity, Rijnhart suddenly turned round and addressed the crowd, saying that he knew for certain that Shahzad Mir had been travelling for six months since he left his home, and that, as the Salars lived comparatively close by, he could not possibly be one of them. This pacified them for a bit, and while they discussed the probability or otherwise of Shahzad Mir being a Salar we quickly left the city and turned into the suburb, which was comparatively quiet; and the only result of the disturbance was that our faithful Duffadar was confined to the inn during the remainder of our stay in that place, while we ourselves never entered the city itself unless accompanied either by Lumberg or Rijnhart.

CHAPTER XXIX.

MISSIONARY YARNS—CHEAP LIVING—ON THE YELLOW RIVER AGAIN—CASH.

THE room we occupied in our inn, which was the only one available, could not have been more than twelve feet by eight feet, and half this space was occupied by the indispensable k'ang. Not having, as yet, acquired the Chinese art of squatting cross-legged on the k'ang, and eating off a little stool about eight inches high, we were obliged to squash ourselves into the remaining space, which just enabled Esau to bring our dinner to the door and hand it in to one of us—there was no room for him inside till one of us went out. Nevertheless we managed to enjoy ourselves immensely, Lumberg forming a pleasant addition to our party. He and Rijnhart managed to keep us very much amused with stories of the mistakes they and others had made in talking Chinese, soon after landing in the country—mistakes that are rendered even more common by the numerous differences of dialect met with in the different districts.

On one occasion Rijnhart, when preaching in the streets, was exhorting his audience "to taste our religion, and see if it is good," saying, "If you see a pear, and want to know whether it is good or not, you bite it, and taste it, and then, if you find it good, you eat it." He had been going on in this strain for a short time, when he was suddenly interrupted by a bystander, who said, "But, teacher, you people don't eat dogs, do you?" Rijnhart having, unfortunately, used the Chinese for dog instead of that for pear.

There is another story of a famous missionary, who, owing to differences in dialect in a district he had not previously visited, addressed the devil, instead of the Lord, at a public prayer meeting. Similar mistakes are very common, and are bound to be so in a language where the slightest inflection of the voice gives a totally different meaning to the words.

It was quite late that night before we went to bed, but as we had nothing to do the next day, it was a good opportunity for sitting up, talking and hearing about the Chinese people, from men who knew as much about them as our two missionary friends did. We had learnt from our own short experience that living in China was not by any means expensive, but it surprised us not a little to hear that Lumberg and his servant managed on one hundred cash a day (rather under twopence each). I do not suppose there is another country in the world where this could be done.

Next morning we went early into the city to see the market—a very busy scene, as people come in every morning from the country, bringing meat and vegetables, and the streets are crowded; quite different from the previous evening, when they had presented an almost deserted appearance, until the people got suddenly suspicious about Shahzad Mir. Besides this daily market, Chong Wei has another peculiarity. Like every town of importance, it is surrounded by a high wall, but unlike any other place we saw, it has only three gates, for instead of a north gate, a temple has been built, which guards the town from evil spirits, who, as every one knows, always come from the north. We had to lay in stores for our boat journey down the river, and as Mr. Forbes's agent asked us to be sure to have everything ready in ample time, we thought that there was no doubt that we would soon be on our way down the Yellow River. Most of our buying was done by Lumberg's servant, a Christian convert from Ning-Shia-Fu, the cleanest and nicest Chinaman we met on our travels, who saved us an enormous amount of trouble, and got everything much cheaper than we could have done.

By night we were quite ready for departure, and had been assured that we should start by midday at the very latest. Accordingly, next morning, we were on board by 11 A.M., when we heard for the first time that there was no chance of leaving till the next morning, and that we should have to make an eight days' journey across the desert from Shih-Tsui-Tsi to Pao T'eo, as no boats could go so far down the river so late in the year. A pleasant prospect this, with hard frost every night, and no arrangements for camping! Altogether, we did not feel very amiably disposed towards the gentleman who had told us that we must be ready to start by midday. However, remonstrances were useless, and we had to make the best of it.

Next morning our inquiries were always met by the invariable answer that we were going to start at once, but the bill of lading had been incorrectly made out, and had to be rectified. Other delays cropped up, and it was just on 2 P.M. when the skipper appeared and we pushed off into the stream. However, the delay was acceptable in one way, for it enabled Lumberg to come down and see us again, with the welcome news that he had been able to arrange to get rooms in a new inn in the east suburb, and his troubles on that score were at an end.

Once under weigh, we travelled pretty fast. The stream was strong and carried us down grandly, but, after going a couple of hours, the skipper insisted on tying up for the night, saying that there was a nasty place ahead which they could not possibly pass in the dusk; a very feeble excuse, the real reason being that some of the crew lived in a village close by. We had been in hopes of travelling all night, and had certainly been led to believe that we should do so, but nothing, apparently, was further from the intentions of the skipper and his crew. There was nothing for it but to set to work to make ourselves as comfortable as we could in the boat.

These wool-boats on the Yellow River are flat-bottomed,

OUR WOOL BOAT ON THE YELLOW RIVER.

and very clumsily, though strongly built. They are from thirty to forty feet long, and ten or twelve feet wide. The ends are decked over for about nine feet, the remainder of the boat being divided off by partitions. As a rule, they trust to the stream to carry them down, the steering being done with a long sweep, but occasionally they use two other long sweeps to row. Up stream they are obliged to tow. The decked portion in the bows was left free of cargo for our accommodation, while that in the stern was allotted to the crew and to our servants, and in it all the cooking was done. Matters were a good deal simplified by our men and the boatmen all being Mohammedans, with the exception of Esau, who had no religious objection to eating with any one, believer or unbeliever. Besides ourselves, there were three or four Chinese passengers going to different places down the river, their passage-money being the skipper's perquisite. All the remaining available space was piled up with wool, piled up as high as was safe, till the gunwale was only a few inches above the water. But for the danger of sticking on mud banks—a by no means infrequent occurrence—I fancy they would have been loaded even more deeply.

In addition to our own, there were four more boats going down stream in company with us, a circumstance we had reason to regret before very long, as on the very next day, the 6th November, just as we were making most satisfactory progress, one of these boats stuck about half-past three in the afternoon, and we had to wait till she got off. As she was still ashore at sunset, we made no more progress that day, and several valuable hours were lost. Next morning six men went to the other boat and began unloading the wool—a very tedious process—but, about 10.30 A.M., they got her off, and she came down towards us.

While waiting here, we had managed to pass the time watching a ferry plying just below the spot where we were tied up. Mongols, Chinese, camels, sheep, and bullocks, all were piled in promiscuously, and taken across from one side to the other, being washed down a very considerable distance in the transit. All of a sudden a tremendous row started between the parties, apparently as to which had the right to be taken over first. They were fairly evenly divided and equally determined. Abuse was plentiful, and a free fight seemed imminent, when, somewhat

HALTING FOR THE NIGHT ON THE YELLOW RIVER.

to our disappointment, we were called upon to renew our journey, thus being robbed of the one possible compensation for our hours of delay.

About 4 P.M. that day we had to pass the customs-house at the border of the Ning-Shia district, and here our skipper was detected smuggling ten bales of pears; the officials wanted to stop us all night, but a few words from

A FERRY ACROSS THE HUANG HO.

Rijnhart pacified them, and on we went. Unfortunately the pears were not yet ripe, or we would have exacted heavy toll in return for our good offices. We had only managed another ten li, before we stopped for the night, at a small village on the right bank of the river, from which the skipper started off to walk twenty li to his own home. We were sick of the constant delays and stoppages, and as there were several boats tied up along the shore, we landed and tried to find the owners, in hopes of being able to buy or hire a boat for ourselves, to go as far down the river as possible.

After some time we were successful, for a young and enterprising Mohammedan agreed to take us all the way to Pao T'eo, without stopping day or night, for the sum of Ts.70 (somewhere about £13). The price was high, but we returned to the wool-boat with a happy feeling of independence, which was increased when we heard that we should not be able to start the next morning until the other boats came down from the customs-house. We had, at first, been asked Ts.120 for the boat, and told we should have to wait a day, but we insisted on starting the following morning, and having knocked down the price to nearly one half, felt that we had not done badly.

As with riding mules and carts, so with the boat, an agreement was necessary, and this the village schoolmaster drew up for us; but by this time our skipper had returned, and was furious at finding that such a grand opportunity of squeezing the foreigner had slipped through his fingers. He did his best to frighten our new friend into backing out of his bargain, but did not quite succeed, and eventually went off down stream in a towering rage. We still had one more difficulty to overcome, a somewhat serious one, and one we did not quite understand, but eventually it transpired that our new skipper was trying to buy an old boat, not wanting to take his own to Pao T'eo and perhaps get her frozen in there. The owner of the old boat saw his opportunity, and was not slow to take advantage of it, as he would not take less than Ts.30, about three times its value under ordinary circumstances.

At last everything was settled, and about 11 A.M. we started, soon passing the wool-boats, which were tied up as usual. We found our craft pretty leaky, but by laying down a flooring of boughs and straw, and keeping up

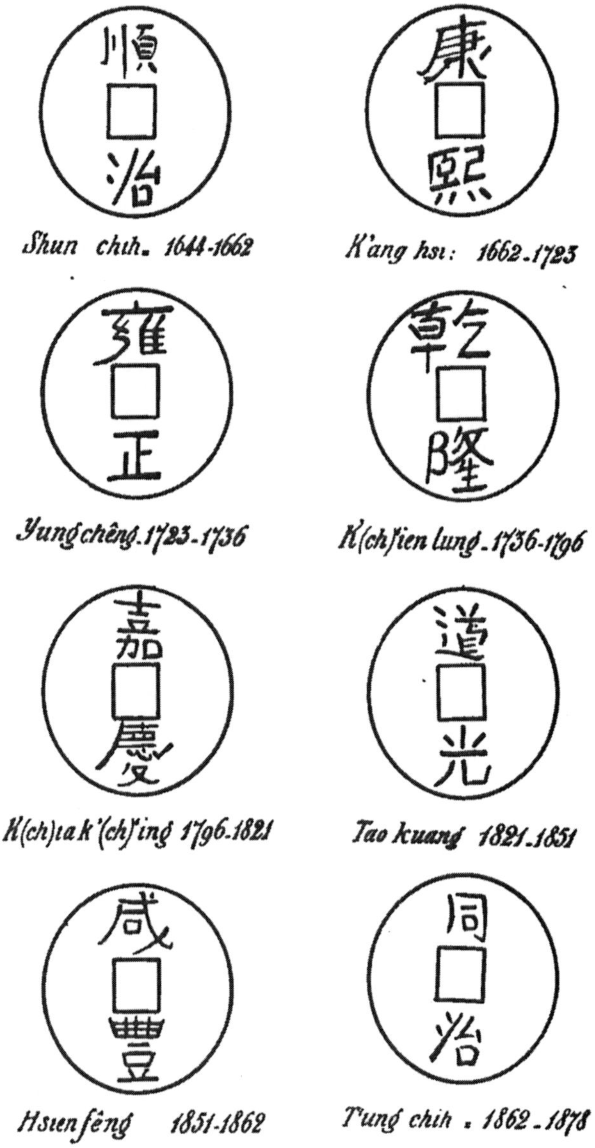

ALL THE "CASH" ISSUED FROM THE FIRST OF THE EMPERORS OF THE TS'ING OR MANCHU DYNASTY.

constant baling, we kept her very comfortable, and after all our chief anxiety was to travel rapidly. Part of our agreement was that we were to stop at Shih-Tsui-Tsi to take in fresh supplies, but that for every unnecessary delay the boatmen were to be fined one tael.

The stream was very strong, and, as the weather was cold, we used to row with the long sweeps to keep ourselves warm during the day, and the boatmen, of whom there were four, including the owner, rowed at night to keep themselves awake. This boat was built exactly the same as the other, but as there was no cargo we had plenty of room, and stood on the partitions to row; another advantage of having no cargo was that we drew very little water, and scarcely ever touched the bottom. The country on either shore was very flat and uninteresting, while the river, sometimes about two miles in width, was a succession of mud banks and shallows.

At five o'clock on the 9th November we got to Shih-Tsui-Tsi, and presented the letter of credit we had received from Chen-Lao-Pan. The agent then kindly gave us a guide, who took us to various shops, where we bought provisions, mostly bread and vegetables, for the rest of the journey to Pao T'eo. We did not, however, succeed in getting any meat, as there was only one sheep available, and that was not worth buying.

Having made our purchases, we returned to the office, where we found our money ready for us; part of this was in silver and part in cash. The latter was of very inferior quality, but, as we were getting it out of civility, and not in the way of business, we could not well say anything. The Chinese cash seems to have been purposely invented to deceive and cheat the unwary; to begin with, every Emperor makes his own cash, but these are not issued from the mint until after his death, and many Emperors have thought fit to economize by issuing inferior coins, which, instead of being about the size of our penny, are rather smaller than a farthing and very roughly made; in fact a very fair estimate of the various Emperors' characters can be drawn from the cash they have issued.

The accompanying diagrams show the cash of all the Emperors of the reigning Ts'ing or Manchu dynasty, but only full-sized specimens have been chosen. These inferior cash may be accepted as current coin in one place, while in the next no one will look at them. Cash are always done up in strings, either of five hundred or a thousand, and look not unlike strings of sausages, each sausage being represented by a hundred cash; and here, again, they have devised a means of fraud, for in some places eighty-five cash count as a hundred, in others ninety, ninety-two, ninety-three, and so on, as the case may be, consequently whenever one arrives at a new town, one has to enquire all about its coinage.

In Tankar they had a very peculiar way of reckoning, for prices were frequently stated in "small cash," a coin that does not exist, but whose value is half that of the current or "street cash." These differences disappeared gradually as we neared Pekin, and signs of a central government became more marked, but in and just around the capital itself we came across a very much larger cash, almost as big as the old English penny, but then, when dollars and cents became the currency, we were very little troubled with these coins. Another difficulty was that, in changing silver in different towns, the rate of exchange would vary as much as three hundred cash for an ounce, and the correct rate always had to be found out in a roundabout way before we presented our silver for exchange. These are only a few of the traps into which a novice may fall when attempting to deal in Chinese coinage. Had we been in the hands of a native interpreter, instead of those of Mr. Rijnhart, we should have been splendid prey for the swindlers.

They told us at Shui-Tsui-Tsi that the price of wool was four cents a pound, but that it was not of such good quality as that which comes from Tankar. Next to the wool business the most important occupation seemed to be iron working, in which a very large portion of the population was engaged. All the way from Chong Wei we had been passing through a district which was very rich in coal, and judging from the number of smithies in Shui-Tsui-Tsi, the district must possess very considerable mineral wealth, which may some day be developed.

By this time it was quite dark, so we hurried back to the boat, and started again after a halt which had lasted just three hours, to make up for which we offered our men an extra Ts.5 if they landed us in Pao T'eo in four days, *i.e.*, by the 9th of the Chinese, or the 13th of the English month. No time was lost in starting, and all night we floated down the mighty stream, but how we avoided the shallows will ever be a mystery to me; a sharp look-out was always kept, and every now and then a shout, followed by violent rowing, would tell us that we had just missed a bank.

Not far below Shui-Tsui-Tsi we passed a village situated in a desolate spot on the left bank, but in spite of its dreary surroundings it was full of life, numbers of boats were lying along the banks, all being filled with saltpetre ; every one was in a hurry to get off before the river should freeze, the whole scene reminding one of coolies at Port Said coaling a ship.

On we went all night and all day floating down the broad stream, the only break in the days being meal-times. The nights and early mornings were very cold, and consequently we spent no inconsiderable part of our time between the blankets, rising late and going early to bed. At twilight numbers of water birds, of all sorts and sizes, used to assemble on the mud banks, uttering weird cries until it was time for them to go to rest.

One night we narrowly escaped a collision, but no damage was done, although we managed, somehow or other, to carry off an oar belonging to the other boat, and had to put ashore to return it. As we got near to Pao T'eo we could see mountains on the north bank gradually closing in towards the river, and about the same place I discovered one of the clearest echoes I have ever heard, which was, moreover, sufficiently distant for three or four words to come back to us across the waters, quite distinct from our own shouts; shouting and an occasional turn at the sweeps was our only form of exercise at this time.

Early on the morning of the 13th November we sighted Pao T'eo, but it was not till 1 P.M. that we reached the termination of our water journey—none too soon, as sleepless nights had quite worn out the crew. Immediately on our arrival the boatmen entered into negotiations for the sale of the rickety old craft which had done us such good service, but no one seemed anxious to buy, boats being a drug in the market just before the river freezes.

CHAPTER XXX.

PAO T'EO—THE SWEDISH MISSION-HOUSE—CHINESE SCHOOLS—CHINESE INNS—CHINESE BURIAL—KUEI HUA CHENG—FRICTION WITH CARTERS—WE LEAVE THE MONGOL COUNTRY—THE GREAT WALL.

THE distance to Pao T'eŏ from the river bank was said to be fifteen li, so we lost no time in starting to walk there, leaving the servants and boatmen to bring our baggage to Messrs. Forbes's office. The fifteen li cannot really have been much more than nine, for, walking quickly, we got to the city gate in a little over three-quarters of an hour. Once inside, we were very much struck by the difference between this and the other cities we had seen; instead of crowded streets, with every available yard of ground within the walls occupied, we here found lanes, almost deserted except by a few children and pigs, and a large bit of waste land inside the walls, absolutely untenanted. Not only had this piece of ground been left severely alone, but two small suburbs, on the south and east sides respectively, had sprung up outside. Why so much ground had been originally enclosed no one could tell us.

While asking our way to the office of the wool firm, the Renki Yang Hong as it was called, we suddenly found ourselves opposite the entrance of the Swedish Mission-house. Needless to say, we went in at once, and were heartily welcomed. While explaining who we were and where we had come from, coffee was prepared by our hostess, and more delicious coffee I have never tasted; but as we were anxious to make all arrangements for starting the next morning, we could not waste time, but had to rush off to the office, accompanied by the missionaries, who showed us the way. Before leaving the house, however, they took us into their school, where we found some five-and-twenty remarkably clean and happy-looking children, who were being brought up to Christianity. When we entered they were deep in study, all reading their lessons at the top of their voices in every imaginable key. This method of committing the task to memory is universal throughout China. As soon as any child has mastered it, he or she holds up a hand, and is then called up to the desk to repeat it to the master. An important difference is now observable between the practice in native and foreign schools, for in the latter they proceed just as we do at home, but the native teacher makes the child stand with his back to the desk and his hands behind him, while the master arms himself with a cane, which descends remorselessly at the slightest slip.

It was not far to the Yang Hong, and old Chen-Lao-Pan's letter was sufficient to ensure us every civility. Money was at once forthcoming, and here, for the first time, we saw and became possessed of a "shoe" of silver, a lump weighing rather more than fifty ounces; we also got some more of the ordinary lumps, weighing from three to five ounces each, for minor current expenses. We had not been long in the office, and had not drunk more than three cups of tea each, when the baggage arrived. One of the Swedes and Malcolm went off with it at once to look for an inn, while Rijnhart and I stayed to complete the arrangements and settle with the boatmen, who said that they had sold their vessel for Ts.5, a considerable loss on the cost price, but which the hire had more than covered.

Malcolm had some difficulty in finding an inn, owing to large numbers of soldiers being in the city at the time, but

ON THE ROAD IN CHINA.

at last he was successful, and also arranged with several carters who were on the look-out for a job to come round to the mission-house to arrange terms. We had long ago found out from Chen-Lao-Pan—who had spent many years in this part of China—how long the cart journey to Pekin should take us and how much we should pay; and, armed with this knowledge, our new friends and Rijnhart were able to get an agreement signed for three carts to do the journey in thirteen days for Ts.19 apiece, a most admirable clause being added to the effect that, should they not arrive up to time, they would only get Ts.9½. Often and often did we have cause to congratulate ourselves on having had this inserted, and I strongly recommend any travellers in China to get some guarantee of this kind whenever possible.

It was with the satisfactory feeling of a good day's work done that we sat down to supper and enjoyed the luxury of an unlimited supply of milk, such as we had not enjoyed since leaving India. After supper we sat up late, our hosts singing in English, as well as in their native tongue and Chinese, accompanying themselves or one another on the guitar, without which no Swedish home is complete; however, we were reluctantly compelled to say good-night, but not good-bye, as our hosts promised to come and see us off on the morrow.

There was the usual hitch in starting, caused this time by the carters discovering that they could not do the distance to Pekin in less than fourteen days, their reason being that some carters who had arrived the previous evening had told them that the road was now very bad. We tried to make them stick to the original agreement, but eventually gave way, and had a fresh one drawn up. Seeing that the usual time occupied in this journey is seventeen days, their request for an extra day was not unreasonable. We also had to change some silver into cash for expenditure on the road, and this we entrusted to our landlord while we took a stroll through the streets.

Pao T'eo does not appear to have any distinctive trade or products of its own. One misses the splendid furs of Lancheo, the coal of Chong Wei, and the forges of Shih-Tsui-Tsi; but one notices very large numbers of Mongols, who bring in wool to the various firms. There were also numbers of copper Mongol kettles, of which we wanted to buy some specimens, but were told we could get them better and cheaper in Pekin. The shops were very much larger and more well-to-do-looking than anything we had hitherto seen, and in one grocer's we bought some first-rate sponge cakes and a sort of apple jam, which was excellent. Eggs were fairly dear, five cash apiece; in some places we had paid five cash for two, but near the capital we had to pay as much as ten cash each. Fancy new-laid eggs at fourpence a dozen in London!

However, the longest delays come to an end at last, and at 11 A.M. on the 14th November we started on the last stage of our journey. The missionaries walked some little way with us to the outskirts of the east suburb, and before leaving they insisted on our promising to visit their countrymen in the various stations we should pass through.

That evening we stopped at a very comfortable inn in a little town called Salaki. Everywhere were signs that we were approaching the capital; the streets were better looked after, and the inn was quite the best we had yet seen.

All Chinese inns seem to be built on the same principle. One passes through a wide entrance, on one side of which is the kitchen, on the other a sort of eating-house, into the courtyard, which varies in size according to the traffic. Opposite the entrance are the best rooms, kept for distinguished guests, and all round are smaller rooms for people of less importance, carters and servants. Every room is furnished with a k'ang or stove bed, and the better class inns have cupboards, tables, and chairs, but only in the best rooms. As long as one can get into these one can make oneself fairly comfortable, but should they be occupied one's lot is not an enviable one. Perhaps the most noticeable sign of civilization was glass windows, which we saw for the first time in Pao T'eo, and always daily afterwards.

ON THE ROAD FROM PAO T'EO TO PEKIN.

It was no longer necessary to carry large stores of provisions—these were obtainable everywhere; but in their place we had to carry an almost equal weight of cash, fifteen thousand of which, weighing no less than ninety pounds, we brought from Pao T'eo.

Next morning we started soon after sunrise. The shopkeepers were just taking down their shutters as we left the inn, and the city was waking up to its daily life; most of the people appeared to be engaged in the silk trade, so I suppose the worm is cultivated somewhere in the neighbourhood. Unfortunately, as we strolled on ahead of the carts we took a wrong turning, and had to retrace our steps almost to the inn before we found out where we had made the mistake. We then hurried after the carts, only to find that their road and ours joined almost at the very spot from which we had turned back. A stern chase is proverbially a long one, and this was no exception to the rule.

Just outside the walls we saw a coffin which was being conveyed to the corpse's native place for interment, and this was the means of our learning a rather interesting Chinese custom. Every Chinaman has three souls, and on death one of these returns to the city temple, one to Hades, and one goes to the grave. With the last of these three a cock is always carried, no matter how far the coffin may have to be conveyed. In Southern China it is always a white cock, but in the north there appears to be no hard-and-fast rule as to colour. When the corpse is finally buried the unfortunate rooster is slain, and his spirit goes to keep company with the soul in the coffin.

Every one has heard of the importance, in the eyes of the Chinaman, of being buried in his own home, and the ships' companies do not fail to take advantage of it, the passage-money for a dead man being many times that of a live one. Before starting on one of these journeys the greatest care is taken to ascertain an auspicious day, months often elapsing before a sufficiently favourable opportunity will occur.

On the 16th November we arrived at Kuei Hua Cheng. As we approached the town we passed a "big man." He was accompanied by three attendants, one riding in front and two behind, and we were told that anybody of importance generally rode in this fashion. Kuei Hua Cheng is a very large town, and is remarkable for the absence of any sort of city wall, a deficiency for which we could discover no reason. Instead of the customary wall we found an extremely dirty entrance, for the road was at least a foot deep in mud. It hardly seems credible that a town of such importance—for besides being a large market it is utilised as the point of departure for numerous caravans—should be so wanting in this most essential respect. If this road were ever supplanted by a railway, Kuei Hua Cheng would become a centre of immense commercial interest. The sun was setting as we entered the town, and we had to make the most of the short time remaining before the shops shut to lay in stores for the next few days, when we should be crossing the Mongolian grass country, and unable to purchase anything. Meat, bread, and kua mien were easily procurable, although the latter was very much dearer than it had been in Kansu, so it was still early when we had finished our supper and turned in for the night. It had been our original intention to visit the missionaries of this place, where I know we should have met with that warm-hearted hospitality which they are ever ready to bestow upon travellers. But supper over, the visions of an early start the next morning and the cold outside our inn were arguments too strong to be thrown aside.

Our carters met many friends at the inn, and determined to enjoy themselves accordingly; much wine was drunk, and one of them indulged in the luxury of a fight, all of which, though perhaps pleasant at the time, tended to prevent a very early start in the morning; further delay being caused by the carters suddenly thinking that they would like to take a pickaxe with them, with which they could improve the road in bad places. This delay enabled me to take a photograph of a very curious Buddhist temple, which stands just at the main eastern entrance to the town. To do this Rijnhart had to give me a leg-up on to the wall, and it was not without some difficulty that I attained my object.

We were sorry not to be able to see more of this town, which has been made famous by Huc and Gabet, Younghusband, and others; but here, as throughout China, "absence without leave" and "reasons in writing" were our bugbears. Especially did we regret not being able to see more of this temple, which is known as "Wu Tai" Temple, and is covered from top to bottom with figures of Buddha ranged in rows, and of a very interesting Manchu city which lies about two miles north-east of Kuei Hua Cheng, and is called Sin Chen, or the "New City." This was the only Manchu city we had a chance of seeing, and its broad streets, planted with trees, and frequented alike by men and women, would have been a strong contrast to the ordinary Chinese town.

While still waiting for the pickaxe a large flock of our old friends the sand-grouse passed over our heads, bringing to our minds the days of plenty and days of hunger we had passed on the Chang. Almost immediately the pickaxe arrived, and we made a fresh start, and for the first time the road showed some signs of having had a little labour expended on it. Previously there had been nothing but rough tracks through or round the fields, or, when this became invisible, the carters would make a road for themselves. The general direction was well known to them, and sooner or later they would strike the track again; nor was it hard to tell when they had done so, as a drop into a rut some eighteen inches deep was an unmistakable sign that we were on the highroad to Pekin, which is, in the opinion of the Chinese, incomparably the finest road in the world. To-day, however, we came across some really neatly-made bridges in excellent repair, but evidently only intended for travellers on foot or on horseback, as, at one end or the other, there was invariably a gap some two feet wide,

BUDDHIST TEMPLE. OUTSIDE KUEI HUA CHENG, CHINA.

effectually stopping wheeled traffic, so that all carts had to go through the water. Ninety li was the day's journey, taking us to Shih-Rong-Wa, where we stopped the night.

Next day was uneventful, but we ascended gradually to a little village called Cha-Ha-Pa-La, 100 li, and got quite into the mountains again, very different country from what we had passed through since leaving Pao T'eo. The soil here appeared very rich, and every available patch of land was cultivated. Every day we used to pass through numerous villages, and in one we were lucky enough to come in for a theatrical entertainment. No village is without its theatre, and performances are frequent in the season; but as it was now the dull time we only saw one. The theatre is always situated close to, generally opposite, the city temple, a great convenience to the Taoist priests, who are also the theatrical managers. The play did not appear exciting, and neither of us understood a word of it, which was perhaps just as well, so we left after a very few minutes. The theatres being in the open, no entrance money is charged. The audience come and go as they please, but are expected to drop a small contribution into a collection box which is continually being handed round. This system has the further advantage of enabling the actors to converse freely with friends below when not otherwise engaged.

From Cha-Ha-Pa-La we made an early start, as we heard that the night's halting-place was to be a fair-sized town, and we wanted to arrive early so as to renew our supplies. We were pretty high up, and as it was now very near the end of November, the mornings were uncommonly cold. Rijnhart, Malcolm, Lassoo, and Esau all started walking, while Shahzad Mir and I followed with the carts. Not far from the village we crossed a low pass into a lovely wide valley, and a little further on the party ahead managed to take a wrong turn. I went on with the carts, and got to our midday halting-place about ten o'clock, and there I had to sit and wait till the others should come up. I managed to make out, by drawings in the dust and other devices, that there was another road to Pekin, which the others must have taken, and by which they would get to our destination in seventeen days. Not thinking they were likely to be quite so long in finding out their mistake, I resolved to have my breakfast and await their arrival. After a couple of hours' waiting I was beginning to get a little bit anxious, and was considering what steps I had better take if, by any chance, they did not arrive before nightfall. However, at about one o'clock they hove in sight, so I immediately had the mules harnessed, while Shahzad Mir warmed up some tea.

In a few minutes Rijnhart and Malcolm were at the inn, but the two men were some way behind, and while waiting for them to come up, I heard how they had managed to miss us. It appeared that, when they missed the road, all the Chinese they had met had misled them by saying that they were right, and it was not till late in the day that they got into the proper road and arrived at the halting-place, after walking fully thirty miles.

We were soon ready for a fresh start, but the carters, anxious for any excuse to back out of their agreement as long as the fault could be laid at our door, were very reluctant, but threats to cut off half their hire prevailed, and we were quickly on the move. The march was a long one, over rolling grassy plains, out of Chinese into Mongolian country. As the sun set a cold wind rose, and for some time we sat shivering on the carts. The carts were travelling very fast, as the going was excellent. We thought we should never get to our destination, but all the time we were buoyed up with the thought that, at all events, we should get to a big place where there was sure to be a good inn. At last they told us that Ho-Lo-Si-T'ai, our goal, was close by, and in a few minutes we saw, not the town with castellated walls that we had imagined, but two miserable wayside inns with large yards full of sheep and camels, as unpromising a spectacle as one could wish to see.

On inquiry, things proved even worse than they had at first appeared, for both inns were crammed full, and we could not find a spot to sleep in. At last we heard that there was a room in a small house close by, so round we went, only to find it tenanted by a man, two women, a sheep, and some children, a fair supply for a place about twelve feet square, but into it we squashed, until we had revived our circulation, and then, after a considerable amount of squabbling, we arranged that we would sleep in the carts, while the carters occupied the already overcrowded room, for the simple reason that the carters flatly refused to take us any further unless they slept inside the house and we outside. Perhaps, after all, the cold blast was preferable to dirt and a close atmosphere.

The following day our road lay over more grassy plains, in which were herds of antelope—called by the Chinese the "yellow sheep"—some sand-grouse, and a few great bustards, none of which we shot. There were several Mongol encampments, with their neat little circular dwelling-places and sheep-folds, much more civilized than those we had seen in the far west.

That evening we left the Mongol country, possibly for ever, and got into the cultivated district again. The change was very sudden, and showed us admirably how the Chinese are slowly, but surely, encroaching upon the country of their pastoral neighbours. Cha-Ha-La-Po, our home for the night, was an insignificant little place, and chiefly to be remembered for the fact that we there managed to get rid of some six hundred very inferior cash, brought from Shih-Tsui-Tsi.

At noon the next day we had to change our axles, the

roads from here being much narrower than they had hitherto been; and while doing so we had a row with the carters. A crowd promptly assembled, but Rijnhart soon managed to get them on our side, and we gained our point. We were now well within our time, and the carters knew that they could fulfil their contract without difficulty, so

MONGOL ENCAMPMENT.

they loitered over the axle changing and made a very short march to a bran-new inn, where we put up in an excellent, clean, and airy room. There was still plenty of daylight left, of which we took advantage to have a real good wash in warm water.

As if to make up for this early halt, we were awakened soon after midnight, and started about 1 A.M.; but this energy, we had every reason to believe, was owing to a desire on the part of our jehus to pass through the next village in the dark, owing to monetary or some other form of trouble they were in there. At first it was very dark, and as our road was very rough we went stumbling along till the moon came out from behind some heavy clouds. Rising rapidly, we were soon on a small pass, where some pious individual, in hopes of future reward, had built a neat little temple. The descent on the far side was steep, and the rocky gorge through which our road lay was very picturesque in the brilliant moonlight.

About daylight we got down to the bed of a stream, which we crossed and recrossed several times till we arrived at the small town of Hsing-Ping-Ho, the gate of which forms part of the Great Wall of China. We had already seen the Great Wall, near Chong Wei, where, however, it is little more than a turf embankment, but as we approached the capital we saw how it gradually improves, both in its original construction and its later preservation; but even now we were very much disappointed, and were unable to realize how it ever managed to gain its world-wide reputation.

At Hsing-Ping-Ho the wall is of earth, faced with brick, generally not more than eight to ten feet high, and quite narrow, very different from the imposing structure one had always pictured it to be, and which we were yet destined to see. But although we could not yet look upon the wall with the respect one had hoped to feel for it, neither of us could help admiring the dogged perseverance with which it has been carried over mountain tops and down valleys, the most forbidding natural obstacles being treated as nought in comparison with the orders of the emperor.

After breakfast our road ran parallel to the stream we had crossed in the morning, which had now grown to a considerable size, and was called the Wo-Ku-Shan-Ho. Every few miles we passed a large walled city, evidently very old, and now almost entirely deserted; they must all have seen better times and been places of importance—probably about the time that the Great Wall was being built. I photographed the walls of one of these cities, and the temple outside tenanted by some wooden figures. The name of the city was Si-Yang Ho.

TEMPLE OUTSIDE SI-YANG HO.

SHOWING STAGES FROM PAO T'EO TO PEKIN.

Date			Stage	Li.
14th	November.—	Pao T'eo to	Tour-tsi	40
,,	,,	,,	Sa-la-ki . . .	50
15th	,,	,,	Mi-tour-chon . .	30
,,	,,	,,	Ta-ri-tsi . . .	80
16th	,,	,,	Peh-sie-ki . . .	50
,,	,,	,,	Kuei Hua Cheng .	70
17th	,,	,,	Shih-Rong-Wa .	90
18th	,,	,,	Cha-Ha-Pa-La .	100
19th	,,	,,	Mongol Camp (long)	50
,,	,,	,,	Ho-Lo-Si-T'ai .	70

SHOWING STAGES FROM PAO T'EO TO PEKIN—*continued.*

Date					Li.
20th	Nov.—Ho-lo-si-tai	to	Mongol Camp (short)		50
,,	,,	,,	Cha-Ha-La-Po	.	80
21st	,,	,,	Cha-ka-ri	. .	60
,,	,,	,,	Teo-tao-keo	.	35
22nd	,,	,,	Hsing-Ping-Ho	.	75
,,	,,	,,	Uen-tsi-tao-ri	.	50
23rd	,,	,,	Io-kia-t'eng	. .	65
,,	,,	,,	Nant-sing-ho	.	75
24th	,,	,,	Shuen-hua-fu	. .	40
,,	,,	,,	Siao-Si-Fu	. .	35
25th	,,	,,	Ki-mio-si	. .	35
,,	,,	,,	Sa-cheng	. .	45
,,	,,	,,	Huai-lai-hsien	.	60
26th	,,	,,	Cha-tao	. .	50
,,	,,	,,	Nan-Kou	. .	45
27th	,,	,,	Sha-ho	. .	50
,,	,,	,,	Pekin	. . .	45

From Pekin to Tien Tsin is 80 miles.

CHAPTER XXXI.

HOW TO MANAGE INN-KEEPERS AND CARTERS—SHUEN-HUA-FU—"SPIRIT'S PAPER"—SHAHZAD MIR LOST AND FOUND—ESAU'S PRESTIGE.

About dusk we got to a very small village, with a most charming little inn. We got two very comfortable little rooms, with excellent furniture, consisting of tables, chairs, and looking-glasses.

This must have been quite one of the longest day's journey we did, but li are very erratic things to go by. As far as we could make out one hour's journey was always counted as ten li, quite irrespective of whether we went fast or slow; thus ten li in one place would be nearly five miles, and in another very little over three.

Delighted as we had been on arrival with our little inn, we were still more so on our departure, for we got off without a word of dispute at the price to be paid for our accommodation. At this time our rule was to pay one hundred cash for each room occupied, and about forty cash each for water and for the use of the fire; when nearer the capital we increased this as the accommodation improved, just as in the rough places further west we had given less. Having a fixed rule like this, which was liberal without being excessive, saved us an infinity of trouble, as the innkeepers saw at once that Rijnhart knew what he was about, and was not likely to be cheated or bluffed into making exorbitant payments. But there was always one thing they could not get over, and that was that Rijnhart always handed them whatever money we took out of the bag and gave him. They saw that we put ourselves in his hands, and could not make out why he exacted no squeezes from us or them; never was such honesty heard of!

This day, the 23rd November, was evidently a very lucky

BRIDAL CHAIR.

one: every one was out visiting friends, dressed in their best, the big ceremonial hat was seen on all sides, and several marriages were in progress. As if to make up for our peaceful morning, we had a most truculent fellow to deal with at breakfast; our cash were all too small and our fees were quite insufficient; in fact, he found a *casus belli* in our every act, and crowned his impertinences by selling us some two dozen real bad eggs, at eight cash apiece.

Sometimes a traveller is apt to find himself in a very awkward position, if his carters and an offensive innkeeper happen to be in league. It may happen that the carters owe the innkeeper money, and the latter threatens to get them punished unless they help him in extorting money from the unfortunate foreigner; the innkeeper then demands a perfectly unreasonable sum from his victim, which the latter refuses; upon this the carters come up and say that they cannot possibly leave till the money is paid, and the helpless traveller finds himself between the devil and the deep sea. Luckily for us, our agreement effectually stopped any nonsense of this kind, for if the carters said they could not go on, we at once replied "All right, please yourselves—but if you do not arrive by the 27th, you lose half your hire."

Every day, now, villages became more numerous, and the country was very thickly cultivated. We stopped a long time at our midday halt at the city of Shuen-Hua-Fu,* as the carters had to change some silver and transact some business before proceeding. After leaving, we passed a very large number of gravestones and memorial stones, with old inscriptions of the rounded characters; the hillsides on the left of the road were studded with them for several miles, and in many places the coffins were sticking out of the ground, where the earth had been washed away from over them. On the road we met a convoy of mules carrying boxes containing tins of oil from Batoum,

* Shuen-Hua-Fu is erroneously called a "Fu," for, strictly speaking, it is a Hsien. A Fu as nearly as possible corresponds to our "city" and a "Hsien" is only equal to a town, while a "Ting" is a place of the third class. A "Fu," properly speaking, means a fort, and appears to be equal to a "Ting" in importance. In some instances a city may have risen or fallen in importance since its title was originally fixed, such as, for instance, the city of Siao-Si-Fu, which is not much larger than a "Ting." In all towns of importance there is a yamen or magistrates' office, and the head civil official there is called a Fut'ai or Hsient'ai, as the case may be. In any large district there is also a higher official called a Taot'ai.

and another with silver; the latter had an escort armed with spears decorated with red tassels, each mule, too, was decorated with a red flag, the whole making quite an imposing show.

Towards evening the road got very bad, and in one place we all had to get out and steady the carts as they passed down a steep, rocky path. Luckily we got down without mishap, but one of the carts was within an ace of slipping down a decline, where there was nothing to stop it for a considerable distance, and where both it and the mules must inevitably have been smashed. As we went down, a string of carts was coming up, two or three teams being hitched on to one cart and then returning for the next. The shouts of the drivers, cracks of whips, and creaking of wheels, made a terrible din, while the motley teams of ponies, mules, donkeys, and bullocks, all straining every nerve and then only managing to progress some ten or fifteen yards without a rest, made a picture. I should very much like to have been able to perpetuate it, but the light had already failed, and I was unable to do so. It was dark when we got down to Siao-Si-Fu and into our inn, but we had really made quite a short day's journey.

Next morning we were up long before it was light, and made a start with lanterns. It was just as well we did so, for our landlord, who was evidently accustomed to foreigners, and looked upon them as fair prey, refused to open the gates of the inn yard unless we paid him far more than was his due; but he reckoned without his host, for as there was no crowd about, and no fear of exciting a disturbance, we were able to threaten, and telling him that if he did not undo the lock, we would blow it open with a revolver, he soon saw that the game was up, and let us go in peace.

The village of Siao-Si-Fu lies just at the entrance of a narrow gorge, through which runs a rapid stream; the road winds along the hillside, generally at a good height above the water, but it has been carefully made, and the going is excellent. We met a large number of camels coming through, mostly carrying tea into the interior; and in one place one of them had managed to slip some distance down the hillside, but did not appear to have hurt himself much—he had been wise in choosing a gradual slope, where he could not fall far.

A GORGE WITH GREAT WALL IN DISTANCE.

The defile lasted nearly ten miles, but we missed most of its beauties, owing to our early start and the darkness, which was also responsible for our party getting separated, Shahzad Mir having somehow managed to lose the rest of us. This did not cause us much anxiety at the time, as we thought that he had merely lagged behind, and would soon be up with us.

When, however, we had made our halt, and breakfast was

being prepared, and there were still no signs of him, we began to get anxious, and in making inquiries, we heard that he had passed our halting-place, and been met by carters coming from the Pekin direction. We still consoled ourselves with the thought that he would soon find out his mistake and retrace his steps, but when it was time to yoko up and make a fresh start, nothing had been seen of him.

We were now very anxious about him, so divided ourselves into two parties, the carts and servants going one road, while we went another, which passed through several small towns and ran parallel to the road taken by the carts. Both parties made inquiries as they went along, and for some thirty li we still heard of him; he seemed to have walked straight ahead, never stopping except to buy some food. His clothes and gait, as well as his dark face, made him very conspicuous, so that the various guards on the town gates always noticed him; but after going about ten miles we lost all trace of our faithful Duffadar, and all we could do was to give notice of his disappearance in different places, and ask the people to show him which way we had gone. The most unlucky part of the business was that he could not speak a solitary word of Chinese, and might get himself into trouble, but fortunately we were in northern, and not central or southern China, so we felt sure that sooner or later he would turn up.*

In some of the towns we passed through we saw quantities of "spirit's paper" lying about the streets, or hanging up in the shops for sale. This spirit's paper is simply round pieces, cut to represent cash, each sheet of paper representing any number, or gilt to represent silver or gold. These are bought by the people and scattered about the houses, or put in holes in walls and tree trunks, where they are found by restless, wandering spirits, who, poor creatures, are easily

* Shahzad Mir, too, knew the direction of Pekin, so was not likely to wander off in a wrong direction.

deceived into thinking them offerings of great value, and consequently refrain from injuring the pious, but economical offerer. They also burn large quantities of this paper money, and effigies of carts, horses, and other signs of worldly wealth, all of which go to improve the social status of their ancestors in the nether world.* The Chinaman, though decidedly superstitious and pious, according to his lights, rarely allows his regard for his ancestors to overcome that for his own pocket.

This was to be another very long day, so we halted for an hour, about 4 o'clock in the afternoon, and fed the animals, we ourselves buying some splendid grapes for forty cash a pound. These are grown south of the town of Shuen-Hua-Fu; also quantities of millet (huang-mi†), which is ground up and eaten like rice by the poor classes.

While wandering round, telling people of Shahzad Mir's disappearance and looking at the various shops, we saw hung up in a cage on the city gate the head of a man who had been found guilty of theft, and next to this gruesome relic were the shoes of several officials, whose ability or zeal in discharge of their duties had merited this special distinction; thus are the best and the worst of men's deeds kept fresh in the minds of the Chinese people.

We were just about to make our third start for the day when two Russian merchants entered our inn. We were much struck by the promptitude with which they extracted their revolvers from the sedan chairs in which they were travelling, and placed them in handy and conspicuous positions on top of their luggage. Curiously enough the only language in which we could converse with them was Chinese, which one man spoke fluently; and it was a great relief

* Huc and Gabet state that Tibetans have a practice of throwing these paper horses to the winds, and they are supposed to help travellers in distress.

† Huang-mi means yellow rice, just as Huang-ho means yellow river.

when we learnt that we need have no fear of the Gulf of Pe Chili being frozen over, for we were still in plenty of time.

We still had sixty li to do before halting for the night at Huai-Lai-Hsien, so we shoved along as fast as the mules could go, but the last twenty li or so were done in pitch darkness and bitter cold. The gates of the suburb were closed when we arrived, but we got them open with some difficulty, after considerably exaggerating the importance of the high official posts we both occupied. We had done nearly fifty miles since morning, so were glad to get an excellent Chinese concoction of eggs, and tumble into our blankets as quickly as might be.

Next morning we had to wait till the main gates were open, as our road lay through the city. The innkeeper coolly demanded 1,160 cash for the use of his rooms, but after a very few moments was more than satisfied with 360, in addition to which we of course gave a *douceur* to the man who had waited on us, as is the custom. A biting cold wind was blowing from the west, and as it was also freezing hard, it was quite the most unpleasant day of the whole journey, but it was not till we got in the open country, outside the walls, that we really felt the full force of the gale. The road was crowded with travellers going to and from Pekin, and one could not but envy the wealthy individuals who, sitting snugly in their neatly-made sedan chairs, could despise both wind and cold. Usually we used to wonder how even a Chinaman could sit all day in one of these conveyances, from which every breath of fresh air was carefully excluded, but to-day I think we would gladly have got into the stuffiest of them had we got the chance.

But if it were bad for us, what must it have been for the people travelling against the wind? Time after time we congratulated ourselves on the wind being at our backs. Several unfortunate Russians whom we met looked as though the wind was nearly cutting them in two, while

Mongols and Chinese sat with their backs towards the heads of their camels or mules as they rode along. One poor man, whose whole attention was fixed on keeping himself warm, was very nearly run over by our carts in spite of all our warning shouts. Somehow, watching the misery of others always makes one forget one's own, and we were able to laugh at the ludicrous though pitiable faces of those we met, and in this way the fifty li to Cha-Tao passed less unpleasantly than it could otherwise have done.

Just before reaching this village we passed through another of the many ramifications of the Great Wall, behind which we cowered until the carts came up, wondering all the time what had happened to the unfortunate Shahzad Mir. Where could he have passed the night? What was he doing now? How would he manage for food? These and many other questions we asked one another, but decided that the only way in which we could help him was to get to Pekin quickly, and give notice at the yamen there of his disappearance.

From the wall to the inn was a very short way, and soon after the carts had come up we found ourselves in a crowded inn, where every one was busy; all the travellers were shivering like ourselves, and all clamouring for hot tea and other luxuries. At length we managed to get something, and had just got well into a substantial meal, when, to our surprise and delight, Shahzad Mir strode into the yard. While some food was being got ready for him he told us his tale. After missing us in the dark, on the morning of the 25th, he had quite made up his mind that we must be ahead, so on and on he went, eventually leaving the right road to his left. By midday he realized that he was lost, but this did not seem to have bothered him in the least. He knew that we were making for Pekin or Peh Chine, as the people call it, and guessed that by repeating that word in an inquiring tone of voice, he would get people to show him the road.

He also knew that Pekin lay pretty well due east, so made up his mind to hold his course in that direction until he got to the sea, if necessary, after which he hoped to fall in with some European who would help him. At nightfall he thought he ought to try and get some food and lodging. He was in a fair-sized town, so walked into the biggest shop he could see, and made the owner understand his

THE GREAT WALL AT CHA-TAO.

wants. Food they gave him willingly, but it was some time before he could get them to let him stay the night, his dark-coloured face apparently filling them with awe; but at last he attained his object, and got not only a good night's rest, but a substantial meal before leaving in the morning, for all of which his host absolutely refused payment.

Somehow or other the dark complexions of our retainers

always struck awe into the minds of the Chinamen, and time after time Rijnhart had to answer questions as to whether these men were "really wild or not." Esau especially, with his flowing Ladakhi locks and earrings, was an object of fear and wonder, being taken for either a woman or a cannibal, greatly to his own disgust, though luckily he could not understand the remarks aroused by his strange appearance, unless they were explained by Rijnhart afterwards.

After breakfast the wind dropped a bit, and the cold was much less than it had been, for which we had reason to be thankful, as about two li beyond Cha-Tao we passed through the Great Wall again, and were able to see it at its best. It is here made of rubble, and splendidly faced with stone; towers are placed at regular intervals, and the top is broad enough for any troops to pass one another without the slightest difficulty or confusion. Just by the gate a flight of steps leads up to the wall, from which we looked down the valley towards Cha-Tao, and I also managed to take a photograph showing the wall as it runs away over the hill tops to the north.

One could now for the first time realize the magnitude of the original design, and had the whole northern frontier of China been divided off from Mongolia by a wall, such as this is near Pekin, and some 1,600 miles in length, there would have been nothing in the world to compare with it. Just behind the wall we found an old cannon, the inscription on which was copied by Rijnhart, as he believed that it proved the gun to be some three thousand years old, but unluckily we had no books at hand to corroborate this idea, or to tell us how old it really was. The name of the Emperor in whose reign it was made was very clear, and a book of dates would show at once between what years the gun was made.

Meanwhile our carts had got some way ahead of us, and

we had to hurry after them. Ascending steadily we reached the summit of the Nan Kou Pass, from which a rapid descent into a warmer climate commenced. The road was at this point by far the best we saw in China, and showed signs of immense labour and no inconsiderable amount of engineering skill having been expended on it. Our road lay down a narrow valley, high on each side of which rose rocky mountains, while along the northern skyline ran the Great Wall.

CHAPTER XXXII.

A TRUCULENT INNKEEPER—A SEDAN CHAIR—CHINESE WOMEN AND THEIR FEET — PEKIN — DEPARTURE OF RIJNHART — CARTERS EARN A BEATING.

As we descended we passed several small shrines and numerous inscriptions cut in the face of the rock, many of which were in ancient Tibetan characters, but more remarkable than these was a large figure of Sakya Muni, cut on a rock, which stands in a very conspicuous position high above the road.

Rijnhart and Malcolm climbed by a steep staircase to a small shrine, some eighty feet above the road ; but although it was evidently very old, they found nothing more remarkable than the names of several Russians and a few Englishmen who had been there in previous years, among others being Grey, Walker, and Allen, 1868 and 1879. We did not add our own to the list.

Still descending, we passed under several arches, which looked as though they had at some time been gates of different fortified camps, and then came to a magnificent Buddhist arch covered with carvings and representations of Buddha ; this must be a great age, and is one of the most interesting relics in Northern China. A short way further on we came to the village of Nan Kou (southern valley), where visitors to the Great Wall almost always stop the night after leaving Pekin. Knowing this, we were quite prepared to pay more than usual for our accommodation,

BUDDHIST ARCHWAY BY NAN KOU.

but the demands with which we were met far exceeded our expectations. In the first place, we could get no fire on which to cook our own food, but must take what the inn provided ; then our servants could not cook their food ; and lastly, we must pay for everything over-night, and not wait till the morning, as had been our invariable custom. Eventually these little difficulties were settled, but not until our landlord had worked himself up into a towering passion, such as only a Chinaman can, and had stamped up and down the room like a mad man.

Now came the great question. We were prepared to settle over-night. But how much were we to pay? "A Chinaman always pays a thousand cash for this room. What are you going to give me?" said Mr. Khe, the innkeeper. "Three hundred cash," we replied, now thoroughly annoyed, and with our liberal intentions all forgotten. "Well, what about the servants?" was his answer. "They are included," was all the reply he got. Never have I seen a man change his demeanour as our friend now did. From the bullying tone he had previously adopted he became quite cringing, and, seeing that we knew the exact amount to which he was entitled, and that we were determined to pay no more, quietly said, "Very well, give me the money," which we did, explaining that but for his insolent behaviour we should have given him about double. This had a most salutary effect on his servants, so that next morning they were all running about with hot water for our tea, and doing other little services, which were rewarded with extra wine money. I was amused to hear later that every one who stays in this inn has a row with the landlord, but it is not every one who gets out of it as well as we did.

Next morning we made a very early start, hoping to reach the capital and get our letters in good time. It was now more than six months since we had heard from home, and we were, naturally, a little anxious as to what news might be awaiting us. For some days the traffic had been rapidly increasing. All night one could hear the camel bells ringing as they passed our inns,* while all day we passed string after string of pack mules and carts. But to-day far surpassed everything we had yet seen. In one hour, just before daybreak, Rijnhart and I counted no less than 765 camels, all carrying tea, sugar, and oil to the interior, while those travelling east were mostly laden with wool.

Just below Nan Kou the road, which for the last few days had lain through rocky mountains, debouched on the wide "Plain of Pe Chili," in which lies Pekin, and where are also the famous "Tombs of the Emperors." As we neared the great city we crossed some fine stone bridges, which must have been quite wonders when originally built in the days of long ago, but, as little care is now taken about keeping them in order, the roadways are very rough. Here it was that we got our best opportunity of studying the crowd that was hurrying to the capital, all bent on business or pleasure.

First and foremost in interest was an important Mongolian prince, decorated with the dark red button and surrounded by an escort whose faces plainly told their nationality. From one of them we learnt that their chief had been hastily summoned into the presence of the Emperor, and was travelling with all possible speed. Just behind his sedan chair came a coffin with its inevitable accompanying rooster, while, indifferent alike to the living prince or the dead commoner, a mass of jostling, bustling humanity, neat little private mule carts, rougher hired ones, country waggons, and people on foot, all hurrying on and looking after themselves alone, crossed the bridge in front of us, a mass of colour and Chinese life worth going a long way to see.

* Each camel man has a string of six animals, to the last of which a bell is attached. The owner has hold of the leading camel, and, as long as he hears the bell, he knows the rest are following all right; if it ceases he knows something is wrong.

CLOSE TO THE CELESTIAL CAPITAL.

Here, too, for the first time, we saw Chinese women with decent sized feet. This is owing to the fact that from mixing with Manchus and other foreigners they have seen the error of their ways, and the younger generation are, to a great extent, forsaking the folly of their ancestors. The treatment necessary to produce a really neat Chinese foot, the best examples of which are to be seen in Lancheo, is absolutely barbarous. First, slits are made between the metatarsal bones to enable the toes, except the big toe, to be bent well under the sole. Then a similar cut is made in the heel, so that it can be bent to nearly meet the toes, the whole foot being tightly bound round and held in position with bandages. The unfortunate child-cripple is now left to walk about on the stumps until the agony becomes unbearable, when the foot is released till the following day. Needless to say, a free, easy gait is an impossibility, and how such deformity can be considered becoming passes all understanding. Shahzad Mir summed up the Chinese race in the words, "All the women are lame, and the men rotten with opium," by no means an unfair description.

Coming from India, the effects of opium on the people strike one perhaps more forcibly than they would do otherwise. In both countries there is a large consumption, but, instead of smoking in the Chinese fashion, the inhabitants of India either eat it or drink a decoction cf it. As was shown before the Opium Commission in 1894, the good effects of the drug in India more than counterbalance the evil effects, but there can be no mistake as to its being an unmitigated curse in China, where many of its slaves would gladly give it up if they could, but the craving it induces is too strong to be combated by nature alone.

Manchu women, with their carefully dressed hair sticking out on either side of the head, and their curious shoes, were the next curiosity to attract our attention, but all these were soon dwarfed into insignificance by the appearance, in the distance, of the west gate of Pekin, but, though still early when first seen, it was three o'clock in the afternoon before we arrived in the suburb.

Here carts had to be changed, as the large country carts are not allowed into the city, and this proved to be another bone of contention between ourselves and our carters, they contending that we ought to get our own carts from the city, while we said it was part of their contract, but this little matter was soon smoothed over, and our belongings were transferred into our new conveyances.

The streets of Pekin were at first a little disappointing, the walls are in many places dilapidated, and drainage there is nil, but at the present time our thoughts were all centred on getting our letters. The drive through the city to the "Hotel de Pekin" took us three quarters of an hour. There we secured most luxurious quarters, and then rushed off to the post office. Here we heard that all our letters had been sent round to the Embassy, so off we went again, but it was not without some difficulty that we obtained admission.

Sergeant Herring,* who for twenty-five years has guarded the portals of the British Minister's residence, looked at us in considerable astonishment, as well he might. Never had he seen in all his experience two such disreputable looking beings. At length we allayed his suspicions, and our names were taken in to Sir Claude Macdonald, who received us with the greatest kindness, but perhaps the strangest sensation of the whole journey was still in store for us when, covered as we were with the grime of our eight months' travel, we suddenly found ourselves in Lady Macdonald's drawing-room, from which we beat a hasty retreat, but not before we had promised to bring our things—

* Sergeant Herring, formerly of the 2nd Life Guards and Metropolitan Police, remembers well the time when he was a member of the mounted escort allowed our ambassador in Pekin in days gone by.

A PORTION OF THE WALLS OF THE CAPITAL.

STREET WHEREIN IS THE ENTRANCE TO THE BRITISH LEGATION.

such things too—over from the hotel in the morning. We had been expected in Pekin in September, and every one had come to the conclusion that we must have returned to India by some other route, so the news of our arrival was promptly telegraphed to London.

Every hour of our short stay in Pekin passed most pleasantly. Unfortunately, the chance of getting frozen in was increasing day by day, and our time was not our own, so we were only able to enjoy a three days' stay in the place which had taken us so long to reach. Nearly all this time we spent wandering about the streets, buying curios of all sorts, but one wants a great deal longer than this to exhaust the sights of China's capital, with its three cities, one within the other, and its narrow, busy streets and bazaars. A walk round the walls and a visit to the Observatory, where the finest bronzes in the world are to be seen, were amongst the good things we missed, but somehow or other the more we got to know the streets the greater attraction they had for us, especially as at this time of year they are free from those appalling smells with which all visitors to China have made us familiar.

During our short stay we met among other Englishmen Sir Robert Hart, who has been for forty-two years in the service of the Chinese Government, with only eighteen months' leave home, and Colonel Brown, who had just come out from home by the Trans-Siberian Railway—a very pleasant but cold journey—to take up the duties of military attaché.

All too soon the day of our departure arrived, and the 1st December saw us again packed in Chinese carts, on the way to Tientsin, where we arrived on the night of the 2nd, our last day's travelling in China having been nearly our longest, as we covered no less than 150 li between 1 A.M. and 6.30 P.M. Greatly did we miss Rijnhart, the cheery companion of our forty days through China. His original intention had been to travel with us by sea to Shanghai, but, at the last moment, he decided to accompany a German traveller, Mr. Eugène Wolf, overland to Hankow, so with real regret we parted from him at Pekin.

We were now without an interpreter, and at Tientsin were unable to find our way to the hotel, so lost considerable time wandering about the streets, asking futile questions from passers-by, and abusing our carters. At last things came to a climax, when one of them drove into a water cart, upsetting it with all its water into the street. Before we really knew what had happened, two of our carters were seized and marched off to the nearest police station.

We were thus left in a fine predicament. There we were in a strange place, unable to speak the language, two of our carters in prison, and the other one refusing to budge till his companions had been released. Such was our first experience of European administration in a Chinese town. There was only one course left to us. We turned carters ourselves, and as we made our way we knew not whither, we fortunately fell in with an intelligent native, who sprang up from somewhere or other, and volunteered to show us the way to an hotel. Driving ourselves, and following our friend in need, we soon arrived at the "Globe Hotel," but here again we were looked upon with the gravest suspicion, and only with the greatest difficulty did we manage to secure one small room between us. A little later, when our landlord found out who we were, he was profuse in his apologies, and anxious to put us into better quarters, explaining that he had at first taken us for robbers. This was rather hard, after having had baths regularly for the last four days, having shaved our beards, and having borrowed clothes from Mr. Hugh Grosvenor at Pekin, but it made us realize what a shock we must have given Lady Macdonald on our first appearance in her drawing-room.

PEKIN.

CHAPTER XXXIII.

BACK TO INDIA — DISILLUSIONMENT OF OUR FOLLOWERS WITH REGARD TO SOME OF THE BLESSINGS OF CIVILIZATION—MILITARY HOSPITALITY—RETURN TO CALCUTTA.

We had just got into our fresh quarters when our carters turned up. They had received a severe beating for their carelessness, and had then been released. We paid them both off, and were not sorry at the thought of having seen the last of the Chinese muleteer.

At dinner that night we met a Mr. Denbigh, who is engaged in large business transactions in Saghalien, Vladivostock, and Japan, and who was now supplying sleepers for the new railway to Pekin. He made a most tempting offer, which we could not accept, namely, that we should accompany him in a ship he had chartered, run over in her to Japan, and then either go on in her to Canton, or change into one of the regular liners to Shanghai and Hong Kong. Next morning, as soon as breakfast was over, we went with Mr. Denbigh to try and fit ourselves out with some new clothes, but we did not succeed in getting much beyond stockings and shoes. We then went to the office of Messrs. Forbes & Co., and presented our letters, showing the amount we had drawn from their various agents, and settled the account in English money.

In the afternoon we met Mr. W. H. Forbes, an Edinburgh man, who told us that our quickest route would be to go by a steamer belonging to Messrs. Butterfield and Swire, called the *Nanchang*, one of the very few running direct to Hong Kong. This would save several days, but would not allow of our seeing Shanghai; but time outweighed all other considerations, and we practically decided at once to adopt this course. In the evening we dined with Surgeon-Major Henston and the mess of the Hong Kong and Shanghai Banking Company, being treated on all hands with the greatest possible kindness.

Next morning we finally decided to go by the *Nanchang* direct to Hong Kong, and, with a view to this, we went round to Messrs. Butterfield and Swire's office. Here we learnt that, by taking the midday train to Tong Ku, we should get on board comfortably before dark. This sounded simple enough, but we still had something to learn with regard to Chinese travelling.

From Tientsin to Tong Ku is about thirty miles, and two trains run daily each way. Ships can come up the river as far as Tientsin, but, at this time of year, they seldom care to run the risk of being frozen in. We arrived at the railway station in good time, and there found a scene of the most horrible confusion. As soon as the train came alongside the platform, there was a general rush for the carriages, and every seat was taken. Not being accustomed to this sort of thing, we got left, but by the kindness of a Dr. Irwin, and a very nice Chinese official, we managed to put our servants and our baggage into an open waggon, while we ourselves travelled in the brake van.*

There was a bitterly cold wind blowing, fortunately at our backs, so we kept the brake door open for fresh air only having to shut it when the train stopped. Had the wind been against us, our servants would have had a very poor time. We found, however, that we had a great pull over

* Our tickets cost sixty-five cents each. This railway had been open eleven years, and was at this time paying fifteen and a half per cent.

people in the carriages, for we had a stove on which we roasted chestnuts the whole way to Tong Ku.

The Chinese gentleman to whom we were indebted for our seat in the train had been educated in America and spoke English fluently; he was a very go-ahead man, and was very anxious that the management of the railway should be put into the hands of foreigners, as the Chinese officials were quite helpless. But, with all his admiration for foreign products, he said that there was one thing he could get in China to suit him, and nowhere else, that was "spectacles." He certainly wore a splendid pair, for which he had given Ts.80—a very heavy price, but the glasses were extraordinarily good.

This was the first railway Esau and Lassoo had ever seen. They had long been looking forward to it, and had asked us many questions as to how the train moved, etc., but I am afraid their first experience was not an encouraging one.

On our arrival at Tong Ku, we heard that the *Nanchang* had gone outside the bar to complete her cargo, but no one could tell us how to get out to her. After walking for about a mile we came to the end of the wharf, and, by pure good luck, found a tug just on the point of leaving. "Where is the *Nanchang?*" we shouted. "I'm going to take a lighter out there at once; look sharp, if you're coming on board," was the reply. The tug began to move, but our repeated shouts brought it to a standstill. The pilot was an impatient man, and our coolies who carried our goods were tardy men, so that we just, and only just, managed to tumble our things and ourselves on board before the tug was in motion again.

As soon as our pilot had tugged us out alongside the lighter, he advised us to go aboard it with our luggage, and as we knew the *Nanchang's* cargo was on board also, we felt we could not be left behind. The pilot, too, promised that if he could not get us alongside the *Nanchang* that night, he would take us ashore to the hotel at Taku. It was bitterly cold as we scrambled from the tug into the lighter, and whilst our servants barricaded themselves from the cruel blast with our boxes and rugs, Malcolm and I gladly stepped below and partook of the small space available, and of the rough though kind hospitality of the uncouth Chinese crew. As we felt ourselves being tugged out to sea it grew colder and colder. At length, soon after nightfall, to our dismay, the pilot faithlessly deserted us. Visions of beds at the Taku Hotel vanished, to be replaced by the flow of wrath we would let the pilot have on the morrow. The only course left to us was to make the best of our situation. As we had made no provision for food, we asked our rough hosts, by signs, what they could give us for dinner. This finally was served up, consisting of tea and monkey-nuts. We smiled at one another as we did ample justice to our last Chinese meal, and prayed that we might never fare worse.

I don't know how long I had slept, but suddenly I awoke. There was considerable hubbub aloft, and somehow I felt that we were dragging our anchor and drifting out to sea. Rushing up on deck, I found the wind was blowing so hard that, instead of an anchor, we were using a bit of a sail, and that after all I had needlessly left the warmth below. Soon after daybreak we saw a tug coming towards us, but, alas! were unable to vent our wrath on our last night's pilot, for this one proved to be another tug. This quickly brought us alongside the *Nanchang*, where we were at first pointed out as being two Russians, but further acquaintance with the hardy and kind-hearted skipper and hospitable officers soon dissolved their first opinion. The *Nanchang* had comfortable quarters for two passengers, with a liberal table. The cargo consisted of Chinese wine, nuts and bones, which latter are utilised for some process in refining sugar. We ourselves never approved of the process, for on a roughish day the odours from these bones were not always welcome.

The following morning, the 6th December, we rose to find ourselves almost blocked in with white drifting masses of ice—quite a Nansenic scene. It seemed as though we could have walked for miles over the sea. Our weather-beaten skipper far from cheered us when he began to narrate how, a year or two ago, he had been caught by the winter just in the same way, and his ship had been blocked for some months. He graphically told us how they used to walk to shore, and of the jolly parties they had at the Taku Hotel! Our heads, however, were turned in a different direction; we were bound to return to India with the least possible delay, and we shuddered to think of our fate. Providentially the weather changed, our last cargo of bones was brought on board, as well as a third and welcome passenger, Mr. Carville, of the Consulate Service. By 5 P.M. we were once more under weigh, steaming some ten knots an hour.

Here, again, Esau and Lassoo began to enjoy a new experience, for they had never seen a big boat. Shahzad Mir had certainly seen one, though he had never made a voyage. Amongst other topics, on cold, still nights, on that vast expanse of unknown land, we had told them of the big ships, and their faces had brightened up as they pictured the leisure, comfort, and ample supply of everything that was in store for them. But, alas! the next morning, with a beam sea on, the three men lay prone, miserable, and unable to eat, while around lay the box of cigars we had provided them with. Poor fellows! they wished they were back again on the Chang, even along the shore of one of those dreary salt lakes. Though smiling at their unfortunate plight, we sincerely pitied them, and felt that it was but a poor return, after all the troubles and privations they had undergone for us. We were heartily glad to find the beam sea was of but short duration, and with its abatement our three men revived sufficiently to enjoy the remainder of the voyage to Hong Kong.

LASSOO AND ESAU.

Landing at Quarry Bay at daybreak on the 12th of December, we then embarked on a small steamer, which speedily carried us up the beautiful harbour to one of the wharfs. From thence we made our way to the Hong Kong Hotel, and learnt there was a boat, the *Suisang*, leaving for Calcutta that very day at noon.

All thoughts of visiting Canton were put aside—before even we had managed to fit ourselves out for this last stage of our travels, we had embarked on board this fine boat; but whatever requirement we had been unable to procure during so short a time our generous skipper, Captain Galsworthy, was only too anxious to provide. Our voyage was as pleasant as it is possible for a voyage at sea to be.

On the 18th of December we touched at Singapore, where we thoroughly enjoyed the ever-ready hospitality of the 1st Battalion Rifle Brigade, who were quartered there. A dinner at mess, a stroll afterwards in the magnificent gardens, as we listened meanwhile to the music of their fine band, told us only too surely that our journey was drawing to a close.

On the 21st we touched at Penang, of well-known beauty, where the hospitality of the detachment of the Rifle Brigade quartered there was only equalled by that we had enjoyed at Singapore.

On Sunday, the 27th December, about 8 A.M., we were waiting for a pilot to come and take us safely up the Hoogly. As we gingerly glided up this changeable river we passed several boats outward bound. From each we endeavoured, by shouting, to learn the latest news, namely, who had won the Viceroy's Cup. Finally, a sportsman from some cargo boat, determined that we should know, shouted out as few men can, for we just heard "Patiala's Sprightly." At evening we had come to anchor, and early the next morning were once more back in India.

It was no small pleasure to Malcolm and me to see the delight of our three faithful followers, as they proudly tramped through the busy streets of Calcutta with money in their pockets to buy whatever their minds should fancy—they were, indeed, a conspicuous little party, with their weather-worn faces, and apparel made up from bits bought at all the places we had been to; with the astonishment, too, depicted on the faces of Esau and Lassoo, and the well-earned swagger that our Duffadar wore, as he explained this and that to his two bewildered companions.

But, apart from their outward appearance, which made them so conspicuous amongst the Calcutta citizens, still greater notice would have been taken of them had it been known how willingly and faithfully they had served us under circumstances and at times which must have been far more trying to them than to ourselves. Like our predecessor, Bower, we found the hardest task of our journey was to part with these three followers. Good fellows, how glad they were to be allowed to keep the enamelled plates which we had carried for so many miles, not so much to eat from as for digging holes in our continual search for water!

Duffadar Shahzad Mir, who all through had worked with unrivalled determination, joined his regiment, the 11th Bengal Lancers, at Nowshera, while Esau and Lassoo returned to their homes in Leh. Wherever they may be, they will at any rate have two friends in the world who can never forget them.

APPENDIX I.

BOTANICAL SPECIMENS COLLECTED IN TIBET BY

CAPTAIN WELLBY AND LIEUT. MALCOLM.

ALLIUM Semenovii, Regel.
Alyssum canescens, D. C.
Androsace tapete, Maxim.
Arenaria musciformis, Wall.
Artemisia minor, Jacquem.
,, nr. A. minor.
Aster altaicus, Willd.
,, Boweri, Hemsl.
,, Heterochæta, Benth.
Astragalus Hendersoni, Baker.
,, nr. A. conferta, Benth.
,, Thomsonianus, Benth.
Braya uniflora, Hook. f. et Thoms.
Callianthemum cachemirianum, Camb.
Capsella Thomsoni, Hook. f.
Carex Moorcroftiana, Boott.
Cochlearia scaposa, Hook. f. et Thoms.
Corydalis Hendersoni, Hemsl.
Crepis glauca, Benth (?)=Thorold, 70.
,, sorocephala, Hemsl.
Delphinium cæruleum, Jacquem.
,, nr. D. brunonianum.
Dilophia salsa, Thoms.
Draba alpina, L.
Dracocephalum heterophyllum, var. (?)=Thorold, 54.
Elymus junceus, Fisch.
,, lanuginosus, Trin.
Erysimum funiculosum, Hook. f. et Thoms.
Erysimum sp. (?)
Festuca sp.
Gentiana tenella, Fries.
Glyceria distans, var. convoluta.
,, ,, var.
Halogeton glomeratus, Camb. (?)
Iris Thoroldii, Baker.
Lagotis brachystachys, Maxim.
Leontopodium alpinum, Cass.
Meconopsis horridula, Hook. f. et Thoms.
Microula Benthami, C. B. Clarke= M. tibetica, Maxim.
Myricaria germanica, Desf., var. prostrata.
Oxytropis chiliophylla, Royle.
,, nr. O. strachyana.
,, nr. O. tatarica=Thorold, 39.
Parrya prolifera, Maxim. (?)
Polygonum sibiricum, Laxm.
Potentilla bifurca, L.
Ranunculus.
Saussurea Aster, Hemsl.
,, Runthiana, Wall.
,, sorocephala, Hook f. et Thoms.
,, sp. nov. (?)
,, subulata, C. B. Clarke.
,, Thomsoni, C. B. Clarke.
,, Thoroldii, Hemsl.
Saxifraga.
Sedum quadrifidum, Pall. (?)
Senecio nr. S. goringensis, Hemsl.
Seseli.
Statice aurea, L.
Stipa orientalis, Trin.
Tanacetum tibeticum, Hook. f. et Thoms.
Thylacospermum rupifragum, Schrenk.
Umbellifera.

APPENDIX II.

ANALYSIS OF THE JOURNEY, WITH READINGS OF BAROMETER AND THERMOMETER.

Date.	Place.	Distance travelled in miles.	Barometers.	Thermometers (Fahr.).	Approximate height in feet above sea level.	Remarks.
	Srinagar	—	25·25	60°	5,250	
*May 4	Leh	0	20·225	48°	11,530	
„ 7	Chumatang ..	89	18·975	44°	13,273	
„ 8	Numa	23½	18·512	46°	14,008	
„ 9	Donlung	26	17·962	38°	14,730	Water boiled at 186·4°, temp. 43°.
„ 10	Shushal, Camp 1	18	18·175	38°	14,448	Water boiled at 187°, temp. 51°.
„ 12	Mun „ 2	25	18·205	47°	14,445	
„ 13	Ludhkong „ 3	15	18·35	38°	14,077	
„ 14	„ 4	22½	17·42	30°	15,440	
„ 15	Niagzu „ 5	21	17·635	31°	15,115	Boiling point 185·6°, temp. 41°. At summit of Ann Pass—Water boiled at 181·4°, temp. 21°.
	Summit of Ann Pass	—	—	—	17,483	
„ 18	Nurtse, Camp 6	19	16·80	36°	16,540	
„ 19	Kona „ 7	15½	16·15	36°	17,635	Boiling point 181·6°, temp. 39°.
„ 20	Lake Treb „ 8	25	16·85	27°	16,200	
„ 21	Tanjun „ 9	10½	15·975	43°	17,960	At summit of Napu La — Water boiled at 179°, temp. 40·6°.
	Summit of Napu La	—	—	—	19,341	
„ 23	Camp 10	13½	16·57	46°	16,867	
„ 24	Kerambutabuk, Camp 11	13	16·835	45°	16,365	
„ 26	„ 12	17	16·30	30°	16,553	
„ 27	„ 13	17	16·55	40°	16,691	
„ 28	Lake Treb, Camp 14	15	16·80	39°	16,215	
„ 29	Lanak La „ 15	11½	16·20	35°	17,314	
„ 31	„ 16	17	16·35	26°	16,878	Boiling point 182·8°, temp. 45°.
June 1	„ 17	14	16·425	36°	16,793	Boiling point 183°, temp. 34°.

* Distances in miles start from Leh.

Date.	Place.	Distance travelled in miles.	Barometers.	Thermometers (Fahr.).	Approximate height in feet above sea level.	Remarks.
June 2	Camp 18	10	16·625	30°	16,349	
" 3	" 19	9½	16·35	38°	16,967	
" 4	" 20	10	16·175	33°	17,193	
" 5	" 21	11	16·425	43°	16,943	
" 7	" 22	14	16·525	28°	16,519	
" 8	" 23	1½	16·525	29°	16,536	
" 9	" 24	4½	16·525	29°	16,646	
" 10	" 25	8½	16·50	32°	16,749	
" 11	" 26	9½	16·625	38°	16,646	
" 12	" 27	10	16·65	44°	16,713	Boiling point 183·5°, temp. 40°.
" 13	" 28	9	16·80	55°	16,588	Boiling point 184°, temp. 59°.
" 14	" 29	12½	16·625	55°	16,848	Boiling point 183·6°, temp. 55°.
" 15	" 30	7½	16·40	51°	17,008	
" 17	" 31	10	16·425	35°	16,628	Boiling point 183·4°, temp. 47°.
" 18	" 32	5	16·275	32°	17,166	
" 19	Camp by Fresh Water Lake..33	7	16·50	43°	17,203	Boiling point 182·7°.
" 21	Camp 34	9½	16·30	53°	17,130	Boiling point 183·1°, temp. 45°.
" 22	" 35	12	16·30	60°	17,341	Boiling point 182·8°, temp. 43°.
" 23	" 36	7	16·60	68°	17,248	Boiling point 183·3°, temp. 60°.
" 24	" 37	9½	16·65	65°	17,106	
" 25	" 38	9½	16·675	55°	16,917	
" 27	" 39	11	16·625	63°	17,159	
" 28	" 40	3	16·60	59°	17,126	
" 29	" 41	13	16·80	64°	16,876	
" 30	" 42	7½	16·80	63°	16,876	
July 1	" 43	11½	16·60	48°	17,109	Boiling point 183·2°, temp. 65°.
" 2	" 44	10½	16·75	61°	16,965	
" 3	" 45	9	17·00	50°	16,382	
" 4	" 46	12½	16·775	61°	16,984	
" 5	" 47	5½	16·95	63°	16,586	Boiling point 184°, temp. 48°.
" 7	" 48	10	16·975	47°	16,400	
" 8	Salt Lake " 49	11½	17·20	53°	16,088	
" 9	" Country " 50	12	17·075	50°	16,237	
" 10	" 51	12	17·05	54°	16,322	
" 11	" 52	7½	17·125	48°	16,086	Boiling point 184·6°, temp. 54°.
" 12	" 53	13½	16·85	55°	16,649	
" 13	" 54	13	16·65	55°	16,983	
" 14	Fresh Lake " 55	12	16·65	56°	16,982	
" 15	" 56	13½	16·75	50°	16,686	
" 16	" 57	8	16·80	49°	16,566	

Date.	Place.	Distance travelled in miles.	Barometers.	Thermometers (Fahr.).	Approximate height in feet above sea level.	Remarks.
July 17	Camp 58	8½	16·90	48°	16,342	Boiling point 184·2°, temp. 48°.
„ 18	„ 59	8½	16·85	48°	16,394	Boiling point 184·1°, temp. 46°.
„ 19	„ 60	15	16·775	52°	16,615	
„ 20	„ 61	14½	16·70	53°	16,790	Boiling point 183·6°, temp. 58°.
„ 21	„ 62	14½	16·925	65°	16,624	
„ 22	„ 63	14½	17·125	63°	16,262	
„ 23	„ 64	13½	16·80	56°	15,612	
„ 24	„ 65	12½	17·05	60	16,367	
„ 25	„ 66	8	17·10	54°	16,183	Boiling point 184·6°, temp. 58°.
„ 26	„ 67	14½	16·[illegible]0	58°	16,542	
„ 27	„ 68	14½	16·80	68	16,831	
„ 28	„ 69	14½	16·90	68	16,690	Boiling point 184·3°, temp. 79°.
„ 29	„ 70	15	16·70	65°	16,922	
„ 30	„ 71	16	16·75	60	16,784	
„ 31	„ 72	11½	17·05	60°	16,282	Boiling point 184·6°, temp. 60°.
Aug. 1	„ 73	10½	17·05	60°	16,168	Boiling point 184·6°, temp. 60°.
„ 2	„ 74	12½	17·00	55°	16,189	
„ 3	„ 75	16	16·90	54	16,346	
„ 4	„ 76	16	17·05	58	15,984	
„ 5	„ 77	16½	17·175	57°	15,836	
„ 6	„ 78	19½	17·125	61°	16,050	
„ 7	„ 79	15	17·05	47°	15,990	
„ 8	„ 80	16	16·85	45°	16,297	Boiling point 184°, temp. 50°.
„ 9	„ 81	16	16·675	47°	16,699	Boiling point 183·4°, temp. 56°.
„ 10	„ 82	16	16·[illegible]5	39°	16,614	Boiling point 183°, temp. 45°.
„ 11	„ 83	5½	16·75	50°	16,474	
„ 12	„ 84	1½	16·825	48°	16,338	
„ 13	„ 85	7	16·95	52°	16,200	
„ 14	„ 86	8	17·05	53°	16,046	
„ 15	„ 87	9	17·075	48°	15,948	
„ 16	„ 88	5	17·075	50°	15,847	
„ 17	„ 89	8½	17·15	50°	15,897	
„ 18	„ 90	7½	17·225	48°	15,765	
„ 19	„ 91	9	17·175	50°	15,897	
„ 20	„ 92	5	17·20	47°	15,832	
„ 22	„ 93	7	17·20	47°	15,849	
„ 23	„ 94	6	17·20	45°	15,829	
„ 24	„ 95	8	17·40	48°	15,582	
„ 25	„ 96	9	17·375	45°	15,659	Boiling point 185·1°, temp. 49°.
„ 26	„ 97	13½	17·40	53°	15,723	Boiling point 185·2°, temp. 53°.

Date.	Place.	Distance travelled in miles.	Barometers.	Thermometers (Fahr.).	Approximate height in feet above sea level.	Remarks.
Aug. 27	Camp 98	8½	17·325	54°	15,674	Boiling point 185·3°, temp. 44°.
„ 28	„ 99	3½	17·325	48°	15,609	
„ 29	„ 100	9	17·30	50°	15,721	Boiling point 185·1°, temp. 51°.
„ 30	„ 101	10	17·375	47°	15,610	
„ 31	„ 102	9	17·40	46°	15,561	
Sept. 1	„ 103	11	17·50	47°	14,714	Boiling point 185·5°, temp. 49°.
„ 2	„ 104	13	17·55	46°	15,234	Boiling point 185·8°, temp. 43°.
„ 3	„ 105	13	17·65	46°	15,119	Boiling point 186°, temp. 46°.
„ 4	„ 106	14½	17·725	48°	15,037	Boiling point 186·2°, temp. 52°.
„ 5	„ 107	13	17·775	44°	14,846	Boiling point 186·4°, temp. 47°.
„ 6	„ 108	7	17·90	45°	14,544	Boiling point 186·9°, temp. 47°.
„ 7	„ 109	12	17·925	42°	14,513	Boiling point 186·9°, temp. 42°.
„ 8	„ 110	15	—	—	—	
„ 9	„ 111	15	—	—	—	
„ 10	„ 112	14	17·275	34°	15,457	
„ 11	„ 113	16	17·525	30°	14,992	
„ 12	„ 114	15	17·75	31°	14,628	
„ 14	„ 115	18	18·85	45°	13,1[illegible]5	Boiling point 189·3°, temp. 45°.
„ 15	„ 116	9	18·80	46°	13,204	
„ 16	„ 117	9	18·75	50°	13,319	
„ 17	„ 118	13	18·70	44°	13,324	
„ 18	„ 119	13	18·35	48°	13,855	Boiling point 188·2°, temp. 50°.
„ 19	„ 120	16	17·75	30°	14,613	Boiling point 186·5°, temp. 30°.
„ 20	„ 121	16	19·05	45°	12,713	Boiling point 190°, temp. 45°.
„ 21	„ 122	16	19·475	57°	12,165	Boiling point 191·2°, temp. 57°.
„ 22	„ 123	12	20·15	45°	11,040	Boiling point 192·8°, temp. 44°.
„ 23	„ 124	17	20·975	50°	9,920	Boiling point 194·8°, temp. 50°.
„ 24	Namoran „ 125	12	21·50	61°	9,453	
„ 26	Ootoo „ 126	14	21·65	60°	9,260	
„ 27	Bayan Gol „ 127	23	21·65	64°	9,311	Boiling point 196·2°, temp. 64°.
Oct. 1	Kanoo „ 128	11	21·625	50°	9,217	
„ 2	Kakohulasun, Camp 129	16	21·525	55°	9,408	
„ 3	Ergetsu „ 130	20	21·475	52°	9,457	
„ 4	Talunturgin „ 131	38	21·55	46°	9,313	

Date.		Place.	Distance travelled in miles.	Barometers.	Thermometers (Fahr.)	Approximate height in feet above sea level.	Remarks.
Oct.	5	Tamnamaga, Camp 132	27	21·60	42°	9,210	
„	6	Tuling Gol „ 133	20	21·05	48°	10,020	
„	7	Thanga Nor, Camp 134	17	20·70	42°	10,412	
„	8	Ootoo „ 135	19	20·15	38°	11,171	
„	9	Bookah „ 136	21	20·65	37°	10,474	
„	10	Hatuturgy Cairn, Camp 137	22	20·85	35°	10,196	
„	11	Koko Nor „ 138	22	20·80	30°	10,208	
„	12	Baga Nor „ 139	38	—	—	—	
„	13	Si-ho „ 140	40	—	—	—	
„	14	Tankar „ 141	16	—	—	—	
			1983				

APPENDIX III.

SOME CONDENSED METEOROLOGICAL OBSERVATIONS.

May.

There were fourteen fine days; five with snow or sleet.

A north wind prevailed during the first half of the month; a west or south-west wind during the latter half.

The coldest night was on the 15th (Camp 5), when 22° Fahr. of frost were registered by the minimum thermometers.

June.

Camps 16 *to* 42.

There were twenty-six fine days.

Snow fell on four days in the first week.

There was no prevailing wind, variable throughout. On some days there was no wind at all, on others there was haze.

The coldest night was on the 16th (Camp 30), with 25° of frost.

The warmest night was on the 24th (Camp 37), with temperature 33° Fahr.

On an average there were 14° of frost.

On the 21st June (Camp 34), the maximum thermometer registered 110° in the sun.

And on the 22nd June (Camp 35), 78° in the tent.

July.

Camps 42 *to* 72.

There were twenty-one fine days and ten stormy or cloudy.

Snow, sleet, or rain fell on ten days or nights.

The prevailing wind was north or north-west.

As a rule there was no wind in the early morning; it generally rose about nine o'clock.

Sometimes dropped again during the early part of the afternoon, and nearly always blew hard again in the evening, only to drop again after dark.

The coldest night was on the 10th July (Camp 51), with 26° of frost.

The warmest night was on the 29th July (Camp 70), with 1° of frost.

On the average there were 11° of frost at night.

August.

Camps 72 *to* 102.

There were eleven fine days and eighteen with rain or snow, the greater portion of which fell during the night. The wind was variable. During the latter part of the month there were several severe storms, and many others passed by north and south of us. These storms generally burst over us in the afternoon or evening, coming up against the wind, from the west.

The coldest night was on the 18th August (Camp 90), with 14° of frost.

The warmest night, 25th August (Camp 96), registered 40° Fahr.

The average temperature at night time was 34° Fahr.

September.

Camps 102 *to* 127.

There were ten fine days and ten days cloudy, with snow or rain, and the last ten days were very fine.

The prevailing wind was west.

The coldest night was on the 11th (Camp 113), when 25° of frost were registered.

The warmest night was on the 5th (Camp 107), when the temperature was 35° Fahr.

The average amount of frost during the night was 12° of frost.

The temperature at 7 P.M. was as high as 64° Fahr. on the 27th (Camp 127).

OCTOBER.

Camps 127 *to* 141 *to SHAPOHTSI.*

There were twenty-seven fine days, two cloudy days, two days with snow.

The prevailing wind was east, often chopping round to west in the evening.

The coldest night was the 10th (Camp 137), when 27° of frost were registered.

The warmest night was the 13th (Camp 140), when 2° of frost were registered.

The average amount of frost at night was 10° of frost.

During November and December we experienced a continuation of bright clear weather with frosty nights.

APPENDIX IV.

EXPLANATION OF SOME UNFAMILIAR WORDS.

AUBERGE	...	A medicine for colds.
Bhoussa	...	Chopped straw.
Boortsa	...	A kind of heather.
Bully beef	...	Tinned beef.
Choudrie	...	Official in a bazaar.
Chuppaties	...	Unleavened bread.
Deghies	...	Cooking-pots.
Ecka	...	A two-wheeled native cart.
Ghi	...	Clarified butter.
Hallal	...	To kill according to Mohammedan form.
Hann	...	A variety of Tibetan vegetable.
K'ang	...	A raised platform used as a bed. There is a fire underneath it.
Kumbuk	...	A variety of Tibetan vegetable.
Numnah	...	Felt saddle-cloth.
Palan	...	A kind of saddle.
Poshteen	...	A fur coat.
Suleetah	...	Saddlebag.
Yakdan	...	Mule trunk.

INDEX.

THE END.